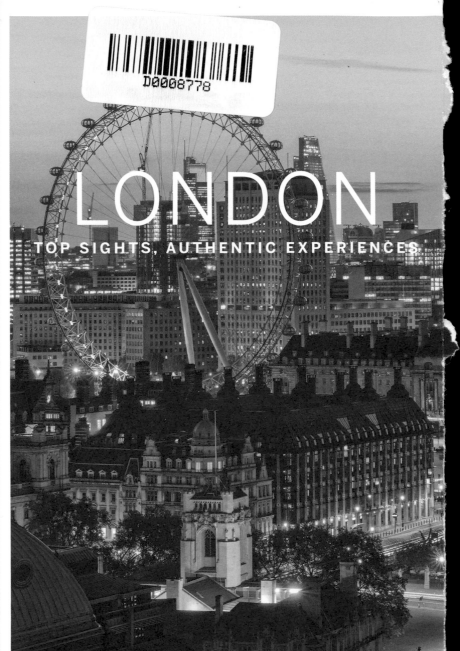

LONDON

TOP SIGHTS, AUTHENTIC EXPERIENCES

Emilie Filou
Peter Dragicevich, Steve Fallon, Damian Harper

Lonely Planet's
London

Welcome to London

One of the world's most visited cities, London has something for everyone, from history and culture to fine wine and good times. Its energy is intoxicating and its sheer diversity inspiring.

With a third of all Londoners foreign born, representing 270 different nationalities, London is marvellously multicultural. These cultures infuse the cuisine, fashion and music offerings of the capital – it's all delightfully international.

A tireless innovator of art and culture, London is a city of ideas and the imagination; the city's creative milieu is streaked with left-field attitude, from ground-breaking theatre to contemporary art, pioneering music, writing and design. No matter how often you come, there is always something new to eat, visit or experience.

Contrasting with the up-to-the-minute restaurant and arts scene, London is also a city immersed in history, with more than its share of mind-blowing antiquity. London's buildings are eye-catching milestones in the city's compelling biography, and its museums have collections as varied as they are magnificent. Of course, London is as much about leafy spaces and wide-open parklands as about high-density, sight-packed exploration and there is always a glorious green escape waiting to soothe the senses.

London is a city immersed in history, with more than its share of mind-blowing antiquity

London skyline

★ LONDON ★

North London
Parks, market
Camden and I
after dark gua
glorious day a
out. *(Map p25*

**Clerkenwell, Shoreditch
& Spitalfields**
Good food and a great
night out in one of London's trendiest areas.
(Map p253)

Kings Cross ◉

◉
St Pancra
Internatio
Euston ◉ (Eurostar

British Museum 🏛

The West End
The beating heart of
London, with iconic
sights, shopping and
nightlife. *(Map p248)*

SOHO ◉

Leiceste
Square ◉

◉ Hyde
Park

National Gallery 🏛 ◉
Trafalgar Square ◉

Buckingham
Palace 🏛

Design
Museum 🏛

Natural History
Museum 🏛

Victoria &
Albert Museum 🏛

Westminster
Abbey

◉ Victoria

Tate
Brita

Kensington & Hyde Park
Three world-class museums and the largest
of the royal parks in
a well-heeled district.
(Map p250)

Plan Your Trip
This Year in London

London

London has a busy year ahead: there are festivals and cultural events galore. A few key sights are reopening after extensive renovations too: whether you have seen them before or not, a visit is definitely in order!

Clockwise from above: New Year's Celebrations at Big Ben (p17); Trooping the Colour (p11); Notting Hill Carnival (p13)

BIKEWORLDTRAVEL/SHUTTERSTOCK ©

2018

MEUNIERD/SHUTTERSTOCK ©

★ Top Events

Trooping the Colour June (p11)

Wimbledon Lawn Tennis Championships June–July (p11)

The Proms July–September (p12)

Notting Hill Carnival August (p13)

New Year's Celebrations December (p17)

MS JANE CAMPBELL/SHUTTERSTOCK ©

Plan Your Trip
This Year in London

January

January in London kicks off with a big bang at midnight. London is in the throes of winter, with short days: light appears at 8am and is all but gone by 4pm.

☆ London International Mime Festival 10 Jan–3 Feb

Held over the month of January, this festival (www.mimelondon.com) is a must for lovers of originality, playfulness, physical talent and the unexpected.

◉ London Art Fair 17–21 Jan

Over 100 major galleries participate in this contemporary art fair (www.londonartfair. co.uk; pictured above), now one of the largest in Europe, with thematic exhibitions, special events and the best emerging artists.

☆ A Night at the Opera Jan

The nights are long and cold so what better way to cosy up than inside the stunning Royal Opera House to revel in world-class opera or ballet? (Plus, it's a great opportunity to dress up.)

◉ Visit the Natural History Museum Jan

The museum (p104) unveiled its new-look Hintze Hall in summer 2017: it now features the skeleton of a blue whale set in dramatic diving position, as well as brand new exhibits.

MANUEL SECHI/SHUTTERSTOCK ©

02

February

February is usually chilly, wet and sometimes even snowy. The Chinese New Year (Spring Festival) is fun and Londoners lark about with pancakes on Shrove Tuesday.

🥞 Pancake Races   13 Feb
On Shrove Tuesday, you can catch pancake races and associated silliness at various venues around town (Old Spitalfields Market, in particular).

🎆 St Valentine's Day   14 Feb
Whether you're single or part of a loved-up group, you'll be able to choose from themed and alternative parties, special movie nights and dedicated menus. Book ahead as it's a popular night.

🎆 Chinese New Year   16 Feb
To usher in the year of the dog, Chinatown fizzes, crackles and pops in this colourful street festival (pictured above), which includes a Golden Dragon parade, eating and partying.

☆ BAFTAs   18 Feb
The British Academy of Film and Television Arts (BAFTA; www.bafta.org) rolls out the red carpet to hand out its annual cinema awards, the BAFTAs (the British Oscars, if you will). Expect plenty of celebrity glamour.

Plan Your Trip
This Year in London

ANDREW COWIE/STRINGER/GETTY IMAGES ©

03

March

March sees spring in the air, with trees beginning to flower and daffodils emerging across parks and gardens. London is getting in the mood to head outdoors again.

🎉 St Patrick's Day Parade & Festival   18 Mar
This is the top festival for the Irish in London, held on the Sunday closest to 17 March (the actual St Patrick's date), with a colourful parade through central London (pictured above) and other festivities in and around Trafalgar Sq.

☆ Flare   late Mar
This LGBT film festival, organised by the British Film Institute (www.bfi.org.uk/flare), runs a packed two-week program of film screenings, along with club nights, talks and events.

👁 Kew's Chinese Pagoda Reopens   Mar
The distinctive 50m octogonal pagoda tower reopens to the public after renovations. Built in 1762, it's been restored to its initial splendour and now features the 80 gold-leafed winged dragons that were part of the initial design.

☆ Head of the River Race   11 Mar
Some 400 crews take part in this colourful boat race, held over a 7km course on the Thames, from Mortlake to Putney.

04

April

April sees London in bloom, with warmer days and a spring in everyone's step. British summer time starts late March, so it's now light until 7pm. Some sights previously shut for winter reopen.

✿ Easter   1 Apr
With Good Friday and Easter Monday both being public holidays, Easter is the longest bank holiday in the UK. Chocolate, which you'll find in many shapes and flavours, is a traditional Easter treat, as are hot cross buns, a spiced, sticky-glazed fruit bun.

☆ Oxford & Cambridge
Boat Race   early Apr
Crowds line the banks of the Thames for the country's two most famous universities going oar-to-oar from Putney to Mortlake (www.theboatraces.org).

☆ London Marathon   mid-Apr
Some 35,000 runners – most running for charity – pound through London in one of the world's biggest road races (www. virginmoneylondonmarathon.com; pictured above), heading from Blackheath to the Mall.

☆ Udderbelly Festival   Apr–Jul
Housed in a temporary venue in the shape of a purple upside-down cow on the South Bank, this festival of comedy, circus and general family fun (www.udderbelly.co.uk) has become a spring favourite. Events run from April to July.

☉ Southbank Centre
Reopens   Apr
Shut for the past two years for extensive refurbishment, the brutalist wing of the Southbank Centre, which contains the Hayward Gallery and Queen Elizabeth Centre, are finally unveiling their shiny new selves, along with the floating glass box linking them to the art-deco-inspired Royal Festival Hall.

Plan Your Trip
This Year in London

May

05

A delightful time to be in London: days are warming up and Londoners begin to start lounging around in parks, popping sunshades on and enjoying the month's two bank holiday weekends (the first and the last).

☆ Shakespeare's Globe Theatre
late Apr–Oct

Watch the work of the world's most famous playwright in a faithful reproduction of a 17th-century theatre (p191). The theatre is outdoors and most of the audience is standing.

◉ Museums at Night
mid-May

For one weekend in May, numerous museums across London open after-hours (www.culture24.org.uk/museumsatnight), with candlelit tours, spooky atmospheres, sleepovers and special events such as talks and concerts.

✿ Chelsea Flower Show
22–26 May

The world's most renowned horticultural event attracts London's green-fingered and flower-mad gardeners. Expect talks, presentations and spectacular displays from the cream of the gardening world.

☆ Regent's Park Open Air Theatre
May

A popular and very atmospheric summertime fixture in London, this 1250-seat outdoor auditorium (www.openairtheatre.com; pictured above) plays host to four productions a year – famous plays (Shakespeare often features), new works, musicals and usually one production aimed at families.

2018

June

The peak season begins with long, warm days (it's light until 10pm), the arrival of Wimbledon and other alfresco events (concerts and music festivals especially).

✳ Trooping the Colour   mid-Jun
The Queen's official birthday (www.trooping-the-colour.co.uk; pictured above) is celebrated with much flag-waving, parades, pageantry and noisy flyovers. The royal family usually attends in force.

☉ London Festival of Architecture   Jun
This month-long celebration of London's built environment (www.londonfestivalofarchitecture.org) explores the significance of architecture and design and how London has become a centre for innovation in those fields.

☉ Open Garden Squares Weekend   mid-Jun
Over one weekend, more than 200 gardens in London that are usually inaccessible to the public fling open their gates for exploration (www.opensquares.org).

☆ Wimbledon Lawn Tennis Championships 27 Jun–10 Jul
For two weeks a year, the quiet South London village of Wimbledon falls under a sporting spotlight as the world's best tennis players gather to battle for the championships (p203).

06

Plan Your Trip
This Year in London

07

July

This is the time to munch on strawberries, drink in beer gardens and join in the numerous outdoor activities, including big music festivals.

⊙ Royal Academy Summer Exhibition mid-Jun–mid-Aug
Beginning in June and running through August, this exhibition at the Royal Academy of Arts (p49) showcases works submitted by artists from all over Britain; the 12,000 or so submissions are distilled to a thousand pieces for the final exhibit.

✿ Pride in London early Jul
The gay community paints the town pink in this annual extravaganza (www.prideinlondon.org; pictured above), featuring a smorgasbord of experiences from talks to live events and culminating in a huge parade across London.

☆ Wireless early Jul
One of London's top music festivals, with an emphasis on dance and R & B, Wireless (www.wirelessfestival.co.uk) takes place in Finsbury Park in northeast London. It is extremely popular, so book in advance.

☆ The Proms mid-Jul–mid-Sep
The BBC Promenade Concerts, or Proms as they are universally known, offer two months of outstanding classical concerts (www.bbc.co.uk/proms) at various prestigious venues, centred on the Royal Albert Hall.

☆ Lovebox mid-Jul
This two-day music extravaganza (www.loveboxfestival.com) in Victoria Park in East London was created by dance duo Groove Armada in 2002. Although its raison d'être is dance music, there are plenty of other genres, too, including indie, pop and hip-hop.

2018

PETER MACDIARMID/STAFF/GETTY IMAGES ©

08

August

Schools have broken up for summer, families are holidaying and the hugely popular annual Caribbean carnival dances into Notting Hill. The last weekend is a bank holiday weekend.

🏃 Outdoor Swimming   Aug
London may not strike you as the place to go for an alfresco swim but you can enjoy a dip in the Serpentine in Hyde Park or in the ponds at Hampstead Heath. The water quality is tested daily and they are extremely popular on warm days.

🍺 Great British Beer Festival   mid-Aug
Organised by CAMRA (Campaign for Real Ale), this boozy festival (www.gbbf.org.uk; pictured above) cheerfully cracks open casks of ale from the UK and abroad at the Olympia exhibition centre.

🎊 Notting Hill Carnival   25–27 Aug
Europe's biggest – and London's most vibrant – outdoor carnival is a celebration of Caribbean London, featuring music, dancing and costumes.

MS JANE CAMPBELL/SHUTTERSTOCK ©

☆ Summer Screen at Somerset House   early Aug
For a fortnight, Somerset House (p63) turns its stunning courtyard into an open-air cinema screening an eclectic mix of film premieres, cult classics and popular requests.

Plan Your Trip
This Year in London

September

The end of summer and start of autumn is a lovely time to be in town, with a chance to look at London properties normally shut to the public.

✿ The Mayor's Thames Festival   Sep

Celebrating the River Thames, this month-long cosmopolitan festival (www.totallythames.org) sees fairs, street theatre, music, food stalls, fireworks and river races, culminating in the superb Night Procession.

◉ Open House London   mid-Sep

For one weekend, the public is invited in to see over 700 heritage buildings throughout the capital that are normally off-limits (www.openhouselondon.org.uk). Some require advance booking.

☆ Great Gorilla Run   mid-Sep

It looks bananas, but this gorilla-costume charity run (www.greatgorillarun.org; pictured above) along an 8km route from the City to Bankside and back again is all in aid of gorilla conservation.

🔒 London Fashion Week   Sep

If you love fashion, don't miss out on this ultimate fashion experience. Highlights include exclusive access to catwalk shows, curated talks, designer shopping and trend presentations.

SVEN HANSCHE/SHUTTERSTOCK ©

10

October

The weather is getting colder, but London's parklands are splashed with gorgeous autumnal colours. Clocks go back to winter time on the last weekend of the month.

✈ Autumn Walks   Oct
London's parks look truly glorious on a sunny day when the trees have turned a riot of yellows and reds. Hyde Park and Greenwich Park are beautiful at this time of year and offer great views of London's landmarks.

☆ Dance Umbrella   mid-Oct
London's annual festival of contemporary dance (www.danceumbrella.co.uk) features two weeks of performances by British and international dance companies at venues across London.

🎨 Affordable Art Fair   mid-Oct
For four days, Battersea Park turns into a giant art fair (www.affordableartfair.com), where more than 100 galleries offer works of art from just £100. There are plenty of talks and workshops too.

☆ London Film Festival   early Oct
The city's premier film event (www.bfi.org.uk/lff) attracts big overseas names and you can catch over 100 British and international films before their cinema release. Masterclasses are given by world-famous directors.

Plan Your Trip
This Year in London

November

London nights are getting longer. It's the last of the parks' autumn colours – enjoy them on a walk and relax by an open fire in a pub afterwards.

✳ Guy Fawkes Night (Bonfire Night) 5 Nov

Bonfire Night commemorates Guy Fawkes' foiled attempt to blow up parliament in 1605. Bonfires and fireworks light up the night across the country. In London, Primrose Hill, Highbury Fields, Alexandra Palace, Clapham Common and Blackheath have the best firework displays.

☆ London Jazz Festival mid-Nov

Musicians from around the world swing into town for 10 days of jazz (www. efglondonjazzfestival.org.uk). World influences are well represented, as are more conventional strands.

✳ Lighting of the Christmas Tree & Lights mid-Nov

A celebrity is normally carted in to switch on all the festive lights that line Oxford, Regent and Bond streets, and a towering Norwegian spruce is set up in Trafalgar Sq.

✳ Lord Mayor's Show mid-Nov

In accordance with the Magna Carta of 1215, the newly elected Lord Mayor of the City of London travels in a state coach from Mansion House to the Royal Courts of Justice to make an oath of allegiance to the Crown. The floats, bands and fireworks that accompany the mayor were added later (www. lordmayorsshow.london; pictured above).

2018

SKATE

12

December

A festive mood reigns as Christmas approaches and shops are dressed up to the nines. Days are increasingly shorter. Christmas Day is the quietest day of the year, with all shops and museums closed and the tube network shut.

🛷 Ice-Skating   mid-Nov–Jan

From mid-November until January, open-air ice-rinks pop up across the city, including one in the exquisite courtyard of Somerset House (p63; pictured above) and another one in the grounds of the Natural History Museum (p104).

🛍 Christmas Shopping   Dec

London has everything you could possibly want and more. Hamleys, with its five storeys of toys, will mesmerise children. Harrods will wow you with its extravagant window display and over-the-top decorations (and prices!). The festive atmosphere should put a spring in your step.

✨ New Year's Celebrations   31 Dec

The famous countdown to midnight with Big Ben is met with terrific fireworks from the London Eye and massive crowds. There are parties in every pub and bar in town.

🛍 Boxing Day   26 Dec

Boxing Day used to be the opening day of the winter sales and one of the busiest days of the year for shops. Pre-Christmas sales have somewhat dampened the rush but it remains a lively day.

Plan Your Trip
Need to Know

Daily Costs

Budget
Less than £85

- Dorm bed: £10–32

- Market-stall lunch: £5; supermarket sandwich: £3.50–4.50

- Many museums: free

- Standby theatre tickets: £5–25

- Santander Cycles daily rental fee: £2

Midrange
£85–185

- Double room in a mid-range hotel: £90–160

- Two-course dinner with a glass of wine: £35

- Theatre ticket: £15–60

Top End
More than £185

- Four-star/boutique hotel room: £200

- Three-course dinner in a top restaurant with wine: £60–90

- Black cab trip: £30

- Top theatre ticket: £65

Advance Planning

Three months before Book weekend performances of top shows; make dinner reservations for renowned restaurants with celebrity chefs; snatch up tickets for must-see temporary exhibitions; book accommodation at boutique properties.

One month before Check listings for fringe theatre, live music and festivals on entertainment sites such as Time Out, and book tickets.

A few days before Check the weather on the Met Office website (www.metoffice.gov.uk).

Useful Websites

- **Lonely Planet** (www.lonelyplanet.com/london) Bookings, traveller forum and more.

- **Time Out London** (www.timeout.com/london) Up-to-date and comprehensive listings.

- **Londonist** (www.londonist.com) A website about London and everything that happens in it.

- **Transport for London** (www.tfl.gov.uk) Essential tool for staying mobile in the capital.

Currency
Pound sterling (£)

Language
English

Visas
Not required for US, Canadian, Australian, New Zealand or South African visitors for stays of up to six months. EU nationals can stay indefinitely for now (Brexit may change that).

Money
ATMs are widespread. Major credit cards are accepted everywhere. The best place to change money is in post office branches, which do not charge a commission.

Mobile Phones
Buy local SIM cards for European and Australian phones, or a pay-as-you-go phone. Set other phones to international roaming.

Time
London is on GMT; during British Summer Time (BST; late March to late October), London clocks are one hour ahead of GMT.

Tourist Information
Visit London (p232) can fill you in on everything you need to know.

When to Go

Summer is peak season: days are long and festivals are afoot, but expect crowds. Spring and autumn are cooler, but delightful. Winter is cold, but quieter.

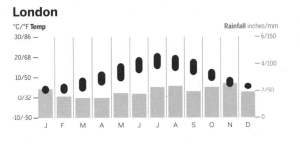

London

°C/°F **Temp**

Rainfall inches/mm

Arriving in London

Heathrow Airport Trains, London Underground (tube) and buses to central London from just after 5am to before midnight (night buses run later and 24-hour tube runs Friday and Saturday) £5.70 to £21.50; taxi £45 to £85.

Gatwick Airport Trains to central London from 4.30am to 1.35am £10 to £20; hourly buses to central London around the clock from £5; taxi £100.

Stansted Airport Trains to central London from 5.30am to 1.30am £23.40; round-the-clock buses to central London from £12; taxi from £130.

Luton Airport Trains to central London from 7am to 10pm from £14; round-the-clock buses to central London £10; taxi £110.

London City Airport DLR trains to central London from 5.30am to 12.30am Monday to Saturday, 7am to 11.15pm Sunday from £2.80; taxi around £30.

St Pancras International Train Station In central London (for Eurostar train arrivals from Europe) and connected by many Underground lines to other parts of the city.

Digital London

There are scores of cool apps for travellers. Here are some of our favourite free ones – from inspirational to downright practical. Many museums and attractions also have their own.

○ Streetmuseum Historical images (photographs, paintings, drawings etc) superimposed on modern-day locations.

○ Street Art Tours London Hand-picked graffiti and other street-art locations.

○ Soho Stories Social history of London's most bohemian neighbourhood, told through poems and extracts from novels and newspapers.

○ CityMapper The best app to work out how to get from A to B.

○ Hailo Summons the nearest black cab right to the curb.

○ Uber A taxi, private car or rideshare at competitive prices.

○ London Bus Live Real-time route finder and bus arrivals for a stop of your choice.

○ Santander Cycles Find a bike, a route and a place to return it.

Sleeping

Hanging your hat (and anything else you care to remove) in London can be painfully expensive and you'll almost always need to book your room well in advance. Decent, central hostels are easy enough to find and also offer reasonably priced double rooms. Bed and breakfasts are a dependable and inexpensive, if rather simple, option. Hotels range from cheap, no-frills chains through boutique choices to luxury five-star historic hotels.

For more, see the **Survival Guide** (p228).

Plan Your Trip
Top Days in London

The West End & the South Bank

Plunge into the heart of the West End for some of London's top sights. This itinerary also spans the River Thames to the South Bank, taking in Westminster Abbey, Buckingham Palace, Trafalgar Square, the Houses of Parliament and the London Eye.

❶ Westminster Abbey (p36)

Begin at Westminster Abbey to steep yourself in British history back to 1066.

➲ Westminster Abbey to Buckingham Palace

🏃 Cross the road to Storey's Gate and walk west along Birdcage Walk.

❷ Buckingham Palace (p46)

Peer through the gates, go on a tour of the interior (summer only) or catch the Changing of the Guard at 11.30am.

➲ Buckingham Palace to Cafe Murano

🏃 Stroll through St James's Park and across the Mall to St James's St.

❸ Lunch at Cafe Murano (p147)

In the heart of St James's, this busy restaurant cooks superb northern Italian fare.

➲ Cafe Murano to Trafalgar Square

🏃 Walk along Jermyn St and down Haymarket to Trafalgar Square.

Day

FENLIOQ / SHUTTERSTOCK ©

❹ Trafalgar Square (p56)

Visit London's epicentre (all distances are measured from here) and explore the National Gallery (p54).

➲ Trafalgar Square to Houses of Parliament

🏃 Walk down Whitehall.

❺ Houses of Parliament (p50)

Dominating the east side of Parliament Sq is the Palace of Westminster, with one of London's ultimate sights, Big Ben.

➲ Houses of Parliament to London Eye

🏃 Cross Westminster Bridge.

❻ London Eye (p94)

Hop on a 'flight' on the London Eye. Pre-book tickets online or grab a fast-track ticket to shorten wait times.

➲ London Eye to Scootercaffe

🏃 Walk down to Waterloo station, cross the Leake St graffiti tunnel under the tracks and turn right on Lower Marsh.

❼ Drinks at Scootercaffe (p179)

Tucked behind Waterloo station, this atmospheric bar is perfect for winding down after traipsing across the city.

From left: Interior of Westminster Abbey (p36); London Eye (p94)

Plan Your Trip
Top Days in London

History, Views & a Spot of Shakespeare

Get set for more of London's top sights – once again on either side of the Thames. Visit the British Museum in Bloomsbury, climb the dome of St Paul's Cathedral, explore the Tower of London and soak up some Shakespeare.

Day

02

❶ British Museum (p42)

Begin with a visit to the British Museum and ensure you tick off the highlights, including the Rosetta Stone, the Egyptian mummies and the Parthenon Marbles.

➲ British Museum to St Paul's Cathedral

⊖ Take the Central Line from Holborn to St Paul's.

❷ St Paul's Cathedral (p86)

Enjoy a light lunch at Café Below (p145) before exploring the cathedral. Don't miss climbing the dome for its astounding views of London and save plenty of time for visiting the fascinating crypt.

➲ St Paul's Cathedral to Tower of London

🚌 Hop on bus 15 from the cathedral to the Tower of London.

❸ Tower of London (p64)

The millennium of history contained within the Tower of London, including the Crown Jewels, Traitors' Gate, the White Tower and its armour collection, and the all-important

resident ravens, deserves at least a couple of hours to fully explore.

➲ Tower of London to Tower Bridge

🏃 Walk along Tower Bridge Approach from the Tower of London to Tower Bridge.

❹ Tower Bridge (p80)

Cross the Thames via elegant Tower Bridge. Check the website for bridge lift times if you want to see it open and close.

➲ Tower Bridge to Oblix at the Shard

🏃 Stroll west along the river to the Shard; the entrance is on St Thomas St.

❺ Drinks at Oblix (p179)

Round off the day with drinks, live music and fabulous views of London from the 32nd floor of the Shard, London's most spectacular skyscraper.

➲ Oblix at the Shard to Shakespeare's Globe

🏃 Walk through Borough Market and then follow the Thames west to Shakespeare's Globe.

❻ A Play at Shakespeare's Globe (p191)

Watch one of Shakespeare's famous plays in a theatre as it would have been in Shakespeare's day: outdoors in summer months in the Globe, or by candlelight in the Playhouse.

From left: Tower Bridge (p80); Shakespeare's Globe (p191)

Plan Your Trip
Top Days in London

Kensington Museums, Knightsbridge Shopping & the West End

Passing through some of London's most attractive and well-heeled neighbourhoods, this route takes in three of the city's best museums and a world-famous department store before delivering you to the bright lights of the West End.

Day
03

❶ Victoria & Albert Museum (p100)

Start your day in South Kensington, home to several of the best museums in the city. Cross off some of the Victoria & Albert's 146 galleries, but leave a little time for the huge Natural History Museum (p104) or the interactive Science Museum (p107).

➡ Victoria & Albert Museum to Kensington Gardens & Hyde Park

🚶 Walk north along Exhibition Rd to Kensington Gardens.

❷ Kensington Gardens & Hyde Park

Follow the museums with an exploration of Kensington Gardens (p99) and Hyde Park (p96). Make sure you take a look at the Albert Memorial (p99), take a peek inside Kensington Palace (p98) and stroll along the Serpentine.

➡ Kensington Gardens & Hyde Park to Magazine

🚶 Stroll through Hyde Park to Magazine, in the middle of the park by the Serpentine Sackler Gallery.

ANTHONY SHAW PHOTOGRAPHY / SHUTTERSTOCK ©

❸ Lunch at Magazine (p141)

Dine on lovely modern European food in the other-wordly undulating building designed by the late prize-winning architect Zaha Hadid. Afternoon tea is another great option.

◗ Magazine to Harrods

🏃 Walk down West Carriage Dr and then across Knightsbridge to reach Harrods.

❹ Harrods (p160)

A visit to Harrods is both fun and fascinating, even if you don't plan to buy anything. The food court is a great place for edible souvenirs.

◗ Harrods to Piccadilly Circus

🚇 Walk to Knightsbridge station, then take the Piccadilly Line three stops to Piccadilly Circus.

❺ Piccadilly Circus (p108)

Jump off the tube at this busy roundabout to have a look at the famous statue (Eros' brother) and enjoy a night out in Soho (p131).

◗ Piccadilly Circus to Yauatcha

🏃 Walk up Shaftesbury Ave and turn left onto Rupert St, which becomes Berwick St, then left into Broadwick St.

❻ Dinner at Yauatcha (p147)

For the most sophisticated and exquisite dim sum, Yauatcha is unrivalled. The selection of tea is second to none. Bookings are essential.

◗ Yauatcha to LAB

🏃 Turn right on Broadwick St, then right on Wardour St, then left on Old Compton St to Swift.

❼ Drinks at Swift (p181)

Ease further into the evening with drinks at this new cocktail bar.

From left: Hyde Park (p96); Statue of Anteros at Piccadilly Circus (p108)

Plan Your Trip
Top Days in London

Greenwich to Camden

You don't want to neglect sights further afield and this itinerary makes a big dent in what's on offer. Lovely Greenwich has a whole raft of stately sights, while a visit to the East End and Camden will help to develop a feel for Londoners' London.

❶ Royal Observatory & Greenwich Park (p114)

Start the day in riverside Greenwich and make sure you visit Greenwich Park and the Royal Observatory, checking out the Cutty Sark (p117) clipper ship. A browse through Greenwich Market (p159) always turns up surprises.

➡ Greenwich Park & Royal Observatory to Tayyabs

🚌 & 🚇 Take the DLR from Cutty Sark station to Bow Church and change for the District or Hammersmith & City underground lines to Whitechapel.

❷ Lunch at Tayyabs (p139)

Dip into the multicultural East End with lunch at this classic Punjabi restaurant. After your meal, wander around Whitechapel, soaking up its atmosphere and visiting the ground-breaking Whitechapel Gallery (p72).

➡ Tayyabs to Old Spitalfields Market

🏃 Walk north from Whitechapel Rd up Osborn St and Brick Lane to Old Spitalfields Market.

Day 04

ELENA ROSTUNOVA / SHUTTERSTOCK ©

❸ Old Spitalfields Market (p71)

Wander along Brick Lane and explore absorbing Georgian Spitalfields before browsing through Old Spitalfields Market. The best days for the market are Thursday, Friday and Sunday.

◗ Old Spitalfields Market to Worship St Whistling Shop

🏃 Walk west from the market along Spital Sq, then north up Bishopgate to Worship St.

❹ Worship St Whistling Shop (p175)

Sample the edgy, creative and offbeat Shoreditch atmosphere: drop in on this basement drinking den to try one of their curious cocktails (Undyed Bloodshed, anyone?).

◗ Worship St Whistling Shop to Market

🚇 Stroll to Old St station, then jump on a Northern Line tube to Camden Town.

❺ Dinner at Market (p143)

End the day in North London by dining on modern British cuisine at the excellent Market before turning to the riveting choice of local bars, pubs and live-music venues in this invigorating neighbourhood.

From left: View of Canary Wharf from Greenwich Park (p115); A stall at Old Spitalfields Market (p71)

Plan Your Trip
Hotspots For...

GLITZ & GLAMOUR

👁 **Buckingham Palace** Pomp, pageantry and a lot of gilded ceilings in the Queen's main residence. (p46)

☆ **Royal Opera House** Ballet or opera in the glittering surroundings of London's premier opera house. (p194)

☆ **Ronnie Scott's** Legendary jazz venue where all the big names have played. (p194)

🛍 **Harrods** Egyptian-themed elevator, stratospheric prices and opulent displays – it's London's most extravagant department store. (p160; pictured above)

🍸 **Dukes Bar** Drink where Ian Fleming of James Bond fame drank. (p179)

CULTURE VULTURES

👁 **V&A** Fashion, sculpture, jewellery, photography – there isn't a decorative art the V&A doesn't cover. (p100)

👁 **Royal Observatory** Learn how 18th-century luminaries solved the longitude problem and how GMT came to be. (p114; pictured below)

☛ **Thames River Services** Hop on a boat for a scenic and informative cruise about London's highlights. (p200)

🍴 **Dinner by Heston Blumenthal** Splendid gastronomy blending traditional and experimental techniques. (p141)

🍷 **Draughts** Spend a night at London's first board-game bar – there are some 500 games to choose from. (p176)

HISTORY BUFFS

👁 **Tower of London** From executions to the dazzling Crown Jewels, the Tower has seen it all. (p64)

👁 **Westminster Abbey** Virtually every monarch has been crowned here since 1066, and many are also buried here. (p36)

🍷 **Ye Olde Mitre** One of the city's oldest pubs, with no music to spoil the drinking and chatting. (p174)

☞ **Guide London** Hire a Blue Badge guide for a tailor-made historical tour of the capital. (p200)

🍷 **Princess Louise** A Victorian stunner of fine tiles, etched mirrors and a horse-shoe bar. (p182)

BARGAIN HUNTERS

👁 **Borough Market** All the free samples will easily make a starter – you can buy the mains from your favourite stall. (p76; pictured above)

👁 **British Museum** Most museums of this calibre charge admission fees, but not this one. Tours are free too. (p42)

🍷 **Sky Pod** For the price of a coffee or cocktail, they throw in the panoramic views and tropical roof gardens. (p143)

🛍 **Burberry Outlet Store** Genuine Burberry, just 30% cheaper. (p159)

🛍 **Sunday UpMarket** Plenty of vintage stalls to browse for that unique piece. Happy haggling! (p158)

NIGHT OWLS

👁 **Tate Modern** This outstanding modern art gallery opens until 10pm on Friday and Saturday nights. (p82; pictured above)

🍷 **XOYO** Regularly open until the small hours and one of the best clubs in town. (p174)

🍴 **Brick Lane Beigel Bake** Whatever the time of day or night, this bagel shop will sort you out. (p71)

🍴 **Duck & Waffle** Eating in style can now be done round the clock. (p145)

☆ **Comedy Store** The 11pm shows on Fridays and Saturdays are just as funny as the 8pm ones. (p194)

Plan Your Trip
What's New

Tate Modern Extension, Switch House

At long last, the Tate Modern (p82) can spread its expansive collection into Switch House. The views from the 10th floor are second to none (and free).

Fourth Plinth Gets Geopolitical

In 2018 artist Michael Rakowitz takes over the Fourth Plinth (p59) on Trafalgar Sq with *The Invisible Enemy Should Not Exist*, a recreation of a sculpture destroyed by Isis.

Architecture for Science

The Science Museum (p107) has unveiled its new mathematics gallery; its stunning look is courtesy of the late and much acclaimed architect Zaha Hadid.

Bigger & Better Design Museum

The Design Museum (p126; pictured above) moved to its new premises in Holland Park, West London, in November 2016. The building itself is a 1960s design icon and the museum has three times more space than in its previous location by the Thames.

Blue Whale Greetings at the Natural History Museum

In summer 2017 the Natural History Museum (p104) unveiled its new look Hintze Hall, the heart of the gallery, which is now spectacularly adorned by the plunging skeleton of a blue whale.

Plan Your Trip
For Free

Museums

The permanent collections of all state-funded museums and galleries are open to the public free of charge; temporary exhibitions cost extra.

Changing of the Guard

London's most famous open-air freebie, the Changing of the Guard in the forecourt of Buckingham Palace (p46) takes place at 11.30am from April to July (and alternate days, weather permitting, August to March). Alternatively, catch the changing of the mounted guard at Horse Guards Parade (p49) at 11am (10am on Sundays).

Houses of Parliament

When parliament (p50) is in session, it's free to attend and watch UK parliamentary democracy in action.

Concerts at St Martin-in-the-Fields

This magnificent church (p59) hosts free concerts at 1pm on Monday, Tuesday and Friday.

Walking in London

Walking around town is possibly the best way to get a sense of the city and its history. Try our walking tours: East End Eras, and Northern Point of View.

Architecture & Interiors

For one weekend in September, **Open House London** opens the doors to more than 700 buildings for free.

Best for Free

- National Gallery (p54; pictured above)
- British Museum (p42)
- Victoria & Albert Museum (p100)
- Natural History Museum (p104)
- Tate Modern (p82)

Plan Your Trip
Family Travel

KOTSOVOLOS PANAGIOTIS / SHUTTERSTOCK ©

Need to Know

o **Babysitters** Find a babysitter or nanny at Greatcare (www.greatcare.co.uk).

o **Cots** Available in most hotels, but always request them in advance.

o **Public transport** Under-16s travel free on buses, under-11s travel free on the tube, and under-5s ride free on trains.

Museums

London's museums are particularly child friendly. You'll find story telling at the National Gallery for children aged three years and over, arts-and-crafts workshops at the Victoria & Albert Museum, train-making workshops at the Transport Museum, plenty of finger-painting opportunities at the Tate Modern and Tate Britain, and performance and handicraft workshops at Somerset House. What's more, they're all free (check websites for details).

Other excellent activities for children include sleepovers at the British, Science and Natural History Museums, though you'll need to book months ahead. The last two are definitive children's museums, with interactive displays and play areas.

Other Attractions

Kids love the London Zoo, London Eye and London Dungeon. Ice rinks glitter around London in winter at the Natural History Museum and Somerset House. There's also a seasonal rink further afield at Hampton Court Palace.

In addition there are the exciting climbs up the dome of St Paul's Cathedral or the Monument and watching the performers in Trafalgar Square, Covent Garden Piazza or along the South Bank. Many arts and cultural festivals aimed at adults also cater for children. London's parks burst with possibilities: open grass, playgrounds, wildlife, trees and, in the warmer weather, ice-cream trucks.

Most attractions offer family tickets and discounted entry for kids under 15 or 16 years (children under five usually go free).

Eating & Drinking with Kids

Most of London's restaurants and cafes are child friendly and offer baby-changing facilities and high chairs. Note that high-end restaurants and small, quiet cafes may be less welcoming, particularly if you have toddlers or small babies.

The one place that isn't traditionally very welcoming for those with children is the pub. By law, minors aren't allowed into the main bar (though walking through is fine), but many pubs have areas where children are welcome, usually a garden or outdoor space. Things are more relaxed during the day on Sunday.

Getting Around with Kids

When it comes to getting around, buses are better for children than the tube, which is often very crowded and hot in summer. As well as being big, red and iconic, buses in London are usually the famous double-decker ones; kids love to sit on the top deck and get great views of the city.

Best Activities for Kids

Natural History Museum (p104)

Changing of the Guard (p49)

Hamleys (p129)

Cutty Sark (p117)

Golden Hinde (p79)

Another excellent way to get around is simply to walk.

Hopping on a boat is another way to put fun (and sightseeing!) into getting from A to B.

From left: An animatronic T-rex in the Natural History Museum (p104); Changing of the Guard (p47)

TOP
EXPERIENCES

The very best to see and do

Figure adorning the interior of Westminster Abbey

Westminster Abbey

Westminster Abbey is such an important commemoration site that it's hard to overstate its symbolic value or imagine its equivalent anywhere else in the world. With a couple of exceptions, every English sovereign has been crowned here since William the Conqueror in 1066, and most of the monarchs from Henry III (died 1272) to George II (died 1760) are buried here.

Great For...

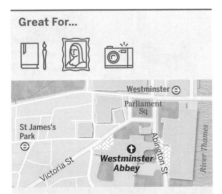

ℹ Need to Know

Map p248; 📞020-7222 5152; www.
westminster-abbey.org; 20 Dean's Yard, SW1;
adult/child £20/9, verger tours £5, cloister
& gardens free; ⏱9.30am-4.30pm Mon,
Tue, Thu & Fri, to 7pm Wed, to 2.30pm Sat;
🚇Westminster

★ **Top Tip**
The abbey gets incredibly busy, even at opening, so come armed with patience.

LIUDMILA KOTVITCKAIA / SHUTTERSTOCK ©

There is an extraordinary amount to see at the Abbey. The interior is chock-a-block with ornate chapels, elaborate tombs of monarchs and grandiose monuments to sundry luminaries throughout the ages. First and foremost, however, it is a sacred place of worship.

A Regal History

Though a mixture of architectural styles, the Abbey is considered the finest example of Early English Gothic (1190–1300). The original church was built in the 11th century by King (later St) Edward the Confessor, who is buried in the chapel behind the sanctuary and main altar. Henry III (r 1216–72) began work on the new building, but didn't complete it; the French Gothic nave was finished by Richard II in 1388. Henry VII's huge and magnificent Lady Chapel was added in 1519.

The Abbey was initially a monastery for Benedictine monks and many of the building's features attest to this collegial past (the octagonal Chapter House, the Quire and four cloisters). In 1536 Henry VIII separated the Church of England from the Roman Catholic Church and dissolved the monastery. The king became head of the Church of England and the Abbey acquired its 'royal peculiar' status, meaning it is administered directly by the Crown and exempt from any ecclesiastical jurisdiction.

North Transept, Sanctuary & Quire

Entrance to the Abbey is via the Great North Door. The North Transept is often referred to as Statesmen's Aisle: politicians

Exterior of Westminster Abbey

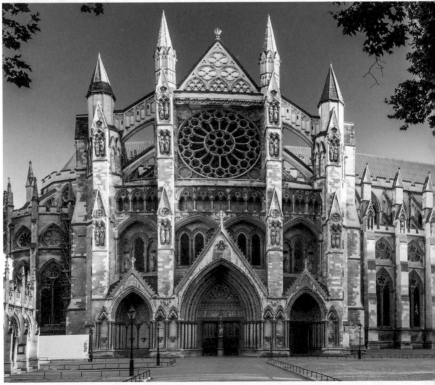

and eminent public figures are commemorated by large marble statues and imposing marble plaques.

At the heart of the Abbey is the beautifully tiled **sanctuary** (or sacrarium), a stage for coronations, royal weddings and funerals. George Gilbert Scott designed the ornate **high altar** in 1873. In front of the altar is the **Cosmati marble pavement** dating back to 1268. It has intricate designs of small pieces of marble inlaid into plain marble, which predicts the end of the world in AD 19,693. At the entrance to the lovely

GRZEGORZ PAKULA / SHUTTERSTOCK ©

Chapel of St John the Baptist is a sublime Virgin and Child bathed in candlelight.

The **Quire**, a magnificent structure of gold, blue and red Victorian Gothic by Edward Blore, dates back to the mid-19th century. It sits where the original choir for the monks' worship would have been, but bears no resemblance to the original. Nowadays, the Quire is still used for singing, but its regular occupants are the Westminster Choir – 22 boys and 12 'lay vicars' (men) who sing the daily services.

Chapels & Chairs

The sanctuary is surrounded by chapels. **Henry VII's Lady Chapel**, in the easternmost part of the Abbey, is the most spectacular, with its fan vaulting on the ceiling, colourful banners of the Order of the Bath and dramatic oak stalls. Behind the chapel's altar is the elaborate sarcophagus of Henry VII and his queen, Elizabeth of York.

Beyond the chapel's altar is the **Royal Air Force Chapel**, with a stained-glass window commemorating the force's finest hour, the Battle of Britain (1940), and the 1500 RAF pilots who died. A stone plaque on the floor marks the spot where Oliver Cromwell's body lay for two years (1658) until the Restoration, when it was disinterred, hanged and beheaded. Two bodies, believed to be those of the child princes allegedly murdered in the Tower of London in 1483, were buried here almost two centuries later in 1674.

There are two small chapels either side of Lady Chapel with the tombs of famous monarchs: on the left (north) is where **Elizabeth I** and her half-sister

Mary I (aka Bloody Mary) rest. On the right (south) is the tomb of **Mary Queen of Scots**, beheaded on the orders of her cousin Elizabeth.

The vestibule of the Lady Chapel is the usual place for the rather ordinary-looking **Coronation Chair**, upon which every monarch since the early 14th century has been crowned.

Shrine of St Edward the Confessor

The most sacred spot in the Abbey lies behind the high altar; access is generally restricted to protect the 13th-century flooring. St Edward was the founder of the Abbey and the original building was consecrated a few weeks before his death. His tomb was slightly altered after the original was destroyed during the Reformation, but it still contains Edward's remains – the only complete saint's body in Britain. Ninety-minute **verger-led tours** of the Abbey include a visit to the shrine.

Outer Buildings & Gardens

The oldest part of the cloister is the East Cloister (or East Walk), dating to the 13th century. Off the cloister are three museums. The octagonal **Chapter House** has one of Europe's best-preserved medieval tile floors and retains traces of religious murals on the walls. It was used as a meeting place by the House of Commons in the second half of the 14th century. To the right of the entrance to Chapter House is what is claimed to be the oldest door in Britain – it's been there for 950 years.

The adjacent **Pyx Chamber** is one of the few remaining relics of the original Abbey and holds the Abbey's treasures and liturgical objects. It contains the pyx, a chest with standard gold and silver pieces for testing coinage weights in a ceremony called the Trial of the Pyx.

Next door in the vaulted undercroft, the **Westminster Abbey Museum** (Map p248; www.westminster-abbey.org; Westminster Abbey; ⊙10.30am-4pm; ⊖Westminster) exhibits the death masks of generations of royalty, wax

effigies representing Charles II and William III (who is on a stool to make him as tall as his wife, Mary II), armour and stained glass. Highlights include the graffiti-inscribed Mary Chair (used for the coronation of Mary II) and the Westminster Retable, England's oldest altarpiece, from the 13th century.

To reach the 900-year-old **College Garden** (Map p248; ⊙10am-6pm Tue-Thu Apr-Sep, to 4pm Oct-Mar; ⊖Westminster), enter Dean's Yard and the Little Cloisters off Great College St.

South Transept & Nave

The south transept contains **Poets' Corner**, where many of England's finest writers are buried and/or commemorated by monuments or memorials.

Westminster Abbey seen from the cloister

In the nave's north aisle is **Scientists' Corner**, where you will find **Sir Isaac Newton's tomb** (note the putto holding a prism to the sky while another feeds material into a smelting oven). Just ahead of it is the north aisle of the Quire, known as **Musicians' Aisle**, where baroque composers Henry Purcell and John Blow are buried, as well as more modern music-makers such as Benjamin Britten and Edward Elgar.

The two towers above the west door are the ones through which you exit. These were designed by Nicholas Hawksmoor and completed in 1745. Just above the door, perched in 15th-century niches, are the additions to the Abbey unveiled in 1998: 10 stone statues of international 20th-century martyrs who died for their Christian faith. These include American pacifist Dr Martin Luther King, the Polish priest St Maximilian Kolbe, who was murdered by the Nazis at Auschwitz, and Wang Zhiming, publicly executed during the Chinese Cultural Revolution.

New Museum for 2018

In the works are the **Queen's Diamond Jubilee Galleries**, a new museum and gallery space located in the medieval triforium and due to open in 2018.

CLAUDIO DIVIZIA / SHUTTERSTOCK ©

British Museum

Britain's most visited attraction – founded in 1753 when royal physician Hans Sloane sold his 'cabinet of curiosities'– is an exhaustive and exhilarating stampede through 7000 years of human civilisation.

The British Museum offers a stupendous selection of tours, many of them free. There are 15 free 30- to 40-minute eyeOpener tours of individual galleries per day. The museum also has free daily gallery talks, a highlights tour (adult/child £12/free, 11.30am and 2pm Friday, Saturday and Sunday) and excellent multimedia iPad tours (adult/child £5/3.50), offering six themed one-hour tours and a choice of 35-minute children's trails.

Great Court

Covered with a spectacular glass-and-steel roof designed by Norman Foster in 2000, the Great Court is the largest covered public square in Europe. In its centre is the world-famous **Reading Room**, formerly the British Library, which has been frequented by all the big brains of history, from Mahatma Gandhi to Karl Marx. It is currently used for temporary exhibits.

Great For...

☑ **Don't Miss**

The Rosetta Stone, the Mummy of Katebet and the marble Parthenon sculptures.

Bust of Ramesses the Great

British Museum

Holborn

Tottenham Court Rd

New Oxford St

Bloomsbury St

⊙ Need to Know

Map p254; ☑020-7323 8299; www.britishmuseum.org; Great Russell St, WC1; ⊙10am-5.30pm Sat-Thu, to 8.30pm Fri; ⊜Russell Sq or Tottenham Court Rd FREE

✕ Take a Break

Just around the corner from the museum in a quiet, picturesque square is one of London's most atmospheric pubs, the Queen's Larder (p181).

★ Top Tip

The museum is huge, so pick your interests and consider the free tours.

Ancient Egypt, Middle East & Greece

The star of the show here is the Ancient Egypt collection. It comprises sculptures, fine jewellery, papyrus texts, coffins and mummies, including the beautiful and intriguing **Mummy of Katebet** (room 63). The most prized item in the collection (and the most popular postcard in the shop) is the **Rosetta Stone** (room 4), the key to deciphering Egyptian hieroglyphics. In the same gallery is the enormous bust of the pharaoh **Ramesses the Great** (room 4).

Assyrian treasures from ancient Mesopotamia include the 16-tonne **Winged Bulls from Khorsabad** (room 10), the heaviest object in the museum. Behind it are the exquisite **Lion Hunt Reliefs from Ninevah** (room 10) from the 7th century BC, which influenced Greek sculpture. Such antiquities

are all the more significant after the Islamic State's bulldozing of Nimrud in 2015.

A major highlight of the museum is the **Parthenon sculptures** (room 18). The marble frieze is thought to be the Great Panathenaea, a blown-out version of an annual festival in honour of Athena.

Roman & Medieval Britain

Upstairs are finds from Britain and the rest of Europe (rooms 40 to 51). Many items go back to Roman times, when the empire spread across much of the continent, such as the **Mildenhall Treasure** (room 49), a collection of pieces of 4th-century Roman silverware from Suffolk with both pagan and early Christian motifs.

Lindow Man (room 50) is the well-preserved remains of a 1st-century man (comically dubbed Pete Marsh) discovered in a bog near Manchester in northern England in 1984. Equally fascinating are artefacts from the **Sutton Hoo Ship-Burial** (room 41), an elaborate Anglo-Saxon burial site from Suffolk dating back to the 7th century.

Perennial favourites are the lovely **Lewis Chessmen** (room 40), 12th-century game pieces carved from walrus tusk and whale teeth that were found on a remote Scottish island in the early 19th century. They served as models for the game of Wizard Chess in the first Harry Potter film.

Enlightenment Galleries

Formerly known as the King's Library, this stunning neoclassical space (room 1) was built between 1823 and 1827 and was the first part of the new museum building as it is seen today. The collection traces how disciplines such as biology, archaeology, linguistics and geography emerged during the Enlightenment of the 18th century.

What's Nearby?

Sir John Soane's Museum   Museum

(Map p245; www.soane.org; 13 Lincoln's Inn Fields, WC2; ⊙10am-5pm Tue-Sat & 6-9pm 1st Tue of month; ⊖Holborn) FREE This little museum is one of the most atmospheric and fascinating in London. The building is the beautiful, bewitching home of architect Sir John Soane (1753–1837), which he left brimming with surprising personal effects and curiosities; the museum represents his exquisite and eccentric taste.

Soane, a country bricklayer's son, is most famous for designing the Bank of England.

The heritage-listed house is largely as it was when Soane died and is itself a main part of the attraction. It has a canopy dome that brings light right down to the crypt, a colonnade filled with statuary and a picture

Great Court

gallery where paintings are stowed behind each other on folding wooden panes. This is where Soane's choicest artwork is displayed, including *Riva degli Schiavoni, looking West* by Canaletto, architectural drawings by Christopher Wren and Robert Adam, and the original *Rake's Progress*, William Hogarth's set of satirical cartoons of late-8th-century London lowlife. Among Soane's more unusual acquisitions are

> ★ **Top Tip**
>
> Check out the outstanding *A History of the World in 100 Objects* radio series (www.bbc.co.uk/podcasts/series/ahow), which retraces two million years of history through 100 objects from the museum's collections.

SONGQUAN DENG / SHUTTERSTOCK ©

an Egyptian hieroglyphic sarcophagus, a mock-up of a monk's cell and slaves' chains.

Squares of Bloomsbury   Square

The Bloomsbury Group, they used to say, lived in squares, moved in circles and loved in triangles. **Russell Square** (Map p254; ⊖Russell Square) sits at the very heart of the district. It was originally laid out in 1800; a striking facelift a decade ago spruced it up and gave the square a 10m-high fountain. The centre of literary Bloomsbury was **Gordon Square** (Map p254; ⊖Russell Sq, Euston Sq), where some of the buildings are marked with blue plaques. Lovely **Bedford Square** (Map p254; ⊖Tottenham Court Rd) is the only completely Georgian square still surviving in Bloomsbury.

At various times, Bertrand Russell (No 57), Lytton Strachey (No 51) and Vanessa and Clive Bell, Maynard Keynes and the Woolf family (No 46) lived in Gordon Sq, and Strachey, Dora Carrington and Lydia Lopokova (the future wife of Maynard Keynes) all took turns living there at No 41.

Charles Dickens Museum   Museum

(Map p254; www.dickensmuseum.com; 48 Doughty St, WC1; adult/child £9/4; ⊙10am-5pm, last admission 4pm; ⊖Chancery Lane or Russell Sq) A £3.5 million renovation made this museum, located in a handsome four-storey house that was the great Victorian novelist's sole surviving residence in London, bigger and better than ever. The museum showcases the family drawing room (restored to its original condition), a period kitchen and a dozen rooms containing various memorabilia.

> ❶ **Did You Know?**
>
> Charles Dickens only spent 2½ years in the house that is now the Charles Dickens Museum but it was here that he wrote many of his most famous works.

LUKASZ PAJOR / SHUTTERSTOCK ©

Buckingham Palace

The palace has been the Royal Family's London lodgings since 1837, when Queen Victoria moved in from Kensington Palace as St James's Palace was deemed too old-fashioned.

Great For...

☑ Don't Miss

Peering through the gates, going on a tour of the interior (summer only) or catching the Changing of the Guard at 11.30am.

The State Rooms are only open in August and September, when Her Majesty is holidaying in Scotland. The Queen's Gallery and the Royal Mews are open year-round however.

State Rooms

The tour starts in the **Grand Hall** at the foot of the monumental **Grand Staircase**, commissioned by George IV in 1828. It takes in John Nash's Italianate **Green Drawing Room**, the **State Dining Room** (all red damask and Regency furnishings), the **Blue Drawing Room** (which has a gorgeous fluted ceiling by Nash) and the **White Drawing Room**, where foreign ambassadors are received.

The **Ballroom**, where official receptions and state banquets are held, was built between 1853 and 1855 and opened with

❶ Need to Know

Map p248; ☑020-7766 7300; www.
royalcollection.org.uk; Buckingham Palace Rd,
SW1; adult/child/under-5 £21.50/12.30/free;
☺9.30am-7.30pm late Jul–Aug, to 6.30pm
Sep; ⊜St James's Park, Victoria or Green Park

✖ Take a Break

During the summer months, you can
enjoy light refreshments in the **Garden
Café** on the Palace's West Terrace.

> ★ **Top Tip**
> Come early for front-row views of the
> Changing of the Guard.

a ball a year later to celebrate the end of
the Crimean War. The **Throne Room** is
rather anticlimactic, with his-and-hers pink
chairs initialled 'ER' and 'P', sitting under a
curtained theatre arch.

Picture Gallery & Garden

The most interesting part of the tour is
the 47m-long Picture Gallery, featuring
splendid works by such artists as Van Dyck,
Rembrandt, Canaletto, Poussin, Claude
Lorrain, Rubens, Canova and Vermeer.

Wandering the 18 hectares of gardens is
another highlight. You'll get beautiful views
of the palace and a peek of its famous lake;
you can also listen to the many birds and
admire some of the 350 species of flowers
and plants.

Changing of the Guard

At 11.30am daily from April to July (on
alternate days, weather permitting, for
the rest of the year), the old guard (Foot
Guards of the Household Regiment) comes
off duty to be replaced by the new guard on
the forecourt of Buckingham Palace.

Crowds come to watch the carefully
choreographed marching and shouting of
the guards in their bright-red uniforms and
bearskin hats. It lasts about 40 minutes
and is very popular, so arrive early if you
want to get a good spot.

Queen's Gallery

Since the reign of Charles I, the Royal
Family has amassed a priceless collection
of paintings, sculpture, ceramics, furniture
and jewellery. The splendid **Queen's Gal-
lery** (Map p248; www.royalcollection.org.uk;
Southern wing, Buckingham Palace, Buckingham
Gate, SW1; adult/child £10.30/5.30, with Royal
Mews £17.70/9.70; ☺10am-5.30pm;

⊙St James's Park, Victoria or Green Park) showcases some of the palace's treasures on a rotating basis.

The gallery was originally designed as a conservatory by John Nash. It was converted into a chapel for Queen Victoria in 1843, destroyed in a 1940 air raid and reopened as a gallery in 1962. A £20-million renovation for Elizabeth II's Golden Jubilee in 2002 added three times as much display space.

Royal Mews

Southwest of the palace, the **Royal Mews** (Map p248; www.royalcollection.org. uk; Buckingham Palace Rd, SW1; adult/child £9.30/5.50, with Queen's Gallery £17.70/9.70; ⊙10am-5pm daily Apr-Oct, to 4pm Mon-Sat Nov-March; ⊙Victoria) started life as a falconry,

but is now a working stable looking after the royals' three dozen immaculately groomed horses, along with the opulent vehicles – motorised and horse-driven – the monarch uses for transport. The Queen is well known for her passion for horses; she names every horse that resides at the mews.

Nash's 1820 stables are stunning. Highlights of the collection include the enormous and opulent Gold State Coach of 1762, which has been used for every coronation since that of George III; the 1911 Glass Coach used for royal weddings and the Diamond Jubilee in 2012; Queen Alexandra's State Coach (1893), used to transport the Imperial State Crown to the official opening of Parliament; and a Rolls-Royce Phantom VI from the royal fleet.

Royal Mews

What's Nearby?

St James's Park — Park

(Map p248; www.royalparks.org.uk; The Mall, SW1; deckchairs per hour/day £1.50/7; ☺5am-midnight, deckchairs daylight hours Mar-Oct; ⊖St James's Park or Green Park) At just 23 hectares, St James's is one of the smallest but best-groomed royal parks in London. It has brilliant views of the London Eye, Westminster, St James's Palace, Carlton Tce and the Horse Guards Parade; the sight of Buckingham Palace from the footbridge spanning the central lake is photo-perfect and the best you'll find.

> **ⓘ Did You Know?**
> The State Rooms represent a mere 19 of the palace's 775 rooms.

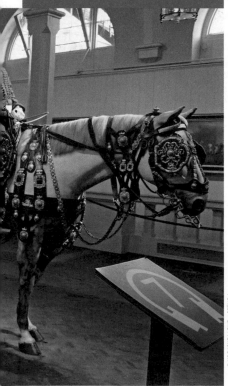

PUN_85 / SHUTTERSTOCK ©

Royal Academy of Arts — Gallery

(Map p248; www.royalacademy.org.uk; Burlington House, Piccadilly, W1; adult/child £10/6, prices vary for exhibitions; ☺10am-6pm Sat-Thu, to 10pm Fri; ⊖Green Park) Britain's oldest society devoted to fine arts was founded in 1768, moving to Burlington House exactly a century later. The collection contains drawings, paintings, architectural designs, photographs and sculptures by past and present Academicians such as Joshua Reynolds, John Constable, Thomas Gainsborough, JMW Turner, David Hockney and Norman Foster.

The famous **Summer Exhibition** (Map p248; Burlington House, Piccadilly, W1; ☺Jun–mid-Aug; ⊖Green Park), which has showcased contemporary art for sale by unknown as well as established artists for nearly 250 years, is the Academy's biggest annual event.

Horse Guards Parade — Historic Site

(Map p248; www.changing-the-guard.com/london-programme.html; Horse Guards Parade, off Whitehall, W1; ☺11am Mon-Sat, 10am Sun; ⊖Westminster or St James's Park) In a more accessible version of Buckingham Palace's **Changing of the Guard** (Map p248; www.royalcollection.org.uk; Buckingham Palace Rd, Buckingham Palace, SW1; ⊖St James's Park or Victoria), the mounted troops of the Household Cavalry change guard here daily, at the official vehicular entrance to the royal palaces. A slightly less pompous version takes place at 4pm when the dismounted guards are changed. On the Queen's official birthday in June, the Trooping the Colour is staged here.

> **ⓘ Did You Know?**
> At the centre of Royal Family life is the Music Room, where four royal babies have been christened – the Prince of Wales (Prince Charles), the Princess Royal (Princess Anne), the Duke of York (Prince Andrew) and the Duke of Cambridge (Prince William) – with water brought from the River Jordan.

Big Ben and the Houses of Parliament

DAN BRECKWOLDT / SHUTTERSTOCK ©

Houses of Parliament

Both the House of Commons and the House of Lords sit in the sumptuous Palace of Westminster, a neo-Gothic confection dating from the mid-19th century.

Great For...

☑ **Don't Miss**

Westminster Hall's hammer-beam roof, the Palace's Gothic Revival interior and Big Ben striking the hours.

Towers

The most famous feature of the Houses of Parliament is the Clock Tower, officially named Elizabeth Tower to mark the Queen's Diamond Jubilee in 2012, but commonly known as **Big Ben** (Map p248; ⊖Westminster). Ben is actually the bell hanging inside and is named after Benjamin Hall, the over-6ft-tall commissioner of works when the tower was completed in 1858. Ben has rung in the New Year since 1924.

At the base of the taller **Victoria Tower** at the southern end is the **Sovereign's Entrance**, which is used by the Queen.

Westminster Hall

One of the most stunning elements of the Palace of Westminster, the seat of the English monarchy from the 11th to the

Sculpture in the Palace of Westminster

KIEV VICTOR / SHUTTERSTOCK©

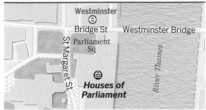

❶ Need to Know

Map p248; www.parliament.uk; Parliament Sq, SW1; ⊖Westminster FREE

✕ Take a Break

The **Jubilee Café** (10am-5:30pm Mon-Fri, to 6pm Sat) near the north door of Westminster Hall serves hot drinks and snacks.

★ Top Tip

There is airport-style security to enter the Houses of Parliament.

(1606) and Charles I (1649) all took place here. In the 20th century, monarchs and Sir Winston Churchill lay in state here after their deaths.

House of Commons

The **House of Commons** (Map p248; www. parliament.uk/business/commons; Parliament Sq, SW1; ⊗2.30-10pm Mon & Tue, 11.30am-7.30pm Wed, 10.30am-6.30pm Thu, 9.30am-3pm Fri; ⊖Westminster) is where Members of Parliament (MPs) meet to propose and discuss new legislation and to grill the prime minister and other ministers.

The layout of the Commons Chamber is based on St Stephen's Chapel in the original Palace of Westminster. The chamber, designed by Giles Gilbert Scott, replaced the one destroyed by a 1941 bomb.

Although the Commons is a national assembly of 650 MPs, the chamber has seating for only 437. Government members sit to the right of the Speaker and Opposition members to the left.

early 16th centuries, is Westminster Hall. Originally built in 1099, it is the oldest surviving part of the complex; the awesome hammer-beam roof was added around 1400. It has been described as 'the greatest surviving achievement of medieval English carpentry'. The only other part of the original palace to survive a devastating 1834 fire is the **Jewel Tower** (Map p248; ✆020-7222 2219; www.english-heritage.org.uk/visit/places/jewel-tower; Abingdon St, St James's Park, SW1; adult/child £4.70/2.80; ⊗10am-5pm daily Apr-Oct, 10am-4pm Sat & Sun Nov-Mar; ⊖Westminster), built in 1365 and used to store the monarch's valuables.

Westminster Hall was used for coronation banquets in medieval times and also served as a courthouse until the 19th century. The trials of William Wallace (1305), Thomas More (1535), Guy Fawkes

House of Lords

The **House of Lords** (Map p248; www.parliament.uk/business/lords; Parliament Sq, SW1; ⊘2.30-10pm Mon & Tue, 3-10pm Wed, 11am-7.30pm Thu, 10am-close of session Fri; ⊜Westminster) is visited via the amusingly named Strangers' Gallery. The intricate 'Tudor Gothic' interior led its poor architect, Augustus Pugin (1812–52), to an early death from overwork and nervous strain.

Most of the 780-odd members of the House of Lords are life peers (appointed for their lifetime by the monarch); there is also a small number – 92 at the time of writing – of hereditary peers and a group of 'crossbench' members (numbering 179, not affiliated to the main political parties), and 26 bishops.

Tours

On Saturdays year-round and on most weekdays during Parliamentary recesses including Easter, summer and Christmas, visitors can join a 90-minute **guided tour** (Map p248; ☎020-7219 4114; www.parliament.uk/visiting/visiting-and-tours; adult/child £25.50/11), conducted by qualified Blue Badge Tourist Guides in seven languages, of both chambers, Westminster Hall and other historic buildings.

What's Nearby?

Tate Britain   Gallery

(www.tate.org.uk; Millbank, SW1; ⊘10am-6pm, to 10pm 1st Fri of month; ⊜Pimlico) FREE Splendidly refurbished with a stunning new art-deco inspired staircase and a rehung collection, the more elderly and venerable

Palace of Westminster

of the two Tate siblings celebrates paintings from 1500 to the present, with works from Blake, Hogarth, Gainsborough, Barbara Hepworth, Whistler, Constable and Turner, as well as vibrant modern and contemporary pieces from Lucian Freud, Francis Bacon, Henry Moore and Tracey Emin. Join free 45-minute **thematic tours** (⊙11am) and 15-minute **Art in Focus talks** (Millbank, SW1; ⊙1.15pm Tue, Thu & Sat). Audioguides (£3.50) are also available.

The star of the show at Tate Britain is, undoubtedly, the light-infused visions of JMW Turner. After he died in 1851, his es-

tate was settled by a decree declaring that whatever had been found in his studio – 300 oil paintings and about 30,000 sketches and drawings – would be bequeathed to the nation. The collection at the Tate Britain constitutes a grand and sweeping display of his work, including classics like *The Scarlet Sunset* and *Norham Castle, Sunrise*.

Tate Britain hosts the prestigious and often controversial Turner Prize for contemporary art from October to early December every year.

Churchill War Rooms
Museum

(Map p248; www.iwm.org.uk; Clive Steps, King Charles St, SW1; adult/child £17.25/8.60; ⊙9.30am-6pm, last entry 5pm; ⊕Westminster) Winston Churchill coordinated the Allied resistance against Nazi Germany on a Bakelite telephone from this underground military HQ during WWII. The Cabinet War Rooms remain much as they were when the lights were flicked off in 1945, capturing the drama and dogged spirit of the time, while the multimedia **Churchill Museum** affords intriguing insights into the resolute, cigar-smoking wartime leader.

No 10 Downing Street
Historic Building

(Map p248; www.number10.gov.uk; 10 Downing St, SW1; ⊕Westminster) The official office of British leaders since 1732, when George II presented No 10 to Robert Walpole, this has also been the prime minister's London residence since refurbishment in 1902. For such a famous address, No 10 is a small-looking Georgian building on a plain-looking street, hardly warranting comparison with the White House, for example. Yet it is actually three houses joined into one and boasts roughly 100 rooms plus a 2000-sq-metre garden with a lovely L-shaped lawn.

> **❶ Did You Know?**
> The House of Lords contains Lords Spiritual, linked with the established church, and Lords Temporal, who are both appointed and hereditary.

PATRYK KOSMIDER / SHUTTERSTOCK ©

> **★ Top Tip**
> When Parliament is in session, visitors are welcome to attend the debates in both houses. Enter via Cromwell Green Entrance. Expect queues.

National Gallery

With some 2300 European paintings on display, this is one of the world's richest art collections, including works by Leonardo da Vinci, Michelangelo, Titian, Van Gogh and Renoir.

The National Gallery's collection spans seven centuries of European painting displayed in sumptuous, airy galleries. All are masterpieces, but some stand out for their iconic beauty and brilliance. Don't overlook the astonishing floor mosaics in the main vestibule inside the entrance to the gallery.

Sainsbury Wing

The modern Sainsbury Wing on the gallery's western side houses paintings from 1250 to 1500. Here you will find largely religious paintings commissioned for private devotion, such as the *Wilton Diptych*, as well as more unusual masterpieces, such as Botticelli's *Venus & Mars* and Van Eyck's *Arnolfini Portrait*.

Great For...

☑ Don't Miss

Venus & Mars by Botticelli, *Sunflowers* by Van Gogh and *Rokeby Venus* by Velázquez.

Interior of the National Gallery

ⓘ Need to Know

Map p248; www.nationalgallery.org.uk; Trafalgar Sq, WC2; ⊙10am-6pm Sat-Thu, to 9pm Fri; ⊖Charing Cross **FREE**

✕ Take a Break

The **National Dining Rooms** (Map p248; ☏020-7747 2525; www.peytonandbyrne.co.uk; 1st fl, Sainsbury Wing, National Gallery, Trafalgar Sq, WC2; mains £14.50-21.50; ⊙10am-5.30pm Sat-Thu, to 8.30pm Fri; ☞; ⊖Charing Cross) have high-quality British food and splendid afternoon teas.

★ Top Tip

Take a free tour to learn the stories behind the gallery's most iconic works.

West Wing & North Wing

Works from the High Renaissance (1500–1600) embellish the West Wing where Michelangelo, Titian, Raphael, Correggio, El Greco and Bronzino hold court; Rubens, Rembrandt and Caravaggio grace the North Wing (1600–1700). Notable are two self-portraits of Rembrandt (age 34 and 63) and the beautiful *Rokeby Venus* by Velázquez.

East Wing

Many visitors flock to the East Wing (1700–1900), where they can see works by 18th-century British artists such as Gainsborough, Constable and Turner, and seminal Impressionist and post-Impressionist masterpieces by Van Gogh, Renoir and Monet.

Visiting

The comprehensive audio guides (£4) are highly recommended, as are the free one-hour taster tours that leave from the information desk in the Sainsbury Wing daily.

What's Nearby?

National Portrait Gallery   Gallery
(Map p248; www.npg.org.uk; St Martin's Pl, WC2; ⊙10am-6pm Sat-Wed, to 9pm Thu & Fri; ⊖Charing Cross or Leicester Sq) **FREE** What makes the National Portrait Gallery so compelling is its familiarity; in many cases you'll have heard of the subject (royals, scientists, politicians, celebrities) or the artist (Andy Warhol, Annie Leibovitz, Lucian Freud). Highlights include the famous 'Chandos' portrait of William Shakespeare, the first artwork the gallery acquired (in 1856) and believed to be the only likeness made during the playwright's lifetime, and a touching sketch of novelist Jane Austen by her sister.

Trafalgar Square

In many ways Trafalgar Sq is the centre of London, where tens of thousands congregate for anything from Christmas celebrations to political protests. The great square was neglected over many years, until a scheme was launched in 2000 to pedestrianise it and transform it into the kind of space John Nash had intended when he designed it in the 19th century.

Great For...

Trafalgar Square
Duncannon St
Strand
Trafalgar Sq
Whitehall
Charing Cross

❶ Need to Know

Map p248; ⊖Charing Cross

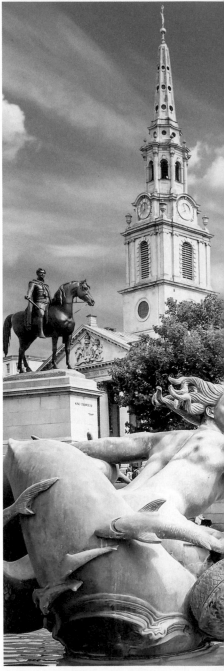

★ **Top Tip**

Check www.london.gov.uk for events happening in the square during your stay, from street artists to open-air screens.

The Square

The square commemorates the 1805 victory of the British navy at the Battle of Trafalgar against the French and Spanish navies during the Napoleonic wars. The main square contains two beautiful fountains, which are dramatically lit at night. At each corner of the square is a plinth; three are topped with statues of military leaders and the fourth, in the northeast corner, is now an art space called the Fourth Plinth.

Note the much overlooked, if not entirely ignored, 19th-century brass plaques recording the precise length of imperial units – including the yard, the perch, pole, chain and link – set into the stonework and steps below the National Gallery (p55).

Nelson's Column

Standing in the centre of the square since 1843, the 52m-high Dartmoor granite Nelson's Column honours Admiral Lord Horatio Nelson, who led the fleet's heroic victory over Napoleon. The good (sandstone) admiral gazes down Whitehall toward the Houses of Parliament, his column flanked by four enormous bronze statues of lions sculpted by Sir Edwin Landseer and only added in 1867. The battle plaques at the base of the column were cast with seized Spanish and French cannons.

The Fourth Plinth

Three of the four plinths at Trafalgar Sq's corners are occupied by notables: King George IV on horseback and military men General Sir Charles Napier and Major

The Trafalgar Square Christmas tree

General Sir Henry Havelock. The fourth, originally intended for a statue of William IV, has largely remained vacant for the past 150 years (although some say it is reserved for an effigy of Queen Elizabeth II, on her death).

The Royal Society of Arts conceived the unimaginatively titled **Fourth Plinth Project** (Map p248; www.london.gov.uk/fourthplinth) in 1999, deciding to use the empty space for works by contemporary artists. They commissioned three works: *Ecce Homo* by Mark Wallinger (1999), a life-size statue of Jesus, which appeared

tiny in contrast to the enormous plinth; Bill Woodrow's *Regardless of History* (2000); and Rachel Whiteread's *Monument* (2001), a resin copy of the plinth, turned upside down.

The mayor's office has since taken over what's now called the Fourth Plinth Commission, continuing with the contemporary-art theme. In 2018 the plinth will be occupied by *The Invisible Enemy Should Not Exist*, by Michael Rakowitz, a recreation of a sculpture destroyed by Isis.

Admiralty Arch

To the southwest of Trafalgar Sq stands Admiralty Arch, from where the ceremonial Mall leads to Buckingham Palace. It is a grand Edwardian monument, a triple-arched stone entrance designed by Aston Webb in honour of Queen Victoria in 1910 and earmarked for transformation into a five-star hotel. The large central gate is opened only for royal processions and state visits.

What's Nearby?
St Martin-in-the-Fields   Church
(Map p248; ☎020-7766 1100; www.stmartin-in-the-fields.org; Trafalgar Sq, WC2; ⊙8.30am-1pm & 2-6pm Mon, Tue, Thu & Fri, 8.30am-1pm & 2-5pm Wed, 9.30am-6pm Sat, 3.30-5pm Sun; ⊖Charing Cross) The 'royal parish church' is a delightful fusion of classical and baroque styles. It was completed by James Gibbs in 1726 and serves as a model for many churches in New England. The church is well known for its excellent classical music concerts, many by candlelight, and its links to the Chinese community (services in English, Mandarin and Cantonese). It usually closes for one hour at 1pm.

☑ Don't Miss

Every year, Norway gives London a huge Christmas tree, which is displayed on Trafalgar Sq, to commemorate Britain's help during WWII.

DIEGO SHRUBERRY / SHUTTERSTOCK ©

✕ Take a Break

Gordon's Wine Bar (p182) has a wonderful selection of wines and serves great platters of cheese and cold meats.

Covent Garden Piazza (p62)

Covent Garden

London's first planned square is now mostly the preserve of visitors, who flock here to shop among the quaint old arcades, enjoy the many street artists' performances or visit some of the excellent nearby sights.

Great For...

ℹ Need to Know

Map p248; ⊖ Covent Garden

★ **Top Tip**

Covent Garden tube station gets unpleasantly busy at weekends – walk to Leicester Sq instead.

History

Covent Garden was originally pastureland that belonged to a 'convent' associated with Westminster Abbey in the 13th century. The site was converted in the 17th century by architect Inigo Jones, who designed the elegant Italian-style piazza, which was dominated by a fruit and vegetable market. The market remained here until 1974 when it moved to South London.

The Piazza

Covent Garden seems to heave whatever the time of day or night. The arcades are chock-a-block with boutiques, market stalls, cafes, ice-cream parlours and restaurants. They're a magnet for street artists too.

The streets around the piazza are full of top-end boutiques, including famous British designers. Covent Garden is also home to the Royal Opera House and a number of theatres.

Sights

London Transport Museum

Museum

(Map p248; www.ltmuseum.co.uk; Covent Garden Piazza, WC2; adult/child £17/free; ☉10am-6pm Sat-Thu, 11am-6pm Fri; ☻Covent Garden) This entertaining and informative museum looks at how London developed as a result of better transport. It contains everything from horse-drawn omnibuses, early taxis, underground trains you can drive yourself, a forward look at Crossrail (a high-frequency rail service linking Reading with east London, southeast

London Transport Museum

London and Essex, due to open in 2018), plus everything in between. Check out the museum shop for imaginative souvenirs, including historical tube posters and 'Mind the Gap' socks.

London Film Museum   Museum
(Map p248; www.londonfilmmuseum.com; 45 Wellington St, WC2; adult/child £14.50/9.50; ⊗10am-5pm; ⊖Covent Garden) Recently moved from County Hall, south of the Thames, this museum's star attraction is its signature *Bond in Motion* exhibition. Get shaken and stirred at the largest official collection of 007 vehicles, including Bond's submersible Lotus Esprit (*The Spy Who Loved Me*), the iconic Aston Martin DB5, Goldfinger's Rolls Royce Phantom III and Timothy Dalton's Aston Martin V8 (*The Living Daylights*).

Royal Opera House   Historic Building
(Map p248; ⊘020-7304 4000; www.roh. org.uk; Bow St, WC2; adult/child general tours £9.50/7.50, backstage tours £12/8.50; ⊗general tour 4pm daily, backstage tour 10.30am, 12.30pm & 2.30pm Mon-Fri, 10.30am, 11.30am, 12.30pm & 1.30pm Sat; ⊖Covent Garden) On the northeastern flank of Covent Garden piazza is the gleaming Royal Opera House. The 'Velvet, Gilt & Glamour Tour' is a general 45-minute turn around the auditorium; more distinctive are the 1¼-hour backstage tours taking you through the venue – a much better way to experience the preparation, excitement and histrionics before a performance.

What's Nearby?

Somerset House   Historic Building
(Map p245; www.somersethouse.org.uk; The Strand, WC2; ⊗galleries 10am-6pm, Safra Courtyard 7.30am-11pm; ⊖Charing Cross, Embankment or Temple) Designed by William Chambers in 1775 for royal societies, Somerset House now contains two fabulous galleries. Near the Strand entrance, the **Courtauld Gallery** (Map p245; www. courtauld.ac.uk; Somerset House, The Strand, WC2; adult/child Tue-Sun £7/free, temporary exhibitions an additional £1.50; ⊗10am-6pm; ⊖Charing Cross, Embankment or Temple) displays a wealth of 14th- to 20th-century art, including masterpieces by Rubens, Botticelli, Cézanne, Degas, Renoir, Seurat, Manet, Monet, Léger and others. Downstairs, the Embankment Galleries are devoted to temporary (mostly photographic) exhibitions; prices and hours vary.

> ☑ **Don't Miss**
> Clambering over old tramways at the London Transport Museum, and street artist performances.

GOGABI26 / SHUTTERSTOCK ©

> ✖ **Take a Break**
> Join the tons of noodle diners at Shoryu (p147) and try the *tonkotsu* ramen.

IOAN PANAITE / SHUTTERSTOCK ©

Tower of London

With a history as bleak as it is fascinating, the Tower of London is now one of the city's top attractions, thanks in part to the Crown Jewels.

Great For...

☑ Don't Miss

The colourful Yeoman Warders (or Beefeaters), the spectacular Crown Jewels, the soothsaying ravens and armour fit for a king.

Begun during the reign of William the Conqueror (1066–87), the Tower is in fact a castle containing 22 towers.

Tower Green

The buildings to the west and the south of this verdant patch have always accommodated Tower officials. Indeed, the current constable has a flat in Queen's House built in 1540. But what looks at first glance like a peaceful, almost village-like slice of the Tower's inner ward is actually one of its bloodiest.

Scaffold Site & Beauchamp Tower

Those 'lucky' enough to meet their fate here (rather than suffering the embarrassment of execution on Tower Hill, observed by tens of thousands of jeering and cheering onlookers) numbered but a handful

Royal Armouries, White Tower

❶ Need to Know

Map p245; ☎0844 482 7777; www.hrp.org.
uk/toweroflondon; Tower Hill, EC3; adult/child
£25/12, audio guide £4/3; ⏰9am-5.30pm
Tue-Sat, 10am-5.30pm Sun & Mon Mar-Oct,
9am-4.30pm Tue-Sat, 10am-4.30pm Sun &
Mon Nov-Feb; ⊖Tower Hill

✕ Take a Break

The Wine Library (p145) is a great
place for a light but boozy lunch opposite the Tower.

★ Top Tip

Book online for cheaper rates for the
Tower.

and included two of Henry VIII's wives (and
alleged adulterers), Anne Boleyn and Catherine Howard; 16-year-old Lady Jane Grey,
who fell foul of Henry's daughter Mary I by
attempting to have herself crowned queen;
and Robert Devereux, Earl of Essex, once a
favourite of Elizabeth I.

Just west of the scaffold site is
brick-faced Beauchamp Tower, where
high-ranking prisoners left behind unhappy
inscriptions and other graffiti.

Chapel Royal of St Peter ad Vincula

Just north of the scaffold site is the
16th-century Chapel Royal of St Peter ad
Vincula (St Peter in Chains), a rare example
of ecclesiastical Tudor architecture. The
church can be visited on a Yeoman Warder
tour, or during the first and last hour of
normal opening times.

Crown Jewels

To the east of the chapel and north of the
White Tower is **Waterloo Block**, the home
of the Crown Jewels, which are said to be
worth up to £20 billion but are in a very real
sense priceless. Here, you file past film clips
of the jewels and their role through history,
and of Queen Elizabeth II's coronation in
1953, before you reach the vault itself.

Once inside you'll be greeted by lavishly
bejewelled sceptres, church plates, orbs
and, naturally, crowns. A moving walkway
takes you past the dozen or so crowns
and other coronation regalia, including the
platinum crown of the late Queen Mother,
Elizabeth, which is set with the 106-carat
Koh-i-Noor (Mountain of Light) diamond,
and the State Sceptre with Cross topped
with the 530-carat First Star of Africa
(or Cullinan I) diamond. A bit further on,
exhibited on its own, is the centrepiece:
the Imperial State Crown, set with 2868
diamonds (including the 317-carat Second

Star of Africa, or Cullinan II), sapphires, emeralds, rubies and pearls. It's worn by the Queen at the State Opening of Parliament in May/June.

White Tower

Built in stone as a fortress in 1078, this was the original 'Tower' of London – its name arose after Henry III whitewashed it in the 13th century. Standing just 30m high, it's not exactly a skyscraper by modern standards, but in the Middle Ages it would have dwarfed the wooden huts surrounding the castle walls and intimidated the peasantry.

Most of its interior is given over to a **Royal Armouries** collection of cannon, guns and suits of mail and armour for men and horses. Among the most remarkable exhibits on the entrance floor are Henry VIII's two suits of armour, one made for him when he

was a dashing 24-year-old and the other when he was a bloated 50-year-old with a waist measuring 129cm. You won't miss the oversize codpiece. Also here is the fabulous **Line of Kings**, a late-17th-century parade of carved wooden horses and heads of historic kings. On the 1st floor, check out the 2m suit of armour once thought to have been made for the giant like John of Gaunt and, alongside it, a tiny child's suit of armour designed for James I's young son, the future Charles I. Up on the 2nd floor you'll find the block and axe used to execute Simon Fraser at the last public execution on Tower Hill in 1747.

Medieval Palace & the Bloody Tower

The Medieval Palace is composed of three towers: St Thomas's, Wakefield and Langthorn. Inside **St Thomas's Tower**

(1279) you can look at what the hall and bedchamber of Edward I might once have been like. Here, archaeologists have peeled back the layers of newer buildings to find what went before. Opposite St Thomas's Tower is **Wakefield Tower**, built by Edward's father, Henry III, between 1220 and 1240. Its upper floor is entered from St Thomas's Tower and has been even more enticingly furnished with a replica throne and other decor to give an impression of how it might have looked as an anteroom in

a medieval palace. During the 15th-century Wars of the Roses between the Houses of York and Lancaster, King Henry VI was murdered as (it is said) he knelt in prayer in this tower. A plaque on the chapel floor commemorates this Lancastrian king. The **Langthorn Tower**, residence of medieval queens, is to the east.

Below St Thomas's Tower along Water Lane is the famous **Traitors' Gate**, the portal through which prisoners transported by boat entered the Tower. Opposite Traitors' Gate is the huge portcullis of the Bloody Tower, taking its nickname from the 'princes in the Tower' – Edward V and his younger brother, Richard – who were held here 'for their own safety' and later murdered to annul their claims to the throne. An exhibition inside looks at the life and times of Elizabethan adventurer Sir Walter Raleigh, who was imprisoned here three times by the capricious Elizabeth I and her successor James I.

> **❶ Did You Know?**
> Those beheaded on the scaffold outside the Chapel Royal of St Peter ad Vincula – notably Anne Boleyn, Catherine Howard and Lady Jane Grey – were reburied in the chapel in the 19th century.

East Wall Walk

The huge inner wall of the Tower was added to the fortress in 1220 by Henry III to improve the castle's defences. It is 36m wide and is dotted with towers along its length. The East Wall Walk allows you to climb up and tour its eastern edge, beginning in the 13th-century **Salt Tower**, which was probably used to store saltpetre for gunpowder. The walk also takes in **Broad Arrow Tower** and **Constable Tower**, each containing small exhibits. It ends at the **Martin Tower**, which houses an exhibition about the original coronation regalia. Here you can see some of the older crowns, with their precious stones removed. It was from this tower that Colonel Thomas Blood attempted to steal the Crown Jewels in 1671 disguised as a clergyman. He was caught but – surprisingly – Charles II gave him a full pardon.

ALICE-PHOTO / SHUTTERSTOCK ©

> **❶ Local Knowledge**
> Over the years, the tower has served as a palace, an observatory, an armoury, a mint and even a zoo.

Yeoman Warders

A true icon of the Tower, the Yeoman Warders have been guarding the fortress since at least the early 16th century. There can be up to 40 – they number 37 at present – and, in order to qualify for the job, they must have served a minimum of 22 years in any branch of the British Armed Forces. They all live within the Tower walls and are known affectionately as 'Beefeaters', a nickname they dislike.

There is currently just one female Yeoman Warder, Moira Cameron, who in 2007 became the first woman to be given the post. While officially they guard the Tower and Crown Jewels at night, their main role is as tour guides. Free tours leave from the bridge near the entrance every 30 minutes; the last tour is an hour before closing.

What's Nearby?

All Hallows by the Tower   Church

(Map p245; 020-7481 2928; www.ahbtt. org.uk; Byward St, EC3; ☺8am-5pm Mon-Fri, 10am-5pm Sat & Sun; ⊖Tower Hill) All Hallows (meaning 'all saints'), which dates to AD 675, survived virtually unscathed by the Great Fire, only to be hit by German bombs in 1940. Come to see the church itself, by all means, but the best bits are in the atmospheric undercroft (crypt), where you'll discover a pavement of 2nd-century Roman tiles and the walls of the 7th-century Saxon church.

Monument   Tower

(Map p245; www.themonument.org.uk; Junction of Fish Street Hill & Monument St, EC3; adult/child £4.50/2.30, incl Tower Bridge Exhibition £11/5; ☺9.30am-6pm Apr-Sep, to 5.30pm Oct-Mar; ⊖Monument) Sir Christopher Wren's 1677 column, known simply as the Monument, is a memorial to the Great Fire of London of 1666, whose impact on London's history cannot be overstated. An immense Doric column made of Portland stone, the Monument is 4.5m wide and 60.6m tall – the exact distance it stands from the bakery in Pudding Lane where the fire is thought to have started.

The Monument is topped with a gilded bronze urn of flames that some think looks like a big gold pincushion. Although Lilliputian by today's standards, the Monument would have been gigantic when built, towering over London.

Climbing up the column's 311 spiral steps rewards you with some of the best 360-degree views over London (due to its central location as much as to its height). And after your descent, you'll also be the proud owner of a certificate that commemorates your achievement.

Leadenhall Market   Market

(Map p245; www.cityoflondon.gov.uk/things-to-do/leadenhall-market; Whittington Ave, EC3; ☺10am-6pm Mon-Fri; ⊖Bank or Monument) A visit to this covered mall off Gracechurch St is a step back in time. There's been a mar-

All Hallows by the Tower

ket on this site since the Roman era, but the architecture that survives is all cobblestones and late-19th-century Victorian ironwork. Leadenhall Market appears as Diagon Alley in *Harry Potter and the Philosopher's Stone*; an optician's shop was used for the entrance to the Leaky Cauldron wizarding pub in *Harry Potter and the Goblet of Fire*.

30 St Mary Axe Notable Building
(Gherkin; Map p245; www.30stmaryaxe.info; 30 St Mary Axe, EC3; ⊖Aldgate) Nicknamed 'the Gherkin' for its unusual shape, 30 St Mary Axe is arguably the City's most distinctive skyscraper, dominating the skyline despite actually being slightly smaller than the neighbouring NatWest Tower. Built in 2003 by award-winning Norman Foster, the Gherkin's futuristic exterior has become an emblem of modern London – as recognisable as Big Ben and the London Eye.

The building is closed to the public, though in the past it has opened its doors over the **Open House London** (☎020-7383 2131; www.openhouselondon.org.uk) weekend in September.

ℹ️ **Local Knowledge**

Common ravens, which once feasted on the corpses of beheaded traitors, have been here for centuries. Nowadays, they feed on raw beef and biscuits.

ℹ️ **Did You Know?**

Yeoman Warders are nicknamed Beefeaters. It's thought to be due to the rations of beef – then a luxury food – given to them in the past.

KIT LEONG / SHUTTERSTOCK ©

A stall at Old Spitalfields Market

ELENA ROSTUNOVA / SHUTTERSTOCK ©

A Sunday in the East End

The East End has a colourful and multicultural history. Waves of migrants (French Protestant, Jewish, Bangladeshi) have left their mark on the area, which, added to the Cockney heritage and the 21st-century hipster phenomenon, has created an incredibly vibrant neighbourhood.

On Sundays, this whole area feels like one giant, sprawling market. It is brilliant fun, but pretty exhausting, so pace yourself – there are plenty of cafes and restaurants to sit down, relax and take in the atmosphere.

Great For...

☑ Don't Miss

There is plenty of graffiti to admire in the area but if you'd like to see a famous Banksy artwork, make a small detour to **Cargo** (Map p245; www.cargo-london.com; 83 Rivington St, EC2A; ⊘noon-1am Sun-Thu, to 3am Fri & Sat; ⊖Shoreditch High St).

Columbia Road Flower Market

A wonderful explosion of colour and life, this weekly **market** (Map p253; www.columbiaroad.info; Columbia Rd, E2; ⊘8am-3pm Sun; ⊖Hoxton) sells a beautiful array of flowers, pot plants, bulbs, seeds and everything you might need for the garden. It's a lot of fun and the best place to hear proper Cockney barrow-boy banter ('We got flowers cheap enough for ya muvver-in-law's grave' etc).

The chimney of the Old Truman's Brewery building (p73)

CHRISDORNEY / SHUTTERSTOCK ©

still makes a brisk trade serving dirt-cheap homemade bagels (filled with salmon, cream cheese and/or salt beef).

Old Spitalfields Market

Traders have been hawking their wares here since 1638 and it's still one of London's best markets. Today's covered **market** (Map p253; www.oldspitalfieldsmarket.com; Commercial St, E1; ☺10am-5pm Mon-Fri & Sun, 11am-5pm Sat; ☻Liverpool St) was built in the late 19th century, with the more modern development added in 2006. Sundays are the biggest and best days, but Thursdays are good for antiques and Fridays for independent fashion. There are plenty of food stalls, too.

Brick Lane Great Mosque

After lunch, walk over to this fascinating **mosque** (Brick Lane Jamme Masjid; Map p253; www.bricklanejammemasjid.co.uk; 59 Brick Lane, E1; ☻Liverpool St). No building symbolises the different waves of immigration to Spitalfields quite as well as this one. Built in 1743 as the New French Church for the Huguenots, it was a Methodist chapel from 1819 until it was transformed into the Great Synagogue for Jewish refugees from Russia and central Europe in 1898. In 1976 it changed faiths yet again, becoming the Great Mosque. Look for the sundial, high up on the Fournier St frontage.

Brick Lane Markets

Head south towards **Brick Lane Market** (Map p253; www.visitbricklane.org; Brick Lane, E1; ☺9am-5pm Sun; ☻Shoreditch High St), which spills out into the surrounding streets with everything from household goods to bric-a-brac, secondhand clothes, cheap fashion and ethnic food. The best range and quality of products are to be found in the beautiful Old Truman Brewery's markets: Sunday UpMarket (p158) and Backyard Market (p158), where young designers sell their creations, along with arts and crafts and cracking food stalls.

Brick Lane's Famous Bagel

A relic of the Jewish East End, **Brick Lane Beigel Bake** (Map p253; 159 Brick Lane, E2; bagels £1-4.10; ☺24hr; ☻Shoreditch High St)

Whitechapel Gallery

From Brick Lane Mosque, continue on to **Whitechapel Gallery** (Map p245; 020-7522 7888; www.whitechapelgallery. org; 77-82 Whitechapel High St, E1; 11am-6pm Tue, Wed & Fri-Sun, to 9pm Thu; Aldgate East) FREE. A firm favourite of art students and the avant-garde *cognoscenti*, this ground-breaking gallery doesn't have a permanent collection, but is devoted to hosting edgy exhibitions of contemporary art. It made its name by staging exhibitions by both established and emerging artists, including the first UK shows by Pablo Picasso, Jackson Pollock, Mark Rothko and Frida Kahlo.

What's Nearby?

Geffrye Museum Museum

(Map p253; www.geffrye-museum.org.uk; 136 Kingsland Rd, E2; 10am-5pm Tue-Sun; Hoxton) FREE If you like nosing around other people's homes, you'll love this museum, entirely devoted to middle-class domestic interiors. Built in 1714 as a home for poor pensioners, these beautiful ivy-clad almshouses have been converted into a series of living rooms, dating from 1630 to the present day. The rear garden is also organised by era, mirroring the museum's exploration of domesticity through the centuries. There's also a very impressive walled herb garden, featuring 170 different plants.

Columbia Road Flower Market (p70)

Dennis Severs' House Museum

(Map p253; ☎020-7247 4013; www.
dennissevershouse.co.uk; 18 Folgate St, E1; day/
night £10/15; ⏱noon-2pm & 5-9pm Mon, 5-9pm
Wed & Fri, noon-4pm Sun; ⊖Liverpool St) This
extraordinary Georgian house is set up as if
its occupants had just walked out the door.
There are half-drunk cups of tea, lit candles
and, in a perhaps unnecessary attention
to detail, a full chamber pot by the bed.
More than a museum, it's an opportunity
to meditate on the minutiae of everyday
Georgian life through silent exploration.

> ### ❶ Local Knowledge
> The area's food offering is as diverse
> as its population, from curry houses
> to modern British cuisine.

DAVID BURROWS / SHUTTERSTOCK ©

Old Truman Brewery Historic Building

(Map p253; www.trumanbrewery.com; 91 Brick
Lane, E1; ⊖Shoreditch High St) Founded here
in the 17th century, Truman's Black Eagle
Brewery was, by the 1850s, the largest
brewery in the world. Spread over a series
of brick buildings and yards straddling both
sides of Brick Lane, the complex is now
completely given over to edgy markets,
pop-up fashion stores, vintage clothes
shops, indie record hunters, cafes, bars and
live-music venues. Beer may not be brewed
here any more, but it certainly is consumed.

After decades of decline, Truman's
Brewery finally shut up shop in 1989 –
temporarily as it turned out, with the brand
subsequently resurrected in 2010 in new
premises in Hackney Wick. In the 1990s the
abandoned brewery premises found new
purpose as a deadly cool hub for boozy
Britpoppers and while it may not have
quite the same cachet today, it's still plenty
popular.

Several of the buildings are heritage
listed, including the Director's House at 91
Brick Lane (built in the 1740s); the old Vat
House directly opposite, with its hexagonal
bell tower (c 1800); and the Engineer's
House right next to it (at 150 Brick Lane),
dating from the 1830s.

> ### ✗ Take a Break
> In the evening, check out **93 Feet East**
> (Map p245; www.93feeteast.co.uk; 150
> Brick Lane, E1; ⏱5-11pm Thu, to 1am Fri &
> Sat, 3-10.30pm Sun; ⊖Liverpool St) on Brick
> Lane for DJs and cocktails.

Walking Tour: East End Eras

This route offers an insight into the old and new of East London. Wander through and soak up the unique character of its neighbourhoods.

Start ⊖Bethnal Green
Distance 3.6 miles
Duration 2½ hours

2 On beautifully preserved **Cyprus St** you'll get a taste of what Victorian Bethnal Green would have looked like.

1 The **Old Ford Rd** area was bombed during WWII and tower blocks were subsequently erected on the bomb sites.

3 Just over Regent's Canal lies **Victoria Park**. Take the left path along the lake to the **Dogs of Alcibiades** howling on plinths.

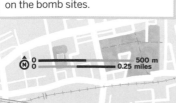

5 Cross Cadogan Tce and pick up the much-graffitied **canal path**; this area is artistic **Hackney Wick**.

6 Cross the canal at the hooped footbridge, follow Roach Rd, then turn left to cross the bridge and enter **Queen Elizabeth Olympic Park**.

Take a Break...
Formans (p139) smokes fish on its premises and serves it in a stunning, panoramic dining room.

Classic photo: The ArcelorMittal Orbit at Queen Elizabeth Park

4 Head to the eastern section of the park and see the **Burdett-Coutts Memorial** drinking fountain (1862). Then, pass **East Lake** and exit at the park's eastern tip.

7 Keep the main stadium on your right, cross the River Lea and walk through the playground towards the **ArcelorMittal Orbit**.

Fresh fruit on display at a Borough Market stall

Borough Market

Overflowing with food lovers, inveterate gastronomes, wide-eyed visitors and Londoners in search of inspiration for their next dinner party, this fantastic market has become a sight in its own right.

Great For...

🍽️ 🥂 📷

ℹ️ Need to Know

Map p245; www.boroughmarket.org.uk; 8 Southwark St, SE1; ⏰10am-5pm Wed & Thu, 10am-6pm Fri, 8am-5pm Sat; ⊖London Bridge

★ **Top Tip**
To avoid the worst of the crowds, avoid lunch times on Friday and Saturday.

Located here in some form or another since the 13th century, 'London's Larder' has enjoyed an astonishing renaissance in the past 15 years.

The market specialises in high-end fresh products, so you'll find the usual assortment of fruit and vegetable stalls, cheesemongers, butchers, fishmongers, bakeries and delis, as well as gourmet stalls selling spices, nuts, preserves and condiments. Prices tend to be high, but many traders offer free samples, a great perk for visitors and locals alike.

Food window-shopping (and sampling) over, you'll be able to grab lunch from one of the myriad takeaway stalls – anything from sizzling gourmet sausages to chorizo sandwiches and falafel wraps. There also seems to be an unreasonable number of cake stalls – walking out without a treat

will be a challenge! Many of the lunch stalls cluster in Green Market (the area closest to Southwark Cathedral). If you'd rather eat indoors, there are some fantastic cafes and restaurants, too.

If you'd like some elbow space to enjoy your takeaway, walk five minutes in either direction along the Thames for river views.

Note that although the full market runs from Wednesday to Saturday, some traders and takeaway stalls do open Mondays and Tuesdays.

What's Nearby?
Southwark Cathedral Church
(Map p245; ☎020-7367 6700; www.cathedral.southwark.anglican.org; Montague Cl, SE1; ◷8am-6pm Mon-Fri, 8.30am-6pm Sat & Sun; ⊖London Bridge) The earliest surviving parts of this relatively small cathedral are

Cupcakes and macaroons for sale at Borough Market

the retrochoir at the eastern end – which contains four chapels and was part of the 13th-century Priory of St Mary Overie – some ancient arcading by the southwest door and an arch that dates to the original Norman church. But most of the cathedral is Victorian. Inside are monuments galore, including a Shakespeare memorial. Catch evensong at 5.30pm on Tuesdays, Thursdays and Fridays, 4pm on Saturdays and 3pm on Sundays.

Shard   Notable Building
(Map p245; www.theviewfromtheshard.com; 32 London Bridge St, SE1; adult/child £30.95/24.95; ⏱10am-10pm; ⊖London Bridge) Puncturing

ANTHONY DELGADO / SHUTTERSTOCK ©

☑ Don't Miss
Grazing on the free samples or eating takeaway by the river.

---

the skies above London, the dramatic splinter like form of the Shard has rapidly become an icon of London. The viewing platforms on floors 68, 69 and 72 are open to the public and the views are, as you'd expect from a 244m vantage point, sweeping, but they come at a hefty price – book online at least a day in advance to save £5.

HMS Belfast   Ship
(Map p245; www.iwm.org.uk/visits/hms-belfast; Queen's Walk, SE1; adult/child £14.50/7.25; ⏱10am-5pm; ⊖London Bridge) HMS *Belfast* is a magnet for naval-gazing kids of all ages. This large, light cruiser – launched in 1938 – served in WWII, helping to sink the German battleship *Scharnhorst* and shelling the Normandy coast on D-Day, and later participated in the Korean War. Her 6in guns could bombard a target 14 land miles distant. Displays offer a great insight into what life on board was like, in peace times and during military engagements.

Golden Hinde   Ship
(Map p245; ☎020-7403 0123; www.goldenhinde.com; St Mary Overie Dock, Cathedral St, SE1; self-guided tours adult/child £6/4.50, events adult/child £7/5; ⏱10am-5.30pm; ♿; ⊖London Bridge) Stepping aboard this replica of Sir Francis Drake's famous Tudor ship will inspire genuine admiration for the admiral and his rather short (average height: 1.6m) crew, which counted between 40 and 60. It was in a tiny five-deck galleon just like this that Drake and his crew circumnavigated the globe from 1577 to 1580. Visitors can explore the ship by themselves or join a guided tour led by a costumed actor – children love these.

✕ Take a Break
Arabica Bar & Kitchen (p145) serves up contemporary Middle Eastern fare.

Tower Bridge

MAPICS / SHUTTERSTOCK ©

Tower Bridge

One of London's most familiar sights, Tower Bridge doesn't disappoint up close. There's something about its neo-Gothic towers and blue suspension struts that makes it quite enthralling.

Great For...

☑ **Don't Miss**

The bridge lifting and the view from the top (as well as down through the new glass floor).

History & Mechanics

Built in 1894 by Horace Jones (who designed many of London's markets) as a much-needed crossing point in the east, Tower Bridge was equipped with a then-revolutionary bascule (see-saw) mechanism that could clear the way for oncoming ships in just three minutes. Although London's days as a thriving port are long over, the bridge still does its stuff, lifting largely for pleasure craft around 1000 times a year.

Tower Bridge Exhibition

Housed within is the **Tower Bridge Exhibition** (Map p245; ☑020-7403 3761; www.towerbridge.org.uk; Tower Bridge, SE1; adult/child £9/3.90, incl Monument £11/5; ⊘10am-6pm Apr-Sep, 9.30am-5.30pm Oct-Mar, last admission 30min before closing; ⊖Tower Hill), which

City Hall

PAJOR PAWEL / SHUTTERSTOCK ©

ℹ Need to Know

Map p245; ⊖Tower Hill

✕ Take a Break

The Watch House (p146), on the South Bank, sells fabulous sandwiches and cakes from local bakers. It does great coffee too.

★ Top Tip

For the best views of the bridge, pop over to the southern bank of the river.

What's Nearby?

City Hall   Notable Building

(Map p245; www.london.gov.uk/city-hall; Queen's Walk, SE1; ⊘8.30am-5.30pm Mon-Fri; ⊖London Bridge) Home to the Mayor of London, bulbous City Hall was designed by Foster and Partners and opened in 2002. The 45m, glass-clad building has been compared to a host of objects – from an onion, to Darth Vader's helmet, a woodlouse and a 'glass gonad'. The scoop amphitheatre outside the building is the venue for a variety of free entertainment in warmer weather, from music to theatre. Parts of the building are open to the public on weekdays.

explains the nuts and bolts of it all. If you're not technically minded, it's still fascinating to get inside the bridge and look along the Thames from its two walkways. A lift takes you to the top of the structure, 42m above the river, from where you can walk along the east- and west-facing walkways, lined with information boards.

The 11m-long glass floor, made of a dozen see-through panels, is stunning – acrophobes can take solace in knowing that each weighs a load-bearing 530kg. There are a couple of stops on the way down before you exit and continue on to the **Victorian Engine Rooms**, which house the beautifully maintained steam engines that powered the bridge lifts, as well as some excellent interactive exhibits and a couple of short films.

Tate Modern

This phenomenally successful gallery combines stupendous architecture and a seminal collection of 20th-century modern art. A huge extension opened in summer 2016, dramatically increasing its display space.

Great For...

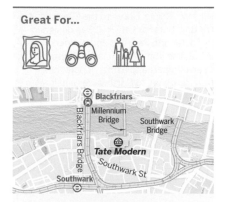

ⓘ Need to Know

Map p245; www.tate.org.uk; Bankside, SE1; ⊘10am-6pm Sun-Thu, to 10pm Fri & Sat; 🚇; ⊖Blackfriars, Southwark or London Bridge `FREE`

★ **Top Tip**

Take the **Tate Boat** (Map p245; www.
tate.org.uk/visit/tate-boat; one-way adult/
child £8/4) **shuttle between Tate Britain
(p52) and Tate Modern.**

Boiler House

The original gallery lies in what was once Bankside Power Station. Now called Boiler House, it is an imposing sight: a 200m-long building, made of 4.2 million bricks. Its conversion into an art gallery was a masterstroke of design.

Turbine Hall

The first thing to greet you as you pour down the ramp off Holland St (the main entrance) is the astounding 3300-sq-metre Turbine Hall. Originally housing the power station's humongous electricity generators, this vast space has become the commanding venue for large-scale installation art and temporary exhibitions.

Switch House

The new Tate Modern extension got its name from the former electrical substation that still occupies the southeast end of the site. To echo its sister building, it is also constructed of brick, although these are slightly lighter and artistically laid out as a lattice to let light in (and out – the building looks stunning after dark).

The Tanks

The three huge subterranean tanks once stored fuel for the power station. These unusual circular spaces are now dedicated to showing live art, performance, installation and film, or 'new art' as the Tate calls it.

Viewing Gallery: Level 10

The views from level 10 are, as you would expect, sweeping. The river views are per-

Switch House

haps not quite as iconic as the full frontal St Paul's view you get from Boiler House, but you get to see Boiler House itself, and a lot more in every direction. The views of the Shard looking east are especially good. And best of all, they are free.

Permanent Collection

Tate Modern's permanent collection is arranged on levels 2 and 4 of Boiler House and levels 0, 2, 3 and 4 of Switch House. The emphasis in the latter is on art from the 1960s onwards.

JANSOS / ALAMY STOCK PHOTO ©

> ☑ **Don't Miss**
>
> Turbine Hall, special exhibitions, the view of St Paul's from the Level 3 balconies of Boiler House and the Viewing Gallery on Level 10 of Switch House.

More than 60,000 works are on constant rotation. The curators have at their disposal paintings by Georges Braque, Henri Matisse, Piet Mondrian, Andy Warhol, Mark Rothko and Jackson Pollock, as well as pieces by Joseph Beuys, Damien Hirst, Rebecca Horn, Claes Oldenburg and Auguste Rodin.

A great place to start is the **Start Display** on level 2 of Boiler House: this small, specially curated 'taster' display features some of the best-loved works in the collection and gives visitors useful pointers for how to go about tackling unfamiliar (and an overwhelming amount of) art.

Special Exhibitions

With the opening of Switch House, the Tate Modern has increased the number of special exhibitions it hosts. You will find them on levels 3 and 4 of Boiler House and level 2 of Switch House; all are subject to an admission charge (£12.50 to £18.50; children go free). Blockbusters to look forward to in 2018 include a retrospective on Amedeo Modigliani and an exhibition looking at Picasso in 1932, a pivotal year for the artist.

What's Nearby?

Shakespeare's Globe
Historic Building

(Map p245; www.shakespearesglobe.com; 21 New Globe Walk, SE1; adult/child £16/9; ⊙9am-5pm; 🚻; ⊖Blackfriars or London Bridge) Unlike other venues for Shakespearean plays, the new Globe was designed to resemble the original as closely as possible, which means having the arena open to the fickle London skies, leaving the 700 'groundlings' to stand in London's spectacular downpours. Visits to the Globe include tours of the theatre (half-hourly, generally in the morning from 9.30am, with afternoon tours on Monday too) as well as access to the exhibition space, which has fascinating exhibits about Shakespeare and theatre in the 17th century.

> ✕ **Take a Break**
>
> Enjoy a taste of Eastern Europe at the exquisite Baltic (p145).

St Paul's Cathedral

St Paul's Cathedral is one of the most majestic buildings in London. Despite the far higher skyscrapers of the Square Mile, it still manages to gloriously dominate the skyline.

Great For...

ⓘ Need to Know

Map p245; ☏ 020-7246 8350; www.stpauls. co.uk; St Paul's Churchyard, EC4; adult/child £18/8; ◷ 8.30am-4.30pm Mon-Sat; ⊖ St Paul's

★ **Top Tip**

A visit to the church's hallowed ground must be made to fully appreciate its sublime architecture.

There has been a place of Christian worship on this site for over 1400 years. St Paul's Cathedral as we know it is the fifth Christian church to be erected here; it was completed in 1711 and sports the largest church dome in the capital.

Dome

Despite the cathedral's rich history and impressive (and uniform) English baroque interior, many visitors are more interested in climbing the dome for one of the best views of London. It actually consists of three parts: a plastered brick inner dome, a nonstructural lead outer dome visible on the skyline and a brick cone between them holding it all together, one inside the other. This unique structure, the first triple dome ever built and second only in size to St Peter's in the Vatican, made the cathedral Christopher Wren's tour de force. It all weighs 59,000 tonnes.

Some 528 stairs take you to the top, but it's a three-stage journey. Through a door on the western side of the southern transept, and some 30m and 257 steps above, you reach the interior walkway around the dome's base. This is the **Whispering Gallery**, so called because if you talk close to the wall it carries your words around to the opposite side, 32m away. Climbing even more steps (another 119) you reach the **Stone Gallery**, an exterior viewing platform 53m above the ground, obscured by pillars and other suicide-preventing measures. The remaining 152 iron steps to the **Golden Gallery** are steeper and narrower than below, but are really worth the effort. From here, 85m above London, you can enjoy superb 360-degree views of the city.

Interior dome of St Paul's Cathedral

Interior

Just beneath the dome is an **epitaph** written for Wren by his son: *Lector, si monumentum requiris, circumspice* (Reader, if you seek his monument, look around you). In the north aisle you'll find the grandiose **Duke of Wellington Memorial** (1912), which took 54 years to complete – the Iron Duke's horse Copenhagen originally faced the other way, but it was deemed unfitting that a horse's rear end should face the altar.

In the north transept chapel is William Holman Hunt's celebrated painting **The**

☑ Don't Miss

Climbing the dome, witnessing the quire ceiling mosaics and visiting the tombs of Admiral Nelson and the Duke of Wellington.

EUGENE REGIS / SHUTTERSTOCK ©

Light of the World, which depicts Christ knocking at a weed-covered door that, symbolically, can only be opened from within. Beyond, in the cathedral's heart, you'll find the spectacular **quire** (or chancel) – its ceilings and arches dazzling with green, blue, red and gold mosaics telling the story of creation – and the **high altar**. The ornately carved choir stalls by Dutch–British sculptor Grinling Gibbons on either side of the quire are exquisite, as are the ornamental wrought-iron gates, separating the aisles from the altar, by Huguenot Jean Tijou (both men also worked on Hampton Court Palace).

Walk around the altar, with its massive gilded oak **baldacchino** – a kind of canopy with barley-twist columns – to the **American Memorial Chapel**, commemorating the 28,000 Americans based in Britain who lost their lives during WWII. Note the Roll of Honour book turned daily, the state flags in the stained glass and American flora and fauna in the carved wood panelling.

In the south quire aisle, Bill Viola's new and very poignant **video installation** *Martyrs (Earth, Air, Fire, Water)* depicts four figures being overwhelmed by natural forces. A bit further on is an **effigy of John Donne** (1573–1631), metaphysical poet and one-time dean of Old St Paul's that survived the Great Fire.

Crypt

On the eastern side of both the north and south transepts are stairs leading down to the crypt and the **OBE Chapel**, where services are held for members of the Order of the British Empire. The crypt has memorials to around 300 of the great and the good, including Florence Nightingale,

✕ Take a Break

The **Crypt Cafe** (Map p245; Crypt, St Paul's Cathedral, EC4; dishes £5.65-8.25; ⊙9am-5pm Mon-Sat, 10am-4pm Sun; ⊜St Paul's) is open for light meals from 9am.

TE Lawrence (of Arabia) and Winston Churchill, while both the Duke of Wellington and Admiral Nelson are actually buried here. On the surrounding walls are plaques in memory of those from the Commonwealth who died in various conflicts during the 20th century, including Gallipoli and the Falklands War.

Wren's tomb is also in the crypt, and many others, notably painters such as Joshua Reynolds, John Everett Millais, JMW Turner and William Holman Hunt, are remembered here, too.

The **Oculus**, in the former treasury, projects four short films onto its walls (you'll need the iPad audio tour to hear the sound). If you're not up to climbing the dome, experience it here audiovisually.

Exterior

Just outside the north transept, there's a simple **monument to the people of London**, honouring the 32,000 civilians killed (and another 50,000 seriously injured) in the city during WWII. Also to the north, at the entrance to Paternoster Sq, is **Temple Bar**, one of the original gateways to the City of London. This medieval stone archway once straddled Fleet St at a site marked by a silver dragon, but was removed to Middlesex in 1877. It was placed here in 2004.

Tours

The easiest way to explore the cathedral is by joining a free 1½-hour guided tour, which grants you access to the Geometric Staircase, the Chapel of St Michael and St George, and the quire. These usually take place four times a day (10am, 11am, 1pm and 2pm) Monday to Saturday – head to the desk just past the entrance to check times and book a place. You can also enquire here about the shorter introductory 15- to 20-minute talks.

What's Nearby?

Museum of London   Museum

(Map p245; www.museumoflondon.org.uk; 150 London Wall, EC2; ☉10am-6pm; ⊖Barbican) FREE One of the capital's best museums, this is a fascinating walk through the various incarnations of the city, from Roman Londinium and Anglo-Saxon Ludenwic to 21st-century metropolis, contained in two-dozen galleries. There are a lot of interactive displays with an emphasis on experience rather than learning.

Highlights include a video on the 1348 Black Death, a section of London's old Roman wall, the graffitied walls of a prison cell (1750), a glorious re-creation of a Victorian street, a 1908 taxi cab, a 1928 art-deco lift from Selfridges and moving WWII testimonies from ordinary Londoners.

Interior of St Paul's Cathedral

Free half-hour highlights tours depart daily at 11am, noon, 3pm and 4pm.

Millennium Bridge
Bridge

(Map p245; ⊖St Paul's or Blackfriars) The elegant steel, aluminium and concrete Millennium Bridge staples the south bank of the Thames, in front of Tate Modern, to the north bank, at the steps of Peter's Hill below St Paul's Cathedral. The low-slung frame designed by Sir Norman Foster and Antony Caro looks spectacular, particularly when lit up at night with fibre optics, and the view of St Paul's from the South Bank has become one of London's iconic images.

St Mary-le-Bow
Church

(Map p245; ☑020-7248 5139; www. stmarylebow.co.uk; Cheapside, EC2; ⊙7.30am-6pm Mon-Wed, to 6.30pm Thu, to 4pm Fri; ⊖St Paul's, Bank) One of Wren's great churches,

St Mary-le-Bow (1673) is famous as the church with the bells that still dictate who is – and who is not – a true Cockney: it's said that a true Cockney has to have been born within earshot of Bow Bells. The church's delicate steeple showing the four classical orders is one of Wren's finest works.

❶ Local Knowledge

The cathedral underwent a major clean-up in 2011. To see the difference, check the section of unrestored wall under glass by the Great West Door.

★ Top Tip

If you'd rather explore on your own, pick up one of the free 1½-hour multi-media tours available at the entrance.

KOTSOVOLOS PANAGIOTIS / SHUTTERSTOCK ©

View of Big Ben from beneath the London Eye (p94)

The South Bank

Ever since the London Eye came up in 2000, the South Bank has become a magnet for visitors and the area is always a buzz of activity. A roll call of riverside sights stretches along the Thames, commencing with the London Eye, running past the cultural enclave of the Southbank Centre and on to the Tate Modern.

Great For...

❶ Need to Know

◉ Waterloo or Southwark

★ **Top Tip**

Book online for the London Eye and London Dungeon to skip queues.

The South Bank has a great vibe. As well as top attractions, there is plenty to take in whilst enjoying a stroll: views of the north bank of London (including great views of the Houses of Parliament and Big Ben), street artists, office workers on their lunchtime run, and boats toing and froing along the Thames.

South Bank Sights

London Eye   Viewpoint

(Map p245; ☎0871-222 4002; www.londoneye. com; adult/child £23.45/18.95; ⊙11am-6pm Sep-May, 10am-8.30pm Jun-Aug; ⊜Waterloo or Westminster) Standing 135m high in a fairly flat city, the London Eye affords views 25 miles in every direction, weather permitting. Interactive tablets provide great information (in six languages) about landmarks as they come up in the skyline. Each rotation takes a gracefully slow 30 minutes. At peak times (July, August and school holidays) it may seem like you'll spend more time in the queue than in the capsule, so save time and money by buying tickets online.

Southbank Centre   Arts Centre

(Map p245; ☎020-7960 4200; www. southbankcentre.co.uk; Belvedere Rd, SE1; ⚐; ⊜Waterloo or Embankment) The flagship venue of the Southbank Centre, Europe's largest centre for performing and visual arts, is the **Royal Festival Hall**. Its gently curved facade of glass and Portland stone is more humane than its 1970s Brutalist neighbours. It is one of London's leading music venues and the epicentre of life on this part of the South Bank, hosting cafes, restaurants, shops and bars.

View from the London Eye

Just north, the austere Queen Elizabeth Hall is a Brutalist icon and the second-largest concert venue in the centre, hosting chamber orchestras, quartets, choirs, dance performances and sometimes opera. Underneath its elevated floor is a graffiti-decorated **skateboarders' hang-out**.

The opinion-dividing 1968 **Hayward Gallery** (Map p245; www.southbankcentre.co.uk; Belvedere Rd, SE1; ⊖Waterloo), another Brutalist beauty, is a leading contemporary-art exhibition space.

The QEH and Hayward Gallery are both closed until April 2018 for 21st-century facelifts.

☑ **Don't Miss**

The astounding views from the London Eye.

PAWEL LIBERA / GETTY IMAGES ©

London Dungeon   Historic Building

(Map p245; www.thedungeons.com/london; County Hall, Westminster Bridge Rd, SE1; adult/child £30/24; ⊗10am-5pm Mon-Fri, to 6pm Sat & Sun; 👶; ⊖Waterloo or Westminster) Older kids tend to love the London Dungeon, as the terrifying queues during school holidays and weekends testify. It's all spooky music, ghostly boat rides, macabre hangman's drop-rides, fake blood and actors dressed up as torturers and gory criminals (including Jack the Ripper and Sweeney Todd). Beware the interactive bits.

What's Nearby?

Roupell Street   Street

(Map p245; Roupell St, SE1; ⊖Waterloo) Waterloo station isn't exactly scenic, but wander around the back streets of this transport hub and you'll find some amazing architecture. Roupell St is an astonishingly pretty row of workers' cottages, all dark bricks and coloured doors, dating back to the 1820s. The street is so uniform it looks like a film set.

Imperial War Museum   Museum

(www.iwm.org.uk; Lambeth Rd, SE1; ⊗10am-6pm; ⊖Lambeth North) FREE Fronted by a pair of intimidating 15in naval guns, this riveting museum is housed in what was the Bethlehem Royal Hospital, also known as Bedlam. Although the museum's focus is on military action involving British or Commonwealth troops largely during the 20th century, it rolls out the carpet to war in the wider sense. The highlight of the collection is the state-of-the-art **First World War Galleries**, opened in 2014 to mark the centenary of the war's outbreak.

The museum is a short tube or bus ride from the South Bank and well worth the effort for anyone interested in WWI or WWII.

✖ **Take a Break**

For tip-top coffee in a bohemian setting, head to Scootercaffe (p179).

The Serpentine

Hyde Park

London's largest royal park spreads itself over 142 hectares of neat gardens, wild grasses and glorious trees. Not only is it a fantastic green space in the middle of London, it is also home to a handful of fascinating sights.

Henry VIII expropriated Hyde Park from the church in 1536, after which it emerged as a hunting ground for kings and aristocrats; later it became a popular venue for duels, executions and horse racing. It was the first royal park to open to the public in the early 17th century, the famous venue of the Great Exhibition in 1851 and became a vast potato bed during WWII. These days, as well as being an exquisite park, it is an occasional concert and music-festival venue.

Green Spaces

The eastern half of the park is covered with expansive lawns, which become one vast picnic-and-frolic area on sunny days. The western half is more untamed, with plenty of trees and areas of wild grass.

Great For...

☑ **Don't Miss**

The Albert Memorial and Kensington Palace.

Albert Memorial (p99)

ℹ Need to Know

Map p250; www.royalparks.org.uk/parks/
hyde-park; ⊙5am-midnight; ⊖Marble Arch,
Hyde Park Corner or Queensway

✕ Take Break

Stop off at the Orangery (p142), in
the grounds of Kensington Palace, for
afternoon tea or a pastry.

★ Top Tip

Being so central, Hyde Park is an ideal
picnic stop between sights.

---

p250; ⊖Knightsbridge or South Kensington), a
small lake.

The Serpentine Galleries

Straddling the Serpentine lake, the
Serpentine Galleries (Map p250; www.
serpentinegalleries.org; Kensington Gardens,
W2; ⊙10am-6pm Tue-Sun; ⊖Lancaster Gate
or Knightsbridge) **FREE** may look like quaint
historical buildings, but they are one of London's most important contemporary-art
galleries. Damien Hirst, Andreas Gursky,
Louise Bourgeois, Gabriel Orozco, Tomoko
Takahashi and Jeff Koons have all exhibited
here.

The original exhibition space is the 1930s
former tea pavillion located in Kensington
Gardens. In 2013 the gallery opened the
Serpentine Sackler Gallery within the Magazine, a former gunpowder depot, across
the Serpentine Bridge in Hyde Park. Built in
1805, it has been augmented with a daring,
undulating extension designed by Pritzker
Prize–winning architect Zaha Hadid.

Speakers' Corner

Frequented by Karl Marx, Vladimir Lenin,
George Orwell and William Morris, **Speak-
ers' Corner** (Map p250; Park Lane; ⊖Marble
Arch) in the northeastern corner of Hyde
Park is traditionally the spot for oratorical
acrobatics and soapbox ranting.

It's the only place in Britain where dem-
onstrators can assemble without police
permission, a concession granted in 1872
after serious riots 17 years before when
150,000 people gathered to demonstrate
against the Sunday Trading Bill before Parliament, only to be unexpectedly ambushed
by police concealed within Marble Arch.

The Serpentine

Hyde Park is separated from Kensington
Gardens by the L-shaped **Serpentine** (Map

Diana, Princess of Wales Memorial Fountain

This **memorial fountain** (Map p250; ⊖Knightsbridge or Lancaster Gate) is dedicated to the late Princess of Wales. Designed by Kathryn Gustafson as a 'moat without a castle', the circular double stream is composed of 545 pieces of Cornish granite, its waters drawn from a chalk aquifer more than 100m below ground. Unusually, visitors are actively encouraged to splash about, to the delight of children.

Gun Salutes

Royal Gun Salutes are fired in Hyde Park on 10 June for the Duke of Edinburgh's birthday and on 14 November for the Prince of Wales' birthday. The salutes are fired at midday and include 41 rounds (21 is stand-ard, but being a royal park, Hyde Park gets a bonus 20 rounds).

What's Nearby?

Kensington Palace   Palace
(Map p250; www.hrp.org.uk/kensingtonpalace; Kensington Gardens, W8; adult/child £16.30/free; ⊘10am-6pm Mar-Oct, to 5pm Nov-Feb; ⊖High St Kensington) Built in 1605, the palace became the favourite royal residence under William and Mary of Orange in 1689 and remained so until George III became king and relocated to St James's Palace. Today, it is still a royal residence, with the likes of the Duke and Duchess of Cambridge (Prince William and his wife Catherine) and Prince Harry living there. A large part of the palace is open to the public, however, including the King's and Queen's State Apartments.

The Serpentine Galleries (p97)

The **King's State Apartments** are the most lavish, starting with the **Grand Staircase**, a dizzying feast of trompe l'oeil. The beautiful **Cupola Room**, once the venue of choice for music and dance, is arranged with gilded statues and a gorgeous painted ceiling. The **Drawing Room** is beyond, where the king and courtiers would entertain themselves with cards.

Visitors can also access **Victoria's apartments** where Queen Victoria (1819–1901) was born and lived until she became Queen. An informative narrative about her life is told through a few personal effects, extracts from her journals and plenty of visual props.

Kensington Gardens — Park

(Map p250; www.royalparks.org.uk/parks/kensington-gardens; ⊘6am-dusk; ⊖Queensway or Lancaster Gate) Immediately west of Hyde Park and across the Serpentine lake, these picturesque 275-acre gardens are technically part of Kensington Palace. The park is a gorgeous collection of manicured lawns, tree-shaded avenues and basins. The largest is the **Round Pond**, close to the palace. Also worth a look are the lovely fountains in the **Italian Gardens** (Map p250; Kensington Gardens; ⊖Lancaster Gate), believed to be a gift from Albert to Queen Victoria.

Albert Memorial — Monument

(Map p250; ✐tours 020-8969 0104; Kensington Gardens; tours adult/concession £8/7; ⊘tours 2pm & 3pm 1st Sun of month Mar-Dec; ⊖Knightsbridge or Gloucester Rd) This splendid Victorian confection on the southern edge of Kensington Gardens is as ostentatious as the subject. Queen Victoria's German husband Albert (1819–61) was purportedly humble. Albert explicitly insisted he did not want a monument; ignoring the good prince's wishes, the Lord Mayor instructed George Gilbert Scott to build the 53m-high, gaudy Gothic memorial in 1872.

☑ Don't Miss

An architect who has never built in the UK is annually commissioned to build a 'Summer Pavilion' (June to October) for the Serpentine Galleries.

RON ELLIS / SHUTTERSTOCK ©

★ Top Tip

Deckchairs are available for hire (1/4 hours £1.60/4.60) throughout the park from March to October.

John Madejski Garden, Victoria & Albert Museum

Victoria & Albert Museum

The Museum of Manufactures, as the V&A was known when it opened in 1852, was part of Prince Albert's legacy to the nation in the aftermath of the successful Great Exhibition of 1851. Its aims were the 'improvement of public taste in design' and 'applications of fine art to objects of utility'. It's done a fine job so far.

Great For...

Victoria & Albert Museum

Exhibition Rd

Thurloe Pl

Cromwell Rd

Thurloe Pl

South Kensington

ℹ Need to Know

V&A; Map p250; www.vam.ac.uk; Cromwell Rd, SW7; ⏱10am-5.45pm Sat-Thu, to 10pm Fri; ⊖South Kensington **FREE**

★ **Top Tip**

The V&A's temporary exhibitions are reliably fantastic, so factor some time to check them out.

Collection

Through 146 galleries, the museum houses the world's greatest collection of decorative arts, from ancient Chinese ceramics to modernist architectural drawings, Korean bronze and Japanese swords, cartoons by Raphael, gowns from the Elizabethan era, ancient jewellery, a Sony Walkman – and much, much more.

Tours

Several free one-hour guided tours leave the main reception area every day. Times are prominently displayed; alternatively, check the website for details.

Level 1

The street level is mostly devoted to art and design from India, China, Japan, Korea and Southeast Asia, as well as European art. One of the museum's highlights is the **Cast Courts** in rooms 46a and 46b, containing staggering plaster casts collected in the Victorian era, such as Michelangelo's *David*, acquired in 1858.

The **T.T. Tsui Gallery** (rooms 44 and 47e) displays lovely pieces, including a beautifully lithe wooden statue of Guanyin seated in *lalitasana* pose from AD 1200; also check out a leaf from the *Twenty Views of the Yuanmingyuan Summer Palace* (1781–86), revealing the Haiyantang and the 12 animal heads of the fountain (now ruins) in Beijing. Within the subdued lighting of the **Japan Gallery** (room 45) stands a fearsome suit of armour in the Domaru style. More than 400 objects are within the **Islamic Middle East Gallery** (room 42), including ceramics, textiles, carpets, glass and woodwork

Ceramics and glass works on display

from the 8th-century up to the years before WWI. The exhibition's highlight is the gorgeous mid-16th-century **Ardabil Carpet**.

For fresh air, the landscaped **John Madejski Garden** is a lovely shaded inner courtyard. Cross it to reach the original **Refreshment Rooms** (Morris, Gamble and Poynter Rooms), dating from the 1860s and redesigned by McInnes Usher McKnight Architects (MUMA), who also renovated the **Medieval and Renaissance galleries** (1350–1600) to the right of the Grand Entrance.

☑ Don't Miss

The temporary exhibitions, Chinese ceramics and Elizabethan gowns.

ANTON_IVANOV / SHUTTERSTOCK ©

Levels 2 & 4

The **British Galleries**, featuring every aspect of British design from 1500 to 1900, are divided between levels 2 (1500–1760) and 4 (1760–1900). Level 4 also boasts the **Architecture Gallery** (rooms 127 to 128a), which vividly describes architectural styles via models and videos, and the spectacular brightly illuminated **Contemporary Glass Gallery** (room 129).

Level 3

The **Jewellery Gallery** (rooms 91 to 93) is outstanding; the mezzanine level – accessed via the glass-and-perspex spiral staircase – glitters with jewel-encrusted swords, watches and gold boxes. The **Photographs Gallery** (room 100) is one of the nation's best, with access to over 500,000 images collected since the mid-19th century. **Design Since 1946** (room 76) celebrates design classics from a 1985 Sony credit-card radio to a 1992 Nike 'Air Max' shoe, Peter Ghyczy's Garden Egg Chair from 1968 and the now-ubiquitous selfie stick.

Level 6

Among the pieces in the **Ceramics Gallery** (rooms 136 to 146) – the world's largest – are standout items from the Middle East and Asia. The **Dr Susan Weber Gallery** (rooms 133 to 135) celebrates furniture design over the past six centuries.

✕ Take a Break

Stop for a coffee at the **V&A Cafe** (Map p250; Victoria & Albert Museum, Cromwell Rd, SW7; mains £6.95-11.50; ⏰10am-5.15pm Sat-Thu, to 9.30pm Fri; 🛜; Ⓔ South Kensington), if only to admire the magnificent Refreshment Rooms, which date from the 1860s.

Natural History Museum

This colossal building is infused with the irrepressible Victorian spirit of collecting, cataloguing and interpreting the natural world. The museum building is as much a reason to visit as the world-famous collection within. Seasonal events and excellent temporary exhibitions complete the package to make this one of the very best museums in London, especially for families.

Great For...

☑ Don't Miss

Its thunderous, animatronic Tyrannosaurus rex, fascinating displays about planet earth, the outstanding Darwin Centre and architecture straight from a Gothic fairy tale.

Hintze Hall

This grand central hall resembles a cathedral nave – quite fitting for a time when the natural sciences were challenging the biblical tenets of Christian orthodoxy. Naturalist and first superintendent of the museum Richard Owen celebrated the building as a 'cathedral to nature'.

Since summer 2017, the hall has been dominated by the skeleton of a blue whale, displayed in a diving position for dramatic effect. It replaced 'Dippy' the diplodocus skeleton cast, which had been the hall's main resident since the 1960s. The hall also features new displays giving a taster of what the museum holds in store.

Blue Zone

Undoubtedly the museum's star attraction, the **Dinosaurs Gallery** takes you on an

Gems in the Vault

DAVE M BENETT / GETTY IMAGES ©

Natural History Museum

Cromwell Rd

Thurloe Pl

South Kensington

❶ Need to Know

Map p250; www.nhm.ac.uk; Cromwell Rd, SW7; ⊙10am-5.50pm; ⊜South Kensington
FREE

✗ Take a Break

The Queen's Arms (p177) beckons with a cosy interior and a right royal selection of ales and ciders on tap.

★ Top Tip

Families can borrow an 'explorer backpack' or buy a themed discover trail (£1).

impressive overhead walkway, past a dro-maeosaurus (a small and agile meat eater) before reaching a roaring animatronic T-rex and then winding its way through skeletons, fossils, casts and fascinating displays about how dinosaurs lived and died.

Another highlight of this zone is the **Mammals & Blue Whale Gallery**, with its life-sized blue whale model and extensive displays on cetaceans.

Green Zone

While children love the Blue Zone, adults may prefer the Green Zone, especially the **Treasures in Cadogan Gallery**, on the 1st floor, which houses the museum's most prized possessions, each with a unique history. Exhibits include a chunk of moon rock, an Emperor Penguin egg collected by Captain Scott's expedition and a 1st

edition of Charles Darwin's *On the Origin of Species*.

Equally rare and exceptional are the gems and rocks held in the **Vault**, including a Martian meteorite and the largest emerald ever found.

Take a moment to marvel at the trunk section of a 1300-year-old **giant sequoia tree** on the 2nd floor: its size is mind boggling.

Back on the ground floor, the **Creepy Crawlies Gallery** is fantastic, delving into every aspect of insect life and whether they are friend or foe (both!).

Red Zone

This zone explores the ever-changing nature of our planet and the forces shaping it. The **earthquake simulator** (in the **Volcanoes & Earthquakes Gallery**), which recreates the 1995 Kobe earthquake in a grocery store (of which you can see footage) is a favourite, as is the **From the Beginning Gallery**, which retraces earth's history.

In **Earth's Treasury**, you can find out more about our planet's mineral riches and how they are being used in our everyday lives – from jewellery to construction and electronics.

Access to most of the galleries in the Red Zone is via **Earth Hall** and a very tall escalator that disappears into a large metal sculpture of earth. The most intact **stegosaurus fossil skeleton** ever found is displayed at the base.

Orange Zone

The **Darwin Centre** is the beating heart of the museum: this is where the museum's millions of specimens are kept and where its scientists work. The top two floors of the amazing '**cocoon**' building are dedicated to explaining the kind of research the museum does (and how) – windows allow you to see the researchers at work.

If you'd like to find out more, pop into the **Attenborough studio** (named after famous naturalist and broadcaster David Attenborough) for one of the daily talks with the museum's scientists. The studio also shows films throughout the day.

Exhibitions

The museum hosts regular exhibitions (admission fees apply), some of them on a recurrent basis. **Wildlife Photographer of the Year** (adult £10.50-13.50, child £6.50-8, family £27-36.90; ☉Oct-Sep), with its show-stopping images, recently celebrated its 50th year, and **Sensational Butterflies**, a tunnel tent on the East Lawn that swarms with what must originally have been called 'flutter-bys', has become a firm summer

Stegosaurus skeleton on display

favourite. In winter, the same lawn turns into a very popular **ice-skating rink**.

Gardens

A slice of English countryside in SW7, the beautiful **Wildlife Garden** next to the West Lawn encompasses a range of British lowland habitats, including a meadow with farm gates and a bee tree where a colony of honey bees fills the air.

In 2018 the eastern grounds are also due to be redesigned to feature a geological and palaeontological walk, with a bronze sculpture of Dippy as well as ferns and cycads.

★ Top Tip

As well as the obligatory dinosaur figurines and animal soft toys, the museum's shop has a fantastic collection of children's books.

ANDREI TUDORAN / SHUTTERSTOCK ©

What's Nearby?

Science Museum   Museum

(Map p250; www.sciencemuseum.org.uk; Exhibition Rd, SW7; ☺10am-6pm; ⊖South Kensington) **FREE** With seven floors of interactive and educational exhibits, this scientifically spellbinding museum will mesmerise adults and children alike, covering everything from early technology to space travel. A perennial favourite is **Exploring Space**, a gallery featuring genuine rockets and satellites and a full-sized replica of *Eagle*, the lander that took Neil Armstrong and Buzz Aldrin to the moon in 1969. The **Making the Modern World Gallery** next door is a visual feast of locomotives, planes, cars and other revolutionary inventions.

The fantastic **Information Age Gallery** on level 2 showcases how information and communication technologies – from the telegraph to smartphones – have transformed our lives since the 19th century. Standout displays include wireless sent by a sinking *Titanic,* the first BBC radio broadcast and a Soviet BESM 1965 supercomputer.

The 3rd-floor **Flight Gallery** (free tours 1pm most days) is a favourite place for children, with its gliders, hot-air balloons and aircraft, including the *Gipsy Moth,* which Amy Johnson flew to Australia in 1930. This floor also features a **Red Arrows 3D flight simulation theatre** (adult/children £6/5) and **Fly 360 degree flight simulator capsules** (£12 per capsule). **Launchpad**, on the same floor, is stuffed with (free) hands-on gadgets exploring physics and the properties of liquids.

If you've got kids under the age of five, pop down to the basement and the **Garden**, where there's a fun-filled play zone, including a water-play area besieged by tots in orange waterproof smocks.

❶ Did You Know?

The museum and its gardens cover a huge 5.7 hectares; the museum contains 80 million specimens from across the natural world.

Statue of Anteros at the centre of Piccadilly Circus

Leicester Square & Piccadilly Circus

This duo of squares make up in buzz what they lack in cultural cachet. It's all flashing signs and crowds, yet no visit to London would be complete without passing through these iconic places.

Great For...

☑ Don't Miss

Celebrity-spotting at film premieres on Leicester Sq.

Piccadilly Circus

John Nash had originally designed Regent St and Piccadilly in the 1820s to be the two most elegant streets in town but, curbed by city planners, couldn't realise his dream to the full. He may be disappointed, but suitably astonished, with Piccadilly Circus today: a traffic maelstrom, deluged with visitors and flanked by flashing advertisement panels.

At the centre of the circus stands the famous aluminium statue, Anteros, twin brother of Eros, dedicated to the philanthropist and child-labour abolitionist Lord Shaftesbury. Through the years, the figure has been mistaken for Eros, the God of Love, and the misnomer has stuck (you'll even see signs for 'Eros' from the Underground).

Leicester Square

❶ Need to Know

Map p245; ⊖Leicester Square or Piccadilly Circus

✕ Take a Break

For delicious Levantine food with attitude, head to Palomar (p147).

★ Top Tip

Tkts Leicester Sq (www.tkts.co.uk/leicester-square; ⊗10am-7pm Mon-Sat, 11am-4.30pm Sun; ⊖Leicester Sq) **is the place to grab bargain tickets to West End performances.**

What's Nearby?
Chinatown   Area

(Map p248; www.chinatownlondon.org; ⊖Leicester Sq) Immediately north of Leicester Sq – but a world away in atmosphere – are Lisle and Gerrard Sts, a focal point for London's growing Chinese community. Although not as big as Chinatowns in many other cities – it's just two streets really – this is a lively quarter with oriental gates, Chinese street signs, red lanterns, restaurants, great Asian supermarkets and shops. The quality of food varies enormously, but there's a good choice of places for dim sum and other cuisine from across China.

To see it at its effervescent best, time your visit for Chinese New Year in mid-February. Twenty years ago you would only hear Cantonese but these days you'll hear Mandarin and other dialects, from places as far afield as Fujian, Sichuan and Shanghai. London's original Chinatown was further east at Limehouse but moved here after heavy bombardments in WWII.

Leicester Square

Although Leicester Sq was very fashionable in the 19th century, more recent decades won it associations with pickpocketing, outrageous cinema-ticket prices and the nickname 'Fester Sq' during the 1979 Winter of Discontent strikes, when it was filled with refuse. As part of the Diamond Jubilee and 2012 Olympics celebrations, the square was given an extensive £15.5 million makeover to turn it once again into a lively plaza. Today a sleek, open-plan design replaces the once-dingy little park.

It retains its many cinemas and nightclubs, and as a glamorous premiere venue it still attracts celebrities and their spotters. Pickpocketing used to be rife around Leicester Sq; things have improved but do keep a very close eye on your belongings.

Day Trip: Hampton Court Palace

London's most spectacular Tudor palace is a 16th-century icon that concocts an imposing sense of history, from the huge kitchens and grand living quarters to the spectacular gardens, complete with a 300-year-old maze. Tag along with a themed tour led by a costumed historian or grab one of the audio tours to delve into Hampton Court and its residents' tumultuous history.

Great For...

ℹ️ Need to Know

www.hrp.org.uk/hamptoncourtpalace; adult/child/family £19/9.50/47; ⊙10am-6pm Apr-Oct, to 4.30pm Nov-Mar; ⌘Hampton Court Palace, ⓡHampton Court

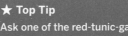

★ **Top Tip**
Ask one of the red-tunic-garbed warders for anecdotes and information.

Hampton Court Palace was built by Cardinal Thomas Wolsey in 1515, but was coaxed from him by Henry VIII just before Wolsey (as chancellor) fell from favour. It was already one of the most sophisticated palaces in Europe when, in the 17th century, Sir Christopher Wren was commissioned to build an extension. The result is a beautiful blend of Tudor and 'restrained baroque' architecture.

Entering the Palace

Passing through the magnificent main gate, you arrive first in the **Base Court** and beyond that the **Clock Court**, named after its 16th-century astronomical clock. The panelled rooms and arched doorways in **Young Henry VIII's Story** upstairs from Base Court provide a rewarding introduction: note the Tudor graffiti on the fireplace.

Henry VIII's Apartments

The stairs inside Anne Boleyn's Gateway lead up to Henry VIII's Apartments, including the stunning **Great Hall**. The **Horn Room**, hung with impressive antlers, leads to the **Great Watching Chamber**, where guards controlled access to the king. Henry VIII's dazzling gemstone-encrusted **crown** has been recreated – the original was melted down by Oliver Cromwell – and sits in the **Royal Pew** (open 10am to 4pm Monday to Saturday and 12.30pm to 1.30pm Sunday), which overlooks the beautiful **Chapel Royal** (still a place of worship after 450 years).

Tudor Kitchens & Great Wine Cellar

Also dating from Henry's day are the delightful Tudor kitchens, once used to rustle

The gardens

up meals for a royal household of some 1200 people. Don't miss the Great Wine Cellar, which handled the 300 barrels each of ale and wine consumed here annually in the mid-16th century.

Cumberland Art Gallery

The Cumberland Suite off Clock Court is the venue for a staggering collection of artworks from the Royal Collection, including Rembrandt's *Self-portrait in a Flat Cap* (1642) and Sir Anthony van Dyck's *Charles I on Horseback* (c 1635–6).

☑ Don't Miss

The Great Hall, the Chapel Royal, William III's apartments, the gardens and maze, and Henry VIII's crown.

PLUSONE / SHUTTERSTOCK ©

William III's & Mary II's Apartments

A tour of William III's Apartments, completed by Wren in 1702, takes you up the grand **King's Staircase**. Highlights include the **King's Presence Chamber**, dominated by a throne backed with scarlet hangings. The sumptuous **King's Great Bedchamber**, with a bed topped with ostrich plumes, and the **King's Closet** (where His Majesty's toilet has a velvet seat) should not be missed. Restored and reopened in 2014, the unique **Chocolate Kitchens** were built for William and Mary in around 1689.

William's wife Mary II had her own apartments, accessible via the fabulous **Queen's Staircase** (decorated by William Kent).

Georgian Private Apartments

The Georgian Rooms were used by George II and Queen Caroline on the court's last visit to the palace in 1737. Do not miss the fabulous Tudor **Wolsey Closet** with its early 16th-century ceiling and painted panels, commissioned by Henry VIII.

Garden & Maze

Beyond the palace are the stunning gardens; keep an eye out for the **Real Tennis Court**, dating from the 1620s. Originally created for William and Mary, the **Kitchen Garden** is a magnificent, recently opened re-creation.

No one should leave Hampton Court without losing themselves in the 800m-long **maze** (adult/child/family £4.40/2.80/13.20; ⏰10am-5.15pm Apr-Oct, to 3.45pm Nov-Mar; 🚢Hampton Court Palace, 🚃Hampton Court), also accessible to those not entering the palace.

★ Top Tip

Between April and September, **Westminster Passenger Services Association** (Map p248; 📞020-7930 2062; www.wpsa.co.uk; return to Hampton Court adult/child £25/12.50; 🚇Westminster) runs boat services between Westminster and Hampton Court.

Royal Observatory

Royal Observatory & Greenwich Park

The Royal Observatory is where the study of the sea, the stars and time converge. The prime meridian charts its line through the grounds of the observatory, dividing the globe into the eastern and western hemispheres. The observatory sits atop a hill within leafy and regal Greenwich Park with fabulous views.

Great For...

☑ Don't Miss

Straddling hemispheres and time zones as you stand astride the actual meridian line in the Meridian Courtyard.

Royal Observatory

Unlike most other attractions in Greenwich, the Royal Observatory contains free-access areas (Weller Astronomy Galleries, Great Equatorial Telescope) and ones you pay for (Meridian Line, Flamsteed House).

Flamsteed House & Meridian Courtyard

Charles II ordered construction of the Christopher Wren–designed Flamsteed House, the original observatory building, on the foundations of Greenwich Castle in 1675 after closing the observatory at the Tower of London. Today it contains the magnificent **Octagon Room** and the rather simple apartment where the Astronomer Royal, John Flamsteed, lived with his family. Here you'll also find the brilliant new **Time Galleries**, explaining how the longitude

The Time Ball at the top of the Royal Observatory

BASPHOTO / SHUTTERSTOCK ©

ℹ️ Need to Know

Map p256; www.rmg.co.uk; Greenwich Park, Blackheath Ave, SE10; adult/child £9.50/5, with Cutty Sark £18.50/8.50; ⏱10am-5pm Sep-Jun, to 6pm Jul-Aug; 🚇DLR Cutty Sark, 🚇DLR Greenwich, 🚉Greenwich

✕ Take a Break

Enjoy a drink with river views on the side at the Cutty Sark Tavern (p177).

★ Top Tip

Get here before 1pm on any day of the week to see the red Time Ball at the top of the Royal Observatory drop.

---

problem – how to accurately determine a ship's east–west location – was solved through astronomical means and the invention of the marine chronometer.

In the Meridian Courtyard, where the globe is decisively sliced into east and west, visitors can delightfully straddle both hemispheres, with one foot on either side of the meridian line. Every day the red **Time Ball** at the top of the Royal Observatory drops at 1pm, as it has done ever since 1833.

Astronomy Centre & Planetarium

The southern half of the observatory contains the highly informative (and free) **Weller Astronomy Galleries**, where you can touch the oldest object you will ever encounter: part of the Gibeon meteorite, a mere 4.5 billion years old. Other engaging exhibits include an orrery (a mechanical

model of the solar system, minus the as-yet-undiscovered Uranus and Neptune) from 1780, astronomical documentaries, a first edition of Newton's *Principia Mathematica* and the opportunity to view the Milky Way in multiple wavelengths. To take stargazing further, pick up a Skyhawk telescope from the shop.

The state-of-the-art **Peter Harrison Planetarium** (Map p256; ☎020-8312 6608; www.rmg.co.uk/whats-on/planetarium-shows; adult/child £7.50/5.50; 🚉Greenwich, 🚇DLR Cutty Sark) – London's only planetarium – can cast entire heavens on to the inside of its roof. It runs at least five informative shows a day. Bookings advised.

Greenwich Park

The **park** (Map p256; www.royalparks.org. uk; King George St, SE10; ⏱6am-6pm winter, to 8pm spring & autumn, to 9pm summer; 🚇DLR Cutty Sark, 🚉Greenwich or Maze Hill) is one of London's loveliest expanses of green, with a rose garden, picturesque walks,

Anglo-Saxon tumuli and astonishing views from the crown of the hill near the Royal Observatory towards Canary Wharf, the financial district across the Thames.

Covering 74 hectares, this is the oldest enclosed royal park and is partly the work of André Le Nôtre, the landscape architect who designed the palace gardens of Versailles.

Ranger's House (Werhner Collection)

This elegant Georgian **villa** (EH; Map p256; 020-8294 2548; www.english-heritage. org.uk; Greenwich Park, Chesterfield Walk, SE10; adult/child £7.60/4.60; guided tours only at 11.30am & 2pm Sun-Wed late Mar-Sep; Greenwich, DLR Cutty Sark), built in 1723, once housed the park's ranger and now

contains a collection of 700 works of fine and applied art (medieval and Renaissance paintings, porcelain, silverware, tapestries) amassed by Julius Wernher (1850–1912), a German-born railway engineer's son who struck it rich in the diamond fields of South Africa in the 19th century.

What's Nearby?

Old Royal Naval College Historic Building

(Map p256; www.ornc.org; 2 Cutty Sark Gardens, SE10; grounds 8am-6pm, to 11pm in summer; DLR Cutty Sark) FREE Designed by Christopher Wren, the Old Royal Naval College is a magnificent example of monumental classical architecture. Parts are now used by the University of Greenwich and Trinity College of Music, but you can still visit the

View of the Royal Observatory from Greenwich Park

chapel and the extraordinary **Painted Hall** (shut until 2019 for renovations), which took artist Sir James Thornhill 19 years to complete. Hour-long, yeomen-led tours (£6) of the complex leave at noon daily, taking in areas not otherwise open to the public.

Cutty Sark
Museum

(Map p256; ☏020-8312 6608; www.rmg.co.uk/cuttysark; King William Walk, SE10; adult/child £13.50/7, with Royal Observatory £18.50/8.50; ☺10am-5pm Sep-Jun, to 6pm Jul-Aug; ☒DLR Cutty Sark) This Greenwich landmark, the last of the great clipper ships to sail between China and England in the 19th

> **❶ Local Knowledge**
>
> In autumn Greenwich Park is one of the best places to collect chestnuts in the capital.

BBA PHOTOGRAPHY / SHUTTERSTOCK ©

century, is now fully operational after six years and £25 million of extensive renovations largely precipitated by a disastrous fire in 2007. The exhibition in the ship's hold tells her story as a tea (and then wool and mixed cargo) clipper at the end of the 19th century.

Launched in 1869 in Scotland, she made eight voyages to China in the 1870s, sailing out with a mixed cargo and coming back with a bounty of tea. As you make your way up, there are films, interactive maps and plenty of illustrations and props to convey what life on board was like. Sleepovers for kids are available.

National Maritime Museum
Museum

(Map p256; www.rmg.co.uk/national-maritime-museum; Romney Rd, SE10; ☺10am-5pm; ☒DLR Cutty Sark) `FREE` Narrating the long and eventful history of seafaring Britain, the museum's exhibits are arranged thematically and highlights include *Miss Britain III* (the first boat to top 100mph on open water) from 1933, the 19m-long golden state barge built in 1732 for Frederick, Prince of Wales, the huge ship's propeller and the colourful figureheads installed on the ground floor. Families will love these, as well as the ship simulator and the children's gallery on the 2nd floor.

Adults are likely to prefer the fantastic (and slightly more serene) galleries such as **Voyagers: Britons and the Sea** on the ground floor, or the award-winning **Nelson, Navy, Nation 1688–1815**, which focuses on the history of the Royal Navy during the conflict-ridden 17th century. It provides an excellent look at the legendary national hero; the coat in which Nelson was fatally wounded during the Battle of Trafalgar takes pride of place.

> **✖ Take a Break**
>
> If you've had enough of sightseeing, pop into the small but atmospheric Greenwich Market (p140) for street food and independent designer stalls.

Granary Square

RON ELLIS / SHUTTERSTOCK ©

King's Cross

Formerly a dilapidated red-light district, King's Cross used to be a place better avoided. Fast forward a couple of decades, though, and the area has metamorphosed, now boasting cool hang-outs and luxury hotels.

Great For...

☑ Don't Miss

The Sir John Ritblatt Gallery at the British Library and the fountain on Granary Square.

Granary Square   Square
(Map p254; www.kingscross.co.uk; Stable St, N1; ⊖King's Cross St Pancras) Positioned by a sharp bend in the Regent's Canal north of King's Cross Station, Granary Sq is at the heart of a major redevelopment of a 27-hectare expanse once full of abandoned freight warehouses. Its most striking feature is a fountain made of 1080 individually lit water jets, which pulse and dance in sequence. On hot spring and summer days, it becomes a busy urban beach.

British Library   Library
(Map p254; www.bl.uk; 96 Euston Rd, NW1; ⊗galleries 9.30am-6pm Mon & Fri, to 8pm Tue-Thu, to 5pm Sat, 11am-5pm Sun; ⊖King's Cross St Pancras) **FREE** Consisting of low-slung redbrick terraces and fronted by a large plaza featuring an oversized statue of Sir Isaac Newton, Colin St John Wilson's British

The Platform 9¾ sign inside King's Cross Station

Library building is a love-it-or-hate-it affair (Prince Charles once famously likened it to a secret-police academy). Completed in 1998 it's home to some of the greatest treasures of the written word, including the *Codex Sinaiticus* (the first complete text of the New Testament), Leonardo da Vinci's notebooks and a copy of the *Magna Carta* (1215).

The most precious manuscripts are held in the **Sir John Ritblatt Gallery**, including the stunningly illustrated Jain sacred texts, explorer Captain Scott's final diary and Shakespeare's *First Folio* (1623). Music fans will love the Beatles' handwritten lyrics and original scores by Bach, Handel, Mozart and Beethoven.

ⓘ Need to Know

Map p245; ⊖King's Cross St Pancras

✕ Take a Break

Grain Store (p143), with its creative European cuisine, is a good example of King's Cross regeneration.

★ Top Tip

Harry Potter fans will want to seek out the Platform 9¾ sign inside King's Cross Station.

St Pancras Station & Hotel
Historic Building

(Map p254; ☑020-8241 6921; info@ luxuryvacationsuk.com; Euston Rd, NW1; ⊖King's Cross St Pancras) Looking at the jaw-dropping Gothic splendour of St Pancras, it's hard to believe that the 1873 Midland Grand Hotel languished empty for years and even faced demolition in the 1960s. Now home to a five-star hotel, 67 luxury apartments and the Eurostar terminal, the entire complex has been returned to its former glory. Tours take you on a fascinating journey through the building's history from its inception as the southern terminus for the Midlands Railway line.

Walking Tour: A Northern Point of View

This walk takes in North London's most interesting locales, including celebrity-infested Primrose Hill and chaotic Camden Town, home to loud guitar bands and the last of London's cartoon punks.

Start ⊖ Chalk Farm
Distance 2.5 miles
Duration 2 hours

Classic photo: London's skyline from atop Primrose Hill

2 In **Primrose Hill**, walk to the top of the park where you'll find a classic view of central London's skyline.

1 Affluent **Regent's Park Rd** is home to many darlings of the women's mags, so keep your eyes open for famous faces.

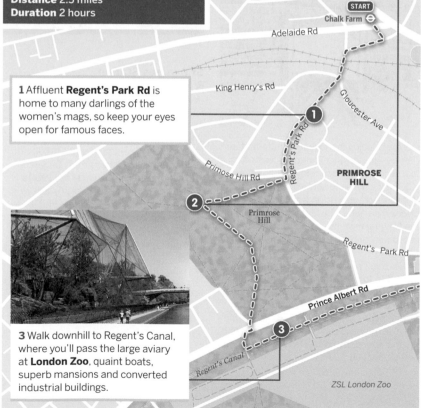

3 Walk downhill to Regent's Canal, where you'll pass the large aviary at **London Zoo**, quaint boats, superb mansions and converted industrial buildings.

0   400 m
0   0.2 miles

4 At **Camden Lock** turn left into buzzing **Camden Lock Market** (p162), with its original fashion, ethnic art and food stalls.

5 Exit onto **Camden High St** and turn right onto bar-lined **Inverness St**, which hosts its own little market.

Chalk Farm Rd

Camden Lock Pl

Camden High St

CAMDEN TOWN

Camden Rd

Regent's Canal

Jamestown Rd

Princes Rd

Gloucester Ave

Gloucester Cres

Inverness St

Oval Rd

6 At **Gloucester Cres** turn left and walk past the glorious Georgian townhouses.

Parkway

Take a Break...
Enjoy excellent British cuisine at **Market** (p143), where a two-course lunch will set you back only £11.50.

Delancey St

FINISH

Mornington Tce

Regent's Park

Albany St

7 Head toward Delancey St and make a beeline for the **Edinboro Castle** (p178), where this walk ends with a well-deserved drink!

2 GEORGE M HILES / SHUTTERSTOCK © 3 RICHARD NEWSTEAD / GETTY IMAGES © 4 CSP / SHUTTERSTOCK ©

Palm House (p124)

Day Trip: Kew Gardens

The 121-hectare gardens at Kew are the finest product of the British botanical imagination and really should not be missed. No worries if you don't know your quiver tree from your alang-alang, a visit to Kew is a journey of discovery for all.

Great For...

❶ Need to Know

www.kew.org; Kew Rd; adult/child £15/3.50; ◷10am-6.30pm Apr-Aug, closes earlier Sep-Mar; 🚤Kew Pier, 🚆Kew Bridge, ⊖Kew Gardens

★ **Top Tip**

Kew is a big place so if you're pressed for time, or getting tired, take the **Kew Explorer** (adult/child £5/2), a hop-on/hop-off road train that takes in the main sights.

ILONGLOVEKING / SHUTTERSTOCK ©

As well as being a public garden, Kew is also a pre-eminent research centre that maintains its reputation as the most exhaustive botanical collection in the world.

Conservatories

Assuming you travel by tube and enter via Victoria Gate, you'll come almost immediately to the enormous and elaborate 700-glass-paned **Palm House**, a domed hothouse of metal and curved sheets of glass dating from 1848, enveloping a splendid display of exotic tropical greenery; an aerial walkway offers a parrot's-eye view of the lush vegetation. Just northwest of the Palm House stands the tiny and irresistibly steamy **Waterlily House** (⊘Mar-Dec), sheltering the gigantic *Victoria cruziana* waterlily, whose vast pads can support the weight of a small adult.

In the southeast of Kew Gardens, **Temperate House** (built in 1860) is the world's largest surviving Victorian glasshouse, covering 4880 sq metres. It has been closed for vital restoration work since 2013 and is set to reopen in 2018.

The angular **Princess of Wales Conservatory** houses plants in 10 different climatic zones – everything from a desert to a mangrove swamp. Look out for stone plants, which resemble pebbles (to deter grazing animals), carnivorous plants, gigantic waterlilies, cacti and a collection of tropical orchids.

Chinese Pagoda

Kew's 49.5m-tall eight-sided Chinese Pagoda (1762), designed by William Chambers (the architect of Somerset House), is one of the gardens' architectural icons. During

Chinese Pagoda

WWII, the pagoda withstood the blast from a stick of Luftwaffe bombs exploding nearby and was also secretly employed by the Ministry of Defence to test bomb trajectories (which involved cutting holes in each floor!).

The pagoda is set to reopen to the public in early 2018 after extensive renovations, which include the reinstatement of 80 winged dragons. They were part of the original design but disappeared shortly after the tower's inauguration.

☑ Don't Miss

The Palm House, Rhizotron and Xstrata Treetop Walkway, Chinese Pagoda, Temperate House and the numerous vistas.

ALEXEY FEDORENKO / SHUTTERSTOCK ©

Kew Palace

The adorable red-brick **Kew Palace** (www.hrp.org.uk/kewpalace; with admission to Kew Gardens; 10.30am-5.30pm Apr-Sep), in the northwest of the gardens was built in 1631 and is the smallest of the royal palaces. This former royal residence was once known as Dutch House. It was the favourite home of George III and his family; his wife, Queen Charlotte, died here in 1818 (you can see the very chair in which she expired). Don't miss the restored **Royal Kitchens** next door.

Rhizotron & Xstrata Treetop Walkway

This fascinating walkway in the **Arboretum** first takes you underground and then 18m up in the air into the tree canopy (a big hit with kids).

Other Highlights

Several long vistas (**Cedar Vista**, **Syon Vista** and **Pagoda Vista**) are channelled by trees from vantage points within Kew Gardens. The idyllic, thatched **Queen Charlotte's Cottage** (11am-4pm Sat & Sun Apr-Sep) in the southwest of the gardens was popular with 'mad' George III and his wife; the carpets of bluebells around here are a drawcard in spring. The **Marianne North Gallery** displays the botanical paintings of Marianne North, an indomitable traveller who roamed the continents from 1871 to 1885, painting plants along the way.

Take a Break

The aptly named **Glasshouse** (020-8940 6777; www.glasshouserestaurant.co.uk; 14 Station Pde, TW9; 2/3-course lunch Mon-Sat £24.50/29.50, 3-course lunch Sun £32.50, 3-course dinner £47.50; noon-2.30pm & 6.30-10.30pm Mon-Sat, 12.30-3pm & 7-10pm Sun; ; Kew Gardens, Kew Gardens) restaurant, with its Michelin star, is the perfect conclusion to a day exploring the gardens.

The central atrium of the Design Museum

EUGENE REGIS / SHUTTERSTOCK ©

Design Museum

Relocated in 2016 from its former Thames location to a stunning new home by Holland Park, this slick museum is a crucial pit stop for anyone with an eye for modern and contemporary aesthetics.

Great For...

☑ **Don't Miss**

The Designer Maker User gallery and the museum's architecture.

Collections & Exhibitions

Dedicated to popularising the importance and influence of design in everyday life, the Design Museum has a revolving program of special exhibitions. Most exhibitions are ticketed (from £10), but the extensive 2nd-floor **Designer Maker User** gallery is free. Exploring the iconography of design classics, the gallery contains almost 1000 objects that trace the history of modern design, from 1980s Apple computers, to water bottles, typewriters, floppy disks and a huge advert for the timeless VW Beetle.

Iconic Building

Until 2016 the museum was housed in a former 1930s banana warehouse that had been given a 1930s modernist makeover by museum founder Terence Conrad. The building, located by the Thames in

Kyoto Garden, Holland Park

EXFLOW / SHUTTERSTOCK ©

ℹ Need to Know

Map p250; ✆020-7940 8790; www.design-museum.org; 224-238 Kensington High St, W8; ◷10am-5.45pm; ⊖High St Kensington

✕ Take a Break

For a delicious, modern take on Greek cuisine, head to Mazi (p151).

★ Top Tip

Choose a sunny day to visit and relax in Holland Park afterwards.

Bermondsey, was a design success but it became too small for the museum's growing collection. For its new home, the museum chose another design jewel: the former Commonwealth Institute building, a listed 1960s beauty, which was given a 21st-century, £83 million facelift for the occasion.

What's Nearby?

Holland Park   Park

(Map p250; Ilchester Pl; ◷7.30am-dusk; ⊖High St Kensington or Holland Park) This handsome park divides into dense woodland in the north, spacious and inviting lawns by Holland House, sports fields for the beautiful game and other exertions in the south, and some lovely gardens, including the restful Kyoto Garden. The park's many splendid peacocks are a gorgeous sight and an

adventure playground keeps kids occupied. Holland House – largely bombed to smithereens by the Luftwaffe in 1940 – is the venue of Opera Holland Park (p195) in summer.

Portobello Road
Market   Clothing, Antiques

(Map p250; www.portobellomarket.org; Portobello Rd, W10; ◷8am-6.30pm Mon-Wed, Fri & Sat, to 1pm Thu; ⊖Notting Hill Gate or Ladbroke Grove) Lovely on a warm summer's day, Portobello Road Market is an iconic London attraction with an eclectic mix of street food, fruit and veg, antiques, curios, collectables, vibrant fashion and trinkets. Although the shops along Portobello Rd open daily and the fruit and veg stalls (from Elgin Cres to Talbot Rd) only close on Sunday, the busiest day by far is Saturday, when antique dealers set up shop (from Chepstow Villas to Elgin Cres).

Oxford St adorned with Christmas decorations

IR STONE / SHUTTERSTOCK ©

Shopping in the West End

Shopping is part and parcel of a trip to London and the West End, with shop-lined Regent St and Oxford St, is probably the most high-profile shopping destination in the capital.

Great For...

☑ **Don't Miss**

The Christmas lights on Regent St and the sheer number of toys at Hamleys.

The shopping nerve centre of the West End are the elegantly curving Regent St and the dead-straight east–west artery of Oxford St.

Regent Street

The handsome border dividing the hoi polloi of Soho from the Gucci-two-shoed of Mayfair, Regent St was designed by John Nash as a ceremonial route linking the Prince Regent's long-demolished city dwelling with the 'wilds' of Regent's Park. Nash had to downscale his plan but Regent St is today a well-subscribed shopping street (as is pedestrian Carnaby St, which runs parallel to it, a block east) and a beautiful curve of listed architecture.

Its most famous tenant is undoubtedly Hamleys, London's premier toy and game store. Regent St is also famous for its

Light installation above Regent St

ⓘ Need to Know

Map p245; ⊖Marble Arch, Bond St, Oxford Circus, Tottenham Court Rd or Piccadilly Circus

✕ Take a Break

Yauatcha (p147) in Soho does the best dim-sum in town; it's not for nothing they have a Michelin star.

★ Top Tip

Shops in the West End open until 9pm on Thursdays (otherwise they usually close at 7pm or 8pm).

Christmas light displays, which get glowing with great pomp earlier and earlier (or so it seems) each year (usually around mid-November).

Hamleys
Toys

(Map p248; www.hamleys.com; 188-196 Regent St, W1; ⊘10am-9pm Mon-Fri, 9.30am-9pm Sat, noon-6pm Sun; ⊖Oxford Circus) Claiming to be the world's oldest (and some say largest) toy store, Hamleys moved to its address on Regent St in 1881. From the ground floor – where staff glide UFOs and foam boomerangs through the air with practised nonchalance – to Lego World and a cafe on the 5th floor, it's a layer cake of playthings.

Liberty
Department Store

(Map p248; www.liberty.co.uk; Great Marlborough St, W1; ⊘10am-8pm Mon-Sat, noon-6pm Sun; ⊖Oxford Circus) An irresistible blend of contemporary styles in an old-fashioned mock-Tudor atmosphere, Liberty has a huge cosmetics department and an accessories floor, along with a breathtaking lingerie section, all at very inflated prices. A classic London souvenir is a Liberty fabric print, especially in the form of a scarf.

We Built This City
Gifts & Souvenirs

(Map p248; www.webuilt-thiscity.com; 56-57 Carnaby St, W1; ⊘10am-7pm Mon-Wed, to 8pm Thu-Sat, noon-6pm Sun; ⊖Oxford Circus) Taking a commendable stand against Union Jack hats and black cab key rings, We Built This City is a shop selling London-themed souvenirs that the recipient might actually want. The products are artistic and thoughtful and celebrate the city's creative side.

Oxford Street

Oxford St is all about chains, from Marks & Spencer to H&M, Top Shop to Gap, with large branches of department stores, the most famous of which is Selfridges. The small lanes heading south towards Mayfair are a favourite for designer boutiques.

Selfridges
Department Store

(Map p250; www.selfridges.com; 400 Oxford St, W1; ⊙9.30am-10pm Mon-Sat, 11.30am-6pm Sun; ⊖Bond St) Selfridges loves innovation – it's famed for its inventive window displays by international artists, gala shows and, above all, its amazing range of products. It's the trendiest of London's one-stop shops, with labels such as Boudicca, Luella Bartley, Emma Cook, Chloé and Missoni. It has an unparalleled food hall and Europe's largest cosmetics department.

Stella McCartney
Fashion & Accessories

(Map p248; ☎020-7518 3100; www.stellamccartney.com; 30 Bruton St, W1;

⊙10am-7pm Mon-Sat; ⊖Bond St) ✦ Stella McCartney's sharp tailoring, floaty designs, accessible style and 'ethical' approach to fashion (no leather or fur) is very of-the-moment. This three-storey terraced Victorian home is a minimalist showcase for the designer's current collections. Depending on your devotion and wallet, you'll either feel at ease or like a trespasser.

Topshop
Clothing

(Map p248; ☎020-7927 0000; www.topshop.co.uk; 214 Oxford St, W1; ⊙9am-9pm Mon-Sat, 11.30am-6pm Sun; ⊖Oxford Circus) The 'it' store when it comes to clothes and accessories, venturing boldly into couture in recent years, Topshop encapsulates London's supreme skill at bringing catwalk fashion to the youth market affordably and quickly.

Selfridges

Browns   Clothing

(Map p250; ☎020-7629 1416; www.
brownsfashion.com; 23-27 South Molton St, W1;
⊙10am-7pm Mon-Wed & Sat, to 8pm Thu & Fri,
noon-6pm Sun; ⊖Bond St) Edgy and exciting,
this parade of shops on upscale South
Molton St is full of natty and individual
clothing ideas, and shoes from Asish, Stella
Jean, Natasha Zinko and other creative
designers.

★ Top Tip

Non-EU visitors should look out for
'tax free' signs in shop windows for
the opportunity to claim back 20%
value-added tax (VAT).

ELENA ROSTUNOVA / SHUTTERSTOCK ©

What's Nearby?

Soho   Area

(Map p248; ⊖Tottenham Court Rd, Leicester
Sq) In a district that was once pastureland,
the name Soho is thought to have evolved
from a hunting cry. While the centre of London nightlife has shifted east and Soho has
recently seen landmark clubs and music
venues shut down, the neighbourhood definitely comes into its own in the evenings
and remains a proud gay neighbourhood.
During the day you'll be charmed by the
area's bohemian side and its sheer vitality.

At Soho's northern end, leafy **Soho
Square** (Map p248; ⊖Tottenham Court Rd,
Leicester Sq) is the area's back garden. It
was laid out in 1681 and originally named
King's Sq; a statue of Charles II stands
in its northern half. In the centre is a tiny
half-timbered mock-Tudor cottage built as
a gardener's shed in the 1870s. The space
below it was used as an underground bomb
shelter during WWII.

South of the square is **Dean Street**,
lined with bars and restaurants. No 28 was
the home of Karl Marx and his family from
1851 to 1856; they lived here in extreme
poverty as Marx researched and wrote *Das
Kapital* in the Reading Room of the British
Museum.

Old Compton Street is the epicentre of
Soho's gay village. It's a street loved by all,
gay or otherwise, for its great bars, risqué
shops and general good vibes.

Seducer and heartbreaker Casanova and
opium-addicted writer Thomas de Quincey
lived on nearby Greek St, while the parallel
Frith Street housed Mozart at No 20 for a
year from 1764.

---

❶ Local Knowledge

Independent music stores find it
difficult to keep going nowadays, but
they seem to thrive in Soho, with its long
rock-and-roll tradition.

DINING OUT

Top-notch restaurants, gastropubs, afternoon tea and more

Dining Out

Once the laughing stock of the cooking world, London has got its culinary act together in the last 20 years and is today an undisputed dining destination. There are plenty of top-notch, Michelin-starred restaurants, but it is the sheer diversity on offer that is head-spinning: from Afghan to Vietnamese, London is a virtual A to Z of world cuisine.

You'll find that there are restaurants to suit every budget – and every occasion. Dinner in a fabulous restaurant is part and parcel of a great trip to London, but make sure you also sample the cheap and cheerful fare on offer in market stalls and sit down in one of the capital's tip-top cafes.

In This Section

Price Ranges & Tipping

These symbols indicate the average cost per main course at the restaurant in question.

£ less than £10

££ £10–20

£££ more than £20

Most restaurants automatically tack a 'discretionary' service charge (12.5%) onto the bill. If you feel the service wasn't adequate, you can tip separately (or not at all).

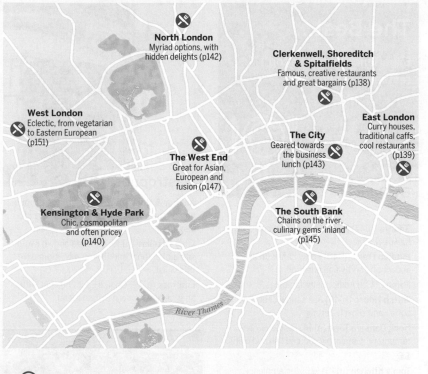

North London
Myriad options, with
hidden delights (p142)

Clerkenwell, Shoreditch
& Spitalfields
Famous, creative restaurants
and great bargains (p138)

West London
Eclectic, from vegetarian
to Eastern European
(p151)

East London
Curry houses,
traditional caffs,
cool restaurants
(p139)

The City
Geared towards
the business
lunch (p143)

The West End
Great for Asian,
European and
fusion (p147)

Kensington & Hyde Park
Chic, cosmopolitan
and often pricey
(p140)

The South Bank
Chains on the river,
culinary gems 'inland'
(p145)

River Thames

Useful Websites

Time Out London (www.timeout.com/ london) Has the most up-to-date listings of restaurants as well as information on harder-to-track pop-up eateries and food trucks.

Open Table (www.opentable.co.uk) Bookings for numerous restaurants, as well as meal deals with excellent discounts.

Wine Pages (www.wine-pages.com) Keeps a useful directory of BYO restaurants.

Classic Dishes

Pie & Mash Once a staple lunch – pie (usually beef) served with mashed potatoes, liquor (a parsley sauce) and jellied eels (we dare you!).

English Breakfast This champion's breakfast usually includes bacon, sausages, eggs, baked beans, tomatoes and mushrooms.

Sunday Roast Your choice of meat (lamb, beef etc) smothered in gravy and served with ballooning Yorkshire pudding, roast potatoes and a smorgasbord of vegetables.

The Best...

Experience London's top restaurants and cafes

By Budget

£

Shoryu (p147) Perfectly executed bowls of *tonkotsu* ramen.

Pimlico Fresh (p140) Perky cafe with an accent on good-value fine food.

Polpo (p138) Addictive Italian tapas.

Watch House (p146) Ace sandwiches, fine coffee and a lovely setting.

Hook Camden Town (p144) Fabulous, contemporary, sustainably sourced fish and chips.

££

Tom's Kitchen (p140) Relaxing ambience, warm staff, excellent food: you can't go wrong.

Palomar (p147) Excellent Jerusalem food for sharing with a foodie friend.

Rabbit (p140) Champions of modern British food and drink.

Baltic (p145) Authentic flavours from Eastern Europe in elegant decor.

Cafe Murano (p147) Northern Italian fare cooked to perfection and without fuss.

£££

Dinner by Heston Blumenthal (p141) A supreme fusion of perfect British food, eye-catching design and celeb stature.

Hawksmoor (p138) An essential destination for carnivores.

Arabica Bar & Kitchen (p145) Forget kebabs and belly-dancers: this is contemporary Middle Eastern cuisine at its best.

Ledbury (p151) A long-standing, scintillating culinary stalwart in West London.

Gastropubs

Anchor & Hope (p146) Flying the gastropub flag on the South Bank for the best part of a decade.

Lady Ottoline (p149; pictured above) Exquisite dining room and thoroughly impressive drinks list.

Empress (p139) Choice East End spot with an excellent modern British menu.

For Views

Duck & Waffle (p145) Hearty British dishes from the top of Heron Tower, round the clock.

Min Jiang (p142) Breathtaking panoramas over Kensington Gardens.

Portrait (p150) Classic views to Nelson's Column and beyond, down Whitehall to Big Ben.

British

St John (p138; pictured above) The restaurant that inspired the revival of British cuisine.

Rabbit (p140) Make it to King's Rd for some of the best British food in London.

Market (p143) A modern British decor for a modern British menu in Camden.

Great Queen St (p150) Quality roasts, stews and other British staples in relaxed atmosphere.

Indian

Tayyabs (p139; pictured above) Long-standing Punjabi favourite in the East End.

Dishoom (p149) Bombay cafe food as it really is served and eaten.

Gymkhana (p149) Splendid club-style Raj environment, top cuisine.

Celebrity Chef Restaurants

Dinner by Heston Blumenthal (p141) Molecular gastronomy at its very best.

Tom's Kitchen (p140; pictured above) Tom Aikens' relaxed Chelsea brasserie remains ever popular.

Cafes

Towpath (p139) Canal-side alfresco lattes: welcome to London.

Sky Pod (p143) The views and surroundings trump the coffee, but how could they not?

Tomtom Coffee House (p141; pictured above) No one takes their coffee more seriously than these guys.

Nude Espresso (p139) Kings of the single-origin coffee.

British Cuisine in a Nutshell

England might have given the world baked beans on toast, mushy peas and chip butties (French fries between two slices of buttered and untoasted white bread), but that's hardly the whole story.

Modern British food has become a cuisine in its own right, by championing traditional (and sometimes underrated) ingredients such as root vegetables, smoked fish, shellfish, game, sausages and black pudding (a kind of sausage stuffed with oatmeal, spices and blood). Dishes can be anything from game served with a traditional vegetable such as Jerusalem artichoke, to seared scallops with orange-scented black pudding, or roast pork with chorizo on rosemary mash.

England does a mean dessert and establishments serving British cuisine revel in these indulgent treats. Favourites include bread-and-butter pudding, sticky toffee pudding (a steamed pudding that contains dates and is topped with a divine caramel sauce), the alarmingly named spotted dick (a steamed suet pudding with currants and raisins), Eton mess (meringue, cream and strawberries mixed into a gooey, heavenly mess) and seasonal musts such as Christmas pudding (a steamed pudding with candied fruit and brandy) and fruity crumbles (rhubarb, apple etc).

Scotch eggs at Maltby Street Market (p146)
ELENACHAYKINAPHOTOGRAPHY / SHUTTERSTOCK ©

Clerkenwell, Shoreditch & Spitalfields

Polpo
Italian £
(Map p253; ☑020-7250 0034; www.polpo.co.uk; 3 Cowcross St, EC1M; dishes £4-12; ⊙11.30am-11pm Mon-Sat, to 4pm Sun; ⊖Farringdon) Occupying a sunny spot on semi-pedestrianised Cowcross St, this sweet little place serves rustic Venetian-style meatballs, *pizzette,* grilled meat and fish dishes. Portions are larger than your average tapas but a tad smaller than a regular main – the perfect excuse to sample more than one of the exquisite dishes. Exceptional value for money.

Hawksmoor
Steak £££
(Map p253; ☑020-7426 4850; www.the-hawksmoor.com; 157 Commercial St, E1; mains £20-50; ⊙noon-2.30pm & 5-10.30pm Mon-Sat, noon-9pm Sun; ☞; ⊖Liverpool St) You could easily miss discreetly signed Hawksmoor, but confirmed carnivores will find it worth seeking out. The dark wood, bare bricks and velvet curtains make for a handsome setting in which to gorge yourself on the best of British beef. The Sunday roasts (£20) are legendary.

Morito
Tapas ££
(Map p253; ☑020-7278 7007; www.morito.co.uk; 32 Exmouth Market, EC1R; dishes £6.50-9.50; ⊙noon-4pm & 5-11pm Mon-Sat, noon-4pm Sun; ☞; ⊖Farringdon) This diminutive eatery is a wonderfully authentic take on a Spanish tapas bar and has excellent eats. Seats are at the bar, along the window, or on one of the small tables inside or out. It's relaxed, convivial and often completely crammed; reservations are taken for lunch, but dinner is first come, first served, with couples generally going to the bar.

St John
British ££
(Map p253; ☑020-7251 0848; www.stjohngroup.uk.com/spitalfields; 26 St John St, EC1M; mains £14.80-24.90; ⊙noon-3pm & 6-11pm Mon-Fri, 6-11pm Sat, 12.30-4pm Sun; ⊖Farringdon) Whitewashed brick walls, high ceilings and simple wooden furniture don't make for a

cosy dining space but they do keep diners free to concentrate on St John's famous nose-to-tail dishes. Serves are big, hearty and a celebration of England's culinary past. Don't miss the signature roast bone marrow and parsley salad (£8.90).

Nude Espresso   Cafe £

(Map p253; www.nudeespresso.com; 26 Hanbury St, E1; dishes £4.50-12; ☉7am-6pm Mon-Fri, 9.30am-5pm Sat & Sun; ☺Liverpool St) A simply styled, cosy cafe serving top-notch coffee (roasted across the street). Along with the standard blend, it has rotating single-origin coffees and filter as well as espresso-based brews. The sweet treats are delicious, as are the cooked breakfasts, brunch items and light lunches.

✪ East London

Empress   Modern British ££

(Map p255; ☎020-8533 5123; www.empresse9. co.uk; 130 Lauriston Rd, E9; mains £16-18; ☉10am-9.30pm Sun, 6-10.15pm Mon, noon-3.30pm & 6-10.15pm Tue-Sat; 🚇277) This up-market pub conversion belts out excellent modern British cuisine in very pleasant surroundings. On Mondays there's a £10 main-plus-drink deal and on weekends it serves an excellent brunch.

Brawn   British, French ££

(Map p253; ☎020-7729 5692; www.brawn.co; 49 Columbia Rd, E2; mains £11.50-28; ☉noon-3pm Tue-Sat, 6-10.30pm Mon-Sat, noon-4pm Sun; ☺Hoxton) There's a Parisian bistro feel to this relaxed corner restaurant, yet the menu walks a fine line between British and French traditions. Hence oxtail and veal kidney pie sits alongside plaice Grenobloise, and souffles are filled with Westcombe cheddar. Try its legendary spicy Scotch-egg starter – a Brit classic delivered with French finesse. The three-course Sunday lunch is £28.

Corner Room   Modern British ££

(Map p255; ☎020-7871 0460; www.townhall-hotel.com/cornerroom; Patriot Sq, E2; mains £13-14, 2-/3-course lunch £19/23; ☉7.30-10am, noon-3pm & 6-9.45pm; ☺Bethnal Green) Some-

one put this baby in the corner, but we're certainly not complaining. Tucked away on the 1st floor of the Town Hall Hotel, this relaxed restaurant serves expertly crafted dishes with complex yet delicate flavours, highlighting the best of British seasonal produce.

Towpath   Cafe £

(Map p253; ☎020-7254 7606; rear 42-44 De Beauvoir Cres, N1; mains £6.50-9; ☉9am-5.30pm Tue-Sun; ☺Haggerston) Occupying four small units on the Regent's Canal towpath, this simple cafe is a super place to sip a cuppa and watch the ducks and narrowboats glide by. The food's excellent too, with delicious frittatas and brownies on the counter and cooked dishes chalked up on the blackboard daily.

Mangal Ocakbasi   Turkish ££

(Map p255; ☎020-7275 8981; www.mangal1.com; 10 Arcola St, E8; mains £8-18; ☉noon-midnight; ☝; ☺Dalston Kingsland) Mangal is the quintessential Turkish *ocakbasi* (open-hooded charcoal grill, the mother of all BBQs): cramped, smoky and serving superb mezze, grilled vegetables, lamb chops, quail and a lip-smacking assortment of kebabs. BYO alcohol.

Formans   Modern British ££

(Map p255; ☎020-8525 2365; www.formans. co.uk; Stour Rd, E3; mains £15-19.50, brunch £6-10; ☉7-11pm Thu & Fri, 10am-3pm & 7-11pm Sat, noon-5pm Sun; ☏; ☺Hackney Wick) Curing fish since 1905, riverside Formans boasts prime views over the Olympic stadium, with a gallery overlooking its smokery. The menu includes a delectable choice of smoked salmon (including its signature 'London cure'), plenty of other seafood and a few nonfishy things, as well as delicious sticky puddings. There's a great selection of British wines and spirits, too.

Tayyabs   Punjabi ££

(☎020-7247 9543; www.tayyabs.co.uk; 83-89 Fieldgate St, E1; mains £5.60-16; ☉noon-11.30pm; ☝; ☺Whitechapel) This buzzing (OK, crowded) Punjabi restaurant is in another league to its Brick Lane equivalents. *Seekh*

🍽️ Celebrity Chefs

London's food renaissance was partly led by a group of telegenic chefs who built food empires around their names and their TV programs. **Gordon Ramsay** is the most (in)famous of the lot and his London venues are still standard-bearers for top-quality cuisine. Other big names include campaigning star **Jamie Oliver; Tom Aikens**, who champions British products; and **Heston Blumenthal** (p141), whose mad-professor-like experiments with food (molecular gastronomy, as he describes it) have earned him rave reviews.

Tom Aikens
HOMER SYKES / ALAMY STOCK PHOTO ©

kebabs, masala fish and other starters served on sizzling hot plates are delicious, as are accompaniments such as dhal, naan and raita. On the downside, it can be noisy, service can be haphazard and queues often snake out the door.

Randy's Wing Bar American £
(Map p255; 📞020-8555 5971; www.randyswingbar.co.uk; 28 East Bay Ln, E15; ⊙noon-11pm Tue-Wed, to 11.30pm Thu-Sun, 6pm-11pm Mon; 🚇Hackney Wick) What began life as a street-food cart has developed into a fully fledged restaurant; happily, the flavours have been unaffected by the presence of a roof. Chicken is the order of the day and, unsurprisingly, the wings are the signature dish, with an excellent variety on offer, from Indian to Korean to good old Americana.

⊗ Greenwich & South London

Greenwich Market Market £
(Map p256; www.greenwichmarketlondon.com/food-and-drink; College Approach, SE10; ⊙9am-5.30pm; 🅿🍴; 🚈DLR Cutty Sark) Perfect for snacking your way through a world atlas of food while browsing the other market stalls. Come here for delicious food to go, from Spanish tapas and Thai curries to sushi, Ethiopian vegetarian, French crêpes, dim sum, Mexican burritos and lots more.

⊗ Kensington & Hyde Park

Rabbit Modern British ££
(Map p250; 📞020-3750 0172; www.rabbit-restaurant.com; 172 King's Rd, SW3; mains £6-24, set lunch £13.50; ⊙noon-midnight Tue-Sat, 6-11pm Mon, noon-6pm Sun; 🍴; ⊖Sloane Sq) Three brothers grew up on a farm. One became a farmer, another a butcher, while the third worked in hospitality. So they pooled their skills and came up with Rabbit, a breath of fresh air in upmarket Chelsea. The restaurant rocks the agri-chic (yes) look and the creative, seasonal modern British cuisine is fabulous.

Tom's Kitchen Modern European ££
(Map p250; 📞020-7349 0202; www.tomskitchen.co.uk/chelsea; 27 Cale St, SW3; mains £16-30, 2-/3-course lunch menu £16.50/19.50; ⊙8am-2.30pm & 6-10.30pm Mon-Fri, 9.30am-3.30pm & 6-10.30pm Sat, to 9.30pm Sun; 🛜🍴; ⊖South Kensington) 🍴 Recipe for success: mix one part relaxed and smiling staff, one part light and airy decor to two parts divine food and voilà, you have Tom's Kitchen. Classics such as grilled steaks, burgers, slow-cooked pork belly and chicken schnitzel are cooked to perfection, whilst seasonal choices such as the homemade ricotta or pan-fried scallops are sublime.

Pimlico Fresh Cafe £
(📞020-7932 0030; 86 Wilton Rd, SW1; mains from £4.50; ⊙7.30am-7.30pm Mon-Fri, 9am-6pm Sat & Sun; ⊖Victoria) This friendly two-room

cafe will see you right whether you need breakfast (French toast, bowls of porridge laced with honey or maple syrup), lunch (homemade quiches and soups, 'things' on toast) or just a good old latte and cake.

Dinner by Heston Blumenthal   Modern British £££

(Map p250; ☑020-7201 3833; www. dinnerbyheston.com; Mandarin Oriental Hyde Park, 66 Knightsbridge, SW1; 3-course set lunch £45, mains £28-44; ⊘noon-2pm & 6-10.15pm Mon-Fri, noon-2.30pm & 6-10.30pm Sat & Sun; ☎; ⊖Knightsbridge) Sumptuously presented Dinner is a gastronomic tour de force, taking diners on a journey through British culinary history (with inventive modern inflections). Dishes carry historical dates to convey context, while the restaurant interior is a design triumph, from the glass-walled kitchen and its overhead clock mechanism to the large windows looking onto the park. Book ahead.

Tomtom Coffee House   Cafe

(Map p250; ☑020-7730 1771; www.tomtom. co.uk; 114 Ebury St, SW1; ⊘8am-5pm Mon-Fri, 9am-6pm Sat & Sun; ☎; ⊖Victoria) Tomtom has built its reputation on its amazing coffee: not only are the drinks fabulously presented (forget ferns and hearts in your latte, here it's peacocks fanning their tails), the selection is dizzying, from the usual espresso-based suspects to filter, and a full choice of beans. You can even spice things up with a bonus tot of cognac or Scotch (£3).

The cafe also serves lovely food throughout the day, from breakfast and toasties on sourdough bread to homemade pies (mains £5 to £10).

Magazine   International ££

(Map p250; ☑020-7298 7552; www.magazine-restaurant.co.uk; Serpentine Sackler Gallery, West Carriage Dr, W2; mains £13-24, 2-/3-course lunch menu £17.50/21.50; ⊘9am-6pm Tue-Sat; ☎; ⊖Lancaster Gate, Knightsbridge) Located in the elegant extension of the Serpentine Sackler Gallery, Magazine is no ordinary museum cafe. The food is as contemporary and elegant as the building, and artworks from current exhibitions add yet another dimension. The afternoon tea (£25, with

Magazine

one cocktail) is particularly original: out with cucumber sandwiches, in with gin-cured sea trout, goat's curd and coconut granita.

Magazine opens for dinner on Fridays and Saturdays from April to September, with the added bonus of live music.

Min Jiang   Chinese £££

(Map p250; ☎020-7361 1988; www.minjiang. co.uk; Royal Garden Hotel, 10th fl, 2-24 Kensington High St, W8; mains £12-68, lunch set menu £40-55, dinner set menu £70-88; ☺noon-3pm & 6-10.30pm; ☯; ⊖High St Kensington) Min Jiang serves up seafood, excellent wood-fired Peking duck (*běijīng kǎoyā*; half/whole £33/60), *dim sum* (from £4.80) and sump-tuously regal views over Kensington Palace and Gardens. The menu is diverse, with a sporadic accent on spice (the Min Jiang is a river in Sichuan).

Orangery   Cafe ££

(Map p250; www.orangerykensingtonpalace. co.uk; Kensington Palace, Kensington Gardens, W8; mains £12.50-16.50, afternoon tea £27.50; ☺10am-5pm; ☯; ⊖Queensway or High St

Kensington) The Orangery, housed in an 18th-century conservatory on the grounds of Kensington Palace (p98), is lovely for a late breakfast or lunch, but the standout experience here is English afternoon tea. Book ahead to bag a table on the beautiful terrace.

⊗ North London

Ottolenghi   Bakery, Mediterranean ££

(☎020-7288 1454; www.ottolenghi.co.uk; 287 Upper St, N1; breakfast £5.50-10.50, mains lunch/ dinner from £12.90/11; ☺8am-10.30pm Mon-Sat, 9am-7pm Sun; ☯; ⊖Highbury & Islington) Mountains of meringues tempt you through the door of this deli-restaurant, where you will be greeted by a sumptuous array of baked goods and fresh salads. Meals are as light and bright as the brilliantly white interior design, with a strong influence from the eastern Mediterranean.

Chin Chin Labs   Ice Cream £

(Map p254; www.chinchinlabs.com; 49-50 Camden Lock Pl, NW1; ice cream £4-5; ☺noon-

Ottolenghi

7pm Sun-Thu, to 10pm Fri & Sat; ⊖Camden Town) This is food chemistry at its absolute best. Chefs prepare the ice-cream mixture and freeze it on the spot by adding liquid nitrogen. Flavours change regularly and match the seasons (spiced hot cross bun, passionfruit and coconut, for instance). Sauces and toppings are equally creative. Try the ice-cream sandwich if you can: ice cream wedged inside gorgeous brownies or cookies.

Grain Store International ££

(Map p254; ☑020-7324 4466; www.grainstore. com; 1-3 Stable St, N1C; mains £13-20.50; ☺10am-11.30pm Mon-Sat, 10.30am-3.30pm Sun; ☑; ⊖King's Cross St Pancras) Fresh seasonal vegetables take top billing at Bruno Loubet's bright and breezy Granary Sq restaurant. Meat does appear but it lurks coyly beneath leaves, or adds crunch to mashes. The creative menu gainfully plunders from numerous cuisines to produce dishes that are simultaneously healthy and delicious.

Caravan International ££

(Map p254; ☑020-7101 7661; www. caravanrestaurants.co.uk; 1 Granary Sq, N1C; mains £7-19.50; ☺8am-10.30pm Mon-Fri, 10am-10.30pm Sat, 10am-4pm Sun; ☂☑; ⊖King's Cross St Pancras) Housed in the lofty Granary Building, Caravan is a vast industrial-chic destination for tasty fusion bites from around the world. You can opt for several small plates to share tapas style, or stick to main-sized plates. The outdoor seating area on Granary Sq is especially popular on warm days.

Market Modern British ££

(Map p254; ☑020-7267 9700; www.marketres-taurant.co.uk; 43 Parkway, NW1; 2-course lunch menu £11.50, mains £15-20; ☺noon-2.30pm & 6-10.30pm Mon-Sat, 11am-3pm Sun; ⊖Camden Town) This fabulous restaurant is an ode to great, simple British food, with a measure of French sophistication thrown in. The light and airy space (bare brick walls, steel tables and basic wooden chairs) reflects this stripped-back approach.

¶◎¶ Afternoon Tea

Afternoon tea has become all the rage in the last few years. This indulgent treat usually includes a selection of savoury sandwiches (such as smoked salmon or cucumber), cakes (anything from macarons to Battenberg), scones (the pièce de résistance) served with jam and clotted cream, and a pot of tea (or, if you're feeling decadent, a glass of sparkling wine).

It's convivial, fun but generally overpriced (£20 to £40 per person). It is usually served in top-end restaurants and hotels at weekends, between 3pm and 6pm. It's best to skip lunch (and you probably won't need much dinner either). Bookings are essential pretty much everywhere, especially in winter.

The best places to try it are Claridge's Foyer & Reading Room (p149), Portrait (p150), Delaunay (p148), Orangery (p142) and Wallace (p150).

Afternoon tea spread
MICHAEL BLANN / GETTY IMAGES ©

✪ The City

Sky Pod Bar

(Map p245; ☑0333-772 0020; http://skygarden. london/sky-pod-bar; 20 Fenchurch St, EC3; ☺7am-1am Mon, 7am-2am Tue-Fri, 8am-2am Sat, 9am-midnight Sun; ⊖Monument) One of the best places in the City to get high is the Sky Pod in the Sky Garden on level 35 of the so-called Walkie Talkie. The views are nothing short of phenomenal – especially from the open-air South Terrace – the gardens

London on a Plate

Cod, plaice or haddock, preferably sustainably sourced.

The batter should be thin and ever-so-slightly crispy.

It's tartar sauce, and tartar sauce only.

Mushy peas are a lovely extra, but we won't judge.

The chips: chunky and lightly salted.

SANITTO/SHUTTERSTOCK ©

Classic Fish & Chips

Fish & Chips in London

Fish and chips isn't fancy and is best enjoyed straight out of the takeaway wrapper while sitting on a park bench on a sunny day. Alternatively, fish and chips 'shops' (as they're usually called) tend to be simple, busy cafes, often offering little more than formica tables and wafts from the deep-fryer. Luckily, London standards are high and the best fish and chips restaurants are rather lovely.

A London fish and chips shop
PAWEL LIBERA / GETTY IMAGES ©

★ Top Three Fish & Chips Restaurants

Hook Camden Town (Map p254; www.hookrestaurants.com; 65 Parkway, NW1; mains £8-12; ⊙noon-3pm & 5-10pm Mon-Thu, noon-10.30pm Fri & Sat, to 9pm Sun; 🏃; ⊖Camden Town) ✦ Works entirely with sustainable small fisheries and local suppliers.

Poppie's (Map p253; www.poppiesfishandchips.co.uk; 6-8 Hanbury St, E1; mains £12.20-15.90; ⊙11am-11pm; ⊖Liverpool St) A glorious re-creation of a 1950s East End chippy.

Geales (Map p250; ☎020-7727 7528; www.geales.com; 2 Farmer St, W8; 2-course express lunch £9.75, mains £9-39.50; ⊙noon-3pm & 6-10.30pm Tue-Fri, noon-10.30pm Sat, noon-4pm Sun; ⊖Notting Hill Gate) **Frying since 1939, Geales has endured with its quiet location on the corner of Farmer St in Hillgate Village.**

are lush and it's the only place where this obstructive and clumsy-looking building won't be in your face.

Enjoy a cocktail or a light meal (breakfast, Bircher muesli £4, sandwiches and salads from £5). More substantial meals are available above in the Sky Garden's **Darwin Brasserie** (level 36) and the **Fenchurch Seafood Bar & Grill** (level 37). But we prefer this cafe and bar where the seating is free and the atmosphere relaxed. The only drawback is that without a restaurant reservation, entry is ticketed (see website) from 10am to 6pm weekdays and 11am to 9pm on Saturday and Sunday. Outside those hours, be prepared to queue (and perhaps be disappointed).

Wine Library   Modern European ££

(Map p245; ☑020-7481 0415; www.winelibrary. co.uk; 43 Trinity Sq, EC3; set meal £18; ⊘10am-6pm Mon, to 8pm Tue-Fri; ⊜Tower Hill) This is a great place for a light but boozy lunch opposite the Tower. Buy a bottle of wine at retail price (no mark-up, £8 corkage fee) from the large selection on offer at the vaulted-cellar restaurant and then snack on a set plate of delicious pâtés, cheeses and salads. Reservations recommended at lunch.

Duck & Waffle   Brasserie ££

(Map p245; ☑020-3640 7310; www.duckandwaf-fle.com; 40th fl, Heron Tower, 110 Bishopsgate, EC2; mains £10-18; ⊘24hr; ☞; ⊜Liverpool St) If you like your views with sustenance round the clock, this is the place for you. Perched atop Heron Tower, just down from Liverpool St station, it serves European and British dishes (shellfish, roast chicken, some unusual seafood concoctions such as pollack meatballs) in small and large sizes by day, waffles by night, and round-the-clocktails.

Café Below   Cafe £

(Map p245; ☑020-7329 0789; www.cafebelow. co.uk; St Mary-le-Bow, Cheapside, EC2; mains £8-15.50; ⊘7.30am-2.30pm Mon-Fri, to 9.30pm Wed-Fri; ☑; ⊜Mansion House or St Paul's) This very atmospheric cafe-restaurant, in the crypt of one of London's most famous

churches, offers excellent value and a tasty range of international fare, with as many vegetarian choices as meat choices. Summer sees tables outside in the shady courtyard. Occasional set dinners are available, but check the website or phone in for details.

⊗ The South Bank

Arabica Bar & Kitchen   Middle Eastern £££

(Map p245; ☑020-3011 5151; www. arabicabarandkitchen.com; 3 Rochester Walk, Borough Market, SE1; dishes £6-14; ⊘11am-11pm Mon-Fri, 8.30am-11.30pm Sat, 11am-9pm Sun; ☑; ⊜London Bridge) Pan–Middle Eastern cuisine is a well-rehearsed classic these days, but Arabica Bar & Kitchen has managed to bring something fresh to its table: the decor is contemporary and bright, the food delicate and light, and there's an emphasis on sharing (two to three small dishes per person). The downside of this tapas approach is that the bill adds up quickly.

Baltic   Eastern European ££

(Map p245; ☑020-7928 1111; www. balticrestaurant.co.uk; 74 Blackfriars Rd, SE1; mains £10.50-19, 2-course lunch menu £17.50; ⊘noon-3pm & 5.30-11.15pm Tue-Sun, 5.30-11.15pm Mon; ☑; ⊜Southwark) In a bright and airy, high-ceilinged dining room with glass roof and wooden beams, Baltic is travel on a plate: dill and beetroot, dumplings and blini, pickle and smoke, rich stews and braised meat. From Polish to Georgian, the flavours are authentic and the dishes beautifully presented. The wine and vodka lists are equally diverse.

Padella   Italian £

(Map p245; www.padella.co; 6 Southwark St, SE1; dishes £5-11; ⊘noon-4pm & 5-10pm Mon-Sat, noon-5pm Sun; ☑; ⊜London Bridge) Yet another fantastic addition to the foodie enclave of Borough Market, Padella is a small, energetic bistro specialising in handmade pasta dishes, inspired by the owners' extensive culinary adventures in Italy. The portions are small, which means that, joy of joys, you can (and should!) have more than one dish. Outstanding.

Watch House   Cafe £

(Map p245; www.watchhousecoffee.com; 193 Bermondsey St, SE1; mains from £4.95; ⊗7am-6pm Mon-Fri, 8am-6pm Sat, 9am-5pm Sun; ✎; ⊝Borough or London Bridge) ✐ Saying that the Watch House nails the sandwich wouldn't really do justice to this tip-top cafe: the sandwiches really are delicious and feature artisan breads from a local baker. There is also great coffee and treats for the sweet-toothed. The small but lovely setting is a renovated 19th-century watch-house from where guards looked out for grave robbers in the cemetery next door.

Anchor & Hope   Gastropub ££

(Map p245; www.anchorandhopepub.co.uk; 36 The Cut, SE1; mains £12-20; ⊗noon-2.30pm Tue-Sat, 6-10.30pm Mon-Sat, 12.30-3pm Sun; ⊝Southwark) A stalwart of the South Bank food scene, the Anchor & Hope is a quintessential gastropub: elegant but not formal, and utterly delicious (European fare with a British twist). The menu changes daily but think salt marsh lamb shoulder cooked for seven hours; wild rabbit with anchovies, almonds and rocket; and panna cotta with rhubarb compote.

Maltby Street Market   Market £

(Map p245; www.maltby.st; Maltby St, SE1; dishes £5-10; ⊗9am-4pm Sat, 11am-4pm Sun; ⊝London Bridge) Started as an alternative to the juggernaut that is Borough Market, Maltby Street Market is becoming a victim of its own success, with brick and mortar shops and restaurants replacing the old workshops, and throngs of visitors. That said, it boasts some original – and all top-notch – food stalls selling smoked salmon from east London, African burgers, seafood and lots of pastries.

Maltby Street Market

ED NORTON / GETTY IMAGES ©

⊗ The West End

Yauatcha   Chinese £

(Map p248; ☏020-7494 8888; www.yauat-
cha.com; 15 Broadwick St, W1; dishes £5-30;
☺noon-11.30pm Mon-Sat, to 10.30pm Sun;
☉Piccadilly Circus, Oxford Circus) London's
most glamorous dim-sum restaurant has
a Michelin star and is divided into two: the
ground-floor dining room offers a delightful
blue-bathed oasis of calm from the chaos
of Berwick St Market, while downstairs has
a smarter feel, with constellations of 'star'
lights. Both serve exquisite dim sum and
have a fabulous range of teas. Cakes here
are creations to die for.

Cafe Murano   Italian ££

(Map p248; ☏020-3371 5559; www.cafemurano.
co.uk; 33 St James's St, SW1; mains £18-25,
2/3-course set meal £19/23; ☺noon-3pm &
5.30-11pm Mon-Sat, 11.30am-4pm Sun; ☉Green
Park) The setting may seem somewhat
demure at this superb and busy restaurant,
but with such a sublime North Italian menu
on offer, it sees no need to be flash and
of-the-moment. You get what you come for
and the lobster linguini, pork belly and cod
with mussels and samphire are as close to
culinary perfection as you'll get.

Palomar   Israeli ££

(Map p248; ☏020-7439 8777; http://thepalomar.
co.uk; 34 Rupert St, W1; mains £7-16.50; ☺noon-
2.30pm & 5.30-11pm Mon-Sat, 12.30-3.30pm &
6-9pm Sun; ☎; ☉Piccadilly Circus) The buzzing
vibe at this good-looking celebration of
modern-day Jerusalem cuisine (in all its
permutations) is infectious, but the noise in
the back dining room might drive you mad.
Choose instead the counter seats at the
front. The 'Yiddish-style' chopped chicken
liver pate, the Jerusalem-style polenta
and the 'octo-hummus' are all fantastic,
but portions are smallish, so you'll need to
share.

Shoryu   Noodles £

(Map p248; ☏none; www.shoryuramen.
com; 9 Regent St, SW1; mains £9.50-14.90;
☺11.15am-midnight Mon-Sat, to 10.30pm Sun;

🍴 Food Markets

The boom in London's eating scene has
extended to its markets, which come
in three broad categories: food stalls
that are part of a broader market and
appeal to visitors keen to soak up the
atmosphere, such as **Old Spitalfields**
(p71), **Borough** (p76) or **Camden** (Map
p254; www.camdenmarket.com; Camden High
St, NW1; ☺10am-6pm; ☉Camden Town or
Chalk Farm); farmers markets, which sell
pricey local and/or organic products
(check out www.lfm.org.uk for a selection of the best); and the many colourful
food markets, where the oranges and
lemons come from who knows where
and the barrow boys and girls speak
with perfect Cockney accents (such as
Berwick St in Soho).

Old Spitalfields Market

☉Piccadilly Circus) Compact, well-mannered
and central noodle-parlour Shoryu draws
in reams of noodle diners to feast at its
wooden counters and small tables. It's
busy, friendly and efficient, with helpful and
informative staff. Fantastic *tonkotsu* pork-
broth ramen is the name of the game here,
sprinkled with *nori* (dried, pressed sea-
weed), spring onion, *nitamago* (soft-boiled
eggs) and sesame seeds. No bookings.

Barrafina   Spanish ££

(Map p248; ☏020-7440 1456; www.barrafina.
co.uk; 10 Adelaide St, WC2; tapas £6.50-15.80;
☺noon-3pm & 5-11pm Mon-Sat, 1-3.30pm & 5.30-
10pm Sun; ☉Embankment or Leicester Sq) With
no reservations, you may need to get in

🍽️ Gastropubs

While not so long ago the pub was where you went for a drink, with maybe a packet of potato crisps to soak up the alcohol, the birth of the gastropub in the 1990s means that today just about every establishment serves full meals. The quality varies widely, from defrosted-on-the-premises to Michelin-star worthy.

A meal in a traditional English pub
EKATERINA POKROVSKY / SHUTTERSTOCK ©

line for an hour or so at this restaurant that does a brisk service in some of the best tapas in town. Divine mouthfuls are served on each plate, from the stuffed courgette flower (£7.80) to the suckling pig's ears (£6.80) and crab on toast (£8), so would-be diners prepare to wait.

There's a maximum group size of four. There are a couple of tables on the pavement.

Spuntino   American £

(Map p248; 📞none; www.spuntino.co.uk; 61 Rupert St, W1; mains £6-12.50; ⏰11.30am-midnight Mon-Wed, to 1am Thu-Sat, to 11pm Sun; 🚇; ⊖Piccadilly Circus) Offering an unusual mix of speakeasy decor and surprisingly creative American food, Spuntino is a delight at every turn. Try old favourites such as macaroni cheese (from £6), cheeseburger with jalapeño peppers (£8) and, as a dessert, peanut butter and jelly sandwich. Seating is at the bar or counters at the back with two-dozen stools.

Delaunay   Brasserie ££

(Map p245; 📞020-7499 8558; www.thedelaunay. com; 55 Aldwych, WC2; mains £7.50-35; ⏰7am-11.30pm Mon-Fri, 8am-midnight Sat, 9am-11pm Sun; 🚇; ⊖Temple, Covent Garden) This smart brasserie southeast of Covent Garden is a kind of Franco-German hybrid, where schnitzels and wieners sit happily beside croque-monsieurs and *choucroute alsacienne* (Alsace-style sauerkraut). Even more relaxed is the adjacent **Counter at the Delaunay** (Map p245; soups & sandwiches £4.5-10; ⏰7am-8pm Mon-Wed, 7am-10.30pm Thu & Fri, 10.30am-10.30pm Sat, 11am-5.30pm Sun), where you can drop in for chicken noodle soup and a New York–style hot dog.

Brunch is from 11am to 5pm at the weekend and afternoon tea (£19.75, or £29.75 with Champagne) is available daily from 3pm.

Kanada-Ya   Noodles £

(Map p248; 📞020-7240 0232; www.kanada-ya. com; 64 St Giles High St, WC2; mains £10.50-14; ⏰noon-3pm & 5-10pm Mon-Sat; ⊖Tottenham Court Rd) With no reservations taken, queues can get impressive outside this tiny and enormously popular canteen, where ramen cooked in *tonkotsu* (pork-bone broth) draws in diners for its three types of noodles delivered in steaming bowls, steeped in a delectable broth and highly authentic flavours. The restaurant also serves up *onigiri* (dried seaweed-wrapped rice balls, £2).

Brasserie Zédel   French ££

(Map p248; 📞020-7734 4888; www. brasseriezedel.com; 20 Sherwood St, W1; mains £13.50-25.75; ⏰11.30am-midnight Mon-Sat, to 11pm Sun; 🚇; ⊖Piccadilly Circus) This brasserie in the renovated art deco ballroom of a former hotel is the Frenchest eatery west of Calais. Favourites include *choucroute alsacienne* (sauerkraut with sausages and charcuterie, £15.50) or a straight-up *steak haché* (chopped steak) with pepper sauce and *frites* (£9.95). Set menus (£9.75/12.75 for two/three courses) and plats du jour (£15.50) offer excellent value in a terrific setting.

Gymkhana

Indian ££

(Map p248; ☑020-3011 5900; www.
gymkhanalondon.com; 42 Albemarle St, W1; mains
£10-38, 2/3-course lunch £25/30; ⏰noon-2.30pm
& 5.30-10.30pm Mon-Sat; ☎; ⊖Green Park) The
rather sombre setting is all British Raj: ceiling
fans, oak ceiling, period cricket photos and
hunting trophies; the menu is lively, bright
and inspiring. For lovers of variety, try the
six-course tasting meat/vegetarian menu
(£70/£65). The bar is open to 1am.

Dishoom

Indian £

(Map p248; ☑020-7420 9320; www.dishoom.
com; 12 Upper St Martin's Lane, WC2; mains
£4.50-16.50; ⏰8am-11pm Mon-Thu, 8am-
midnight Fri, 9am-midnight Sat, 9am-11pm
Sun; ☎; ⊖Covent Garden) This branch of a
highly successful minichain takes the fast-
disappearing Iranian cafe of Bombay and
gives it new life. Distressed with a modern
twist (all ceiling fans, stained mirrors and
sepia photos), you'll find yummy favourites
like *seekh* kebab and spicy chicken
ruby, okra fries and snack foods such as
bhel (Bombay mix and puffed rice with
pomegranate, onion, lime and mint).

Claridge's Foyer & Reading Room

British £££

(Map p250; ☑020-7107 8886; www.claridges.
co.uk; 49-53 Brook St, W1; afternoon tea £68, with
champagne £79; ⏰afternoon tea 2.45-5.30pm;
☎; ⊖Bond St) Extend that pinkie finger to
partake in afternoon tea within the classic
art-deco Foyer and Reading Room of this
landmark hotel, whose gentle clink of
fine porcelain and champagne glasses
could be a defining memory of your trip to
London. The setting is gorgeous and dress
is elegant, smart casual (ripped jeans and
baseball caps won't get served).

Lady Ottoline

Gastropub ££

(Map p254; ☑020-7831 0008; www.theladyottoline.
com; 11a Northington St, WC1; mains £14-17;
⏰noon-11pm Mon-Sat, to 5pm Sun; ⊖Chancery
Lane) Bloomsbury can sometimes seem a bit
of a culinary wasteland, but this gastropub
(named after a patron of the Bloomsbury
Set) is a pleasant exception. You can eat in
the buzzy pub downstairs, but the cosy dining
room above is more tempting. Favourites
such as beer-battered fish and chips and
pork with apple ketchup are excellent.

Delaunay

Vegetarians & Vegans

London has been one of the best places for vegetarians to dine out since the 1970s, initially due mostly to its many Indian restaurants, which, for religious reasons, always cater for people who don't eat meat. A number of dedicated vegetarian restaurants have since cropped up, offering imaginative, filling and truly delicious meals. Most nonvegetarian places generally offer a couple of dishes for those who don't eat meat; vegans, however, will find it harder outside Indian or dedicated establishments.

Some 95 gins are on offer as well as Lady Ottoline's own in-house vermouth.

Wallace   Modern European ££
(Map p250; ☏020-7563 9505; www.
wallacecollection.org/visiting/
thewallacerestaurant; Hertford House, Manchester
Sq, W1; mains £14-22.50; ☺10am-5pm Sun-Thu, to
11pm Fri & Sat; ⊖Bond St) There are few more
idyllically placed restaurants than this spot
in the enclosed courtyard of the **Wallace
Collection** (Map p250; www.wallacecollection.org;
Hertford House, Manchester Sq, W1; ☺10am-5pm;
⊖Bond St) **FREE**. The emphasis is on seasonal
French-inspired dishes, with the daily menu
offering two- or three-course meals for
£22.50/25.50. Afternoon tea is £18.50.

Great Queen Street   British ££
(Map p248; ☏020-7242 0622; www.greatqueen-
streetrestaurant.co.uk; 32 Great Queen St, WC2;
mains £15.80-19.80; ☺noon-2.30pm & 5.30-

10.30pm Mon-Sat, noon-3.30pm Sun; ⊖Holborn)
The menu at one of Covent Garden's best
places to eat is seasonal (and changes
daily), with an emphasis on quality, hearty
dishes and fine ingredients – there are
always delicious stews, roasts and simple
fish dishes. The atmosphere is lively, with
the small **Cellar Bar** (5pm to 11pm Tuesday
to Saturday) open for cocktails and drinks.
Booking is essential.

La Fromagerie   Cafe ££
(Map p250; ☏020-7935 0341; www.lafromagerie.
co.uk; 2-6 Moxon St, W1; mains £7-18; ☺8am-
7.30pm Mon-Fri, 9am-7pm Sat, 10am-6pm Sun;
🛜; ⊖Baker St) ✔ This deli-cafe has bowls of
delectable salads, antipasto, peppers and
beans scattered about the long communal
table. Huge slabs of bread invite you to tuck
in while the heavenly waft from the cheese
room beckons. Cheese boards come
in small and large (£9.25 and £16) and
breakfast is always a good choice.

Pollen Street
Social   Modern European £££
(Map p248; ☏020-7290 7600; www.
pollenstreetsocial.com; 8-10 Pollen St, W1; mains
£33-38; ☺noon-2.45pm & 6-10.45pm Mon-Sat;
⊖Oxford Circus) Jason Atherton's cathedral
to haute cuisine would be beyond reach of
anyone not on a hefty expense account, but
the excellent-value set lunch (£32/37 for
two/three courses) makes it fairly accessible
to all. A generous two-hour slot allows
ample time to linger over such delights as
lime-cured salmon, braised West Country ox
cheek and a choice from the dessert bar.

Portrait   Modern European £££
(Map p248; ☏020-7312 2490; www.npg.org.uk/
visit/shop-eat-drink.php; 3rd fl, National Portrait
Gallery, St Martin's Pl, WC2; mains £19.50-26,
2/3-course menu £27.50/31.50; ☺10-11am,
11.45am-3pm & 3.30-4.30pm daily, 6.30-8.30pm
Thu, Fri & Sat; 🛜; ⊖Charing Cross) This stunningly located restaurant above the excellent National Portrait Gallery (p55) comes
with dramatic views over Trafalgar Sq and
Westminster. It's a fine choice for tantalising
food and the chance to relax after a morning

or afternoon of picture-gazing at the gallery. The breakfast/brunch (10am to 11am) and afternoon tea (3.30pm to 4.30pm) come highly recommended. Booking is advisable.

⊗ West London

Mazi   Greek ££
(Map p250; 📞020-7229 3794; www.mazi. co.uk; 12-14 Hillgate St, W8; mains £9-24; ⏱noon-3pm Tue-Sun, 6.30-10.30pm Mon-Sat & 6.30-10pm Sun; 🛜; ⊖Notting Hill Gate) Where long-standing Costa's Grill did business for decades, Mazi has shaken up the Greek tradition along pretty Hillgate St, concocting a lively menu of modern and innovative (and many of sharing size) platters in a bright and neat setting, with a small back garden (for summer months) and an all-Greek wine list. It's both small and popular, so reservations are important.

Ledbury   French £££
(Map p250; 📞020-7792 9090; www.theledbury. com; 127 Ledbury Rd, W11; 4-course set lunch £70, 4-course dinner £115; ⏱noon-2pm Wed-Sun & 6.30-9.45pm daily; 🛜; ⊖Westbourne Park or Notting Hill Gate) Two Michelin stars and swooningly elegant, Brett Graham's artful French restaurant attracts well-heeled diners in jeans with designer jackets. Dishes – such as hand-dived scallops, Chinese water deer, smoked bone marrow, quince and red leaves or Herdwick lamb with salt-baked turnips, celery cream and wild garlic – are simply triumphant. London gastronomes have the Ledbury on speed-dial, so reservations well in advance are crucial.

Taquería   Mexican £
(Map p250; www.taqueria.co.uk; 139-143 Westbourne Grove; tacos £6.50-9; ⏱noon-11pm Mon-Thu, to 11.30pm Fri & Sat, to 10.30pm Sun; 🛜; ⊖Notting Hill Gate) 🍴 You won't find fresher, limper (they're not supposed to be crispy!) tacos anywhere in London because these ones are made on the premises. Recently refurbished, it's a small casual place with a great vibe. Taquería is also a committed environmental establishment: the eggs, chicken and pork are free-range, the meat British, the fish MSC-certified and the milk and cream organic.

The kitchen of Pollen Street Social

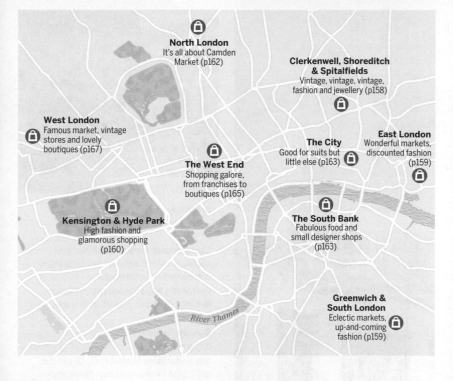

North London
It's all about Camden
Market (p162)

**Clerkenwell, Shoreditch
& Spitalfields**
Vintage, vintage, vintage,
fashion and jewellery (p158)

West London
Famous market, vintage
stores and lovely
boutiques (p167)

The City
Good for suits but
little else (p163)

East London
Wonderful markets,
discounted fashion
(p159)

The West End
Shopping galore,
from franchises to
boutiques (p165)

Kensington & Hyde Park
High fashion and
glamorous shopping
(p160)

The South Bank
Fabulous food and
small designer shops
(p163)

River Thames

**Greenwich &
South London**
Eclectic markets,
up-and-coming
fashion (p159)

Opening Hours

Shops generally open from 9am or
10am to 6pm or 7pm Monday to
Saturday.

The majority of stores in the most
popular shopping strips also open on
Sunday, typically from noon to 6pm but
sometimes from 10am to 4pm.

Shops in the West End open late (to
9pm) on Thursday.

Sales

With the popularity of online shopping,
sales now often start earlier and last
longer, but there are two main sales
seasons in the UK, both of which last
about a month:

Winter sales Start on Boxing Day
(26 December)

Summer sales July

The Best...

Experience London's best shopping

Best Markets

Broadway Market (p159) Local market known for its food but with plenty else besides.

Camden Lock Market (p162; pictured above) Authentic antiques to tourist tat – and everything in between.

Portobello Road Market (p127) Classic Notting Hill sprawl, perfect for vintage everything.

Sunday UpMarket (p158) Up-and-coming designers, cool tees, terrific food and vintage.

Old Spitalfields Market (p71) One of London's best for young fashion designers.

Best Fashion Shops

Selfridges (p130) Everything from streetwear to high fashion under one roof.

Burberry Outlet Store (p159) A slightly cheaper take on the classic Brit brand.

Harvey Nichols (p162) The best denim range in town.

Best for Vintage

Blitz London (p158) A massive selection of just about everything.

Beyond Retro (p159; pictured above) A London vintage empire with a rock 'n' roll heart.

British Red Cross (p162) Kensington cast-offs of exceptional quality.

Best for Music

Rough Trade East (p158; pictured above) An excellent selection of vinyl and CDs, plus in-store gigs.

Sister Ray (p167) Just what you'd expect from a store whose name references the Velvet Underground.

Casbah Records (p160) Classic vinyl and memorabilia.

Reckless Records (p167) A superb selection of secondhand CDs and vinyls.

Best for Books

Hatchards (p165) The oldest, and still one of the best, independent bookshops.

Stanford's (p166) Guidebooks and maps galore, with a great range of books on London.

Foyles (p165; pictured above) Four miles of shelving in light, airy settings; you'll be there for hours.

Gay's The Word (p166) A literary institution for the LGBT community.

Gosh! (p166) A compulsory stop for lovers of graphic novels.

Best Department Stores

Selfridges (p130) Over 100 years of retail innovation.

Liberty (p129; pictured above) Fabric, fashion and much, much more.

Harrods (p160) Enormous, overwhelming and indulgent, with a world-famous food hall.

Fortnum & Mason (p165) A world of food in luxuriously historic surroundings.

Harvey Nichols (p162) Fashion, food, beauty and lifestyle over eight floors.

★ Lonely Planet's Top Choices

Sunday Upmarket (p158) Up-and-coming designers, cool tees and terrific food.

Silver Vaults (p163) The world's largest collection of silver, from cutlery to jewellery.

Fortnum & Mason (p165) The world's most glamorous grocery store.

Harrods (p160) Garish, stylish, kitsch, yet perennially popular department store.

Sister Ray (p167) A top independent music shop, with an ever-changing selection of vinyls and CDs.

ⓐ Clerkenwell, Shoreditch & Spitalfields

Sunday UpMarket   Market
(Map p253; www.sundayupmarket.co.uk; Old Truman Brewery, 91 Brick Lane, E1; ⊘11am-6pm Sat, 10am-5pm Sun; ⊜Shoreditch High St) The Sunday Upmarket (which in fact opens Saturdays and Sundays) sprawls within the beautiful red-brick buildings of the Old Truman Brewery. You'll find young designers in the Backyard Market (p158), a drool-inducing array of food stalls in the Boiler House, antiques and bric-a-brac in the Tea Rooms and a huge range of vintage clothes in the basement across the street.

Rough Trade East   Music
(Map p253; www.roughtrade.com; Old Truman Brewery, 91 Brick Lane, E1; ⊘9am-9pm Mon-Thu, to 8pm Fri, 10am-8pm Sat, 11am-7pm Sun; ⊜Shoreditch High St) It's no longer directly associated with the legendary record label (home to The Smiths, The Libertines and The Strokes, among many others), but this huge record shop is still the best for music of an indie, soul, electronica and alternative persuasion. In addition to an impressive selection of CDs and vinyl, it also dispenses coffee and stages promotional gigs.

Backyard Market   Market
(Map p253; www.backyardmarket.co.uk; 146 Brick Lane, E1; ⊘11am-6pm Sat, 10am-5pm Sun; ⊜Shoreditch High St) Just off Brick Lane, the Backyard Market fills a large brick warehouse (part of the Old Truman Brewery complex) with stalls selling designer clothes, ceramics, jewellery, unique prints and funky furniture titbits.

Blitz London   Vintage
(Map p253; www.blitzlondon.co.uk; 55-59 Hanbury St, E1; ⊘11am-7pm; ⊜Liverpool St) One of the capital's best secondhand clothes stores, with more than 20,000 hand-selected items of men's and women's clothing, shoes and accessories spanning four decades since the 1960s. You'll find anything from mainstream brands such as Nike to designer labels such as Burberry.

John Sandoe Books (p160)

⊕ East London

Broadway Market   Market
(Map p255; www.broadwaymarket.co.uk; Broadway Market, E8; ⊙9am-5pm Sat; 🚌394) There's been a market down this pretty street since the late 19th century. The focus these days is artisan food, arty knick-knacks, books, records and vintage clothing. Stock up on edible treats then head to **London Fields** (Map p255; Richmond Rd, E8; ⊖Hackney Central) for a picnic.

Pringle of Scotland
Outlet Store   Clothing
(Map p255; ☎020-8533 1158; www.pringlescotland.com; 90 Morning Lane; ⊙10am-6.30pm Mon-Sat, 11am-5pm Sun; ⊖Hackney Central) There are proper bargains to be had at this excellent outlet store that stocks seconds and end-of-line items from the Pringle range. Expect high-quality merino, cashmere and lambswool knitwear for both men and women.

Burberry Outlet Store   Clothing
(Map p255; www.burberry.com; 29-31 Chatham Pl, E9; ⊙10am-5pm; ⊖Hackney Central) This outlet shop has excess international stock from the reborn-as-trendy Brit brand's current and last-season collections. Prices are around 30% lower than those in the main shopping centres – but still properly pricey.

Beyond Retro   Vintage
(Map p255; ☎020-7923 2277; www.beyondretro.com; 92-100 Stoke Newington Rd, N16; ⊙10am-7pm Mon-Sat, 11.30am-6pm Sun; ⊖Dalston Kingsland) A riot of colour, furbelow, frill, feathers and flares, this vast store has every imaginable type of vintage clothing for sale, from hats to shoes. When it all gets too overwhelming, retreat to the licensed cafe. There's a smaller but even cheaper outlet branch in **Bethnal Green** (Map p255; ☎020-7613 3636; www.beyondretro.com; 110-112 Cheshire St, E2; ⊙10am-7pm Mon-Sat, 11.30am-6pm Sun; ⊖Shoreditch High St).

🛍 British Designers

British designers are well established in the fashion world, and **Stella McCartney** (p130), Vivienne Westwood, Paul Smith, Burberry and Alexander McQueen (the design house behind Princess Catherine's wedding dress) are now household names. For the best selection, head to Selfridges (p130); otherwise most designers have their own boutique.

Vivienne Westwood store on Bond St
VISITBRITAIN/BRITAIN ON VIEW/GETTY IMAGES ©

Traid   Clothing
(Map p255; ☎020-7923 1396; www.traid.org.uk; 106-108 Kingsland High St, E8; ⊙11am-7pm Mon-Sat, to 5pm Sun; ⊖Dalston Kingsland) Banish every preconception you have about charity shops, for Traid is nothing like the ones you've seen before: big and bright, with not a whiff of mothball. The offerings aren't necessarily vintage but rather quality, contemporary secondhand clothes for a fraction of the usual prices. It also sells its own creations made from offcuts.

⊕ Greenwich & South London

Greenwich Market   Market
(Map p256; www.greenwichmarketlondon.com; College Approach, SE10; ⊙9.30am-5pm; 🚆DLR Cutty Sark) Greenwich Market is one of the smallest of London's ubiquitous markets, but it holds its own in quality. On Tuesdays, Wednesdays, Fridays and weekends, stallholders tend

to be small, independent artists, offering original prints, wholesome beauty products, funky jewellery and accessories, cool fashion pieces and so on. On Tuesdays, Thursdays and Fridays, you'll find vintage, antiques and collectables. Loads of street food too.

Casbah Records   Music

(Map p256; ☏020-8858 1964; www.casbahrecords.co.uk; 320-322 Creek Rd, SE10; ⊙11.30am-6pm Mon, 10.30am-6pm Tue-Fri, 10.30am-6pm Sat & Sun; ☒DLR Cutty Sark) This funky meeting ground of classic, vintage and rare vinyl (Bowie, Rolling Stones, soul, rock, blues, jazz, indie etc) – as well as CDs, DVDs and memorabilia – originally traded at Greenwich Market before upgrading to this highly browsable shop.

Arty Globe   Gifts & Souvenirs

(Map p256; ☏020-7998 3144; www.artyglobe.com; 15 Greenwich Market, SE10; ⊙11am-6pm; ☒DLR Cutty Sark) The unique fisheye-view drawings of various areas of London (and other cities, including New York, Paris and Berlin) by architect Hartwig Braun are works of art and appear on the shopping bags, place mats, notebooks, coasters, mugs and jigsaws available in this tiny shop. They make excellent gifts.

⊕ Kensington & Hyde Park

Harrods   Department Store

(Map p250; ☏020-7730 1234; www.harrods.com; 87-135 Brompton Rd, SW1; ⊙10am-9pm Mon-Sat, 11.30am-6pm Sun; ☒Knightsbridge) Garish and stylish in equal measures, perennially crowded Harrods is an obligatory stop for visitors, from the cash-strapped to the big spenders. The stock is astonishing, as are many of the price tags. High on kitsch, the 'Egyptian Elevator' resembles something out of an Indiana Jones epic, while the memorial fountain to Dodi and Di (lower ground floor) merely adds surrealism.

Many visitors don't make it past the ground floor where designer bags, the myriad scents from the perfume hall and the mouth-watering counters of the food hall provide plenty of entertainment. The latter actually makes for an excellent, and surprisingly affordable, option for a picnic in nearby Hyde Park. From 11.30am to midday on Sunday, it's browsing time only.

John Sandoe Books   Books

(Map p250; ☏020-7589 9473; www.johnsandoe.com; 10 Blacklands Tce, SW3; ⊙9.30am-6.30pm Mon-Sat, 11am-5pm Sun; ☒Sloane Sq) The perfect antidote to impersonal book superstores, this atmospheric three-storey bookshop in 18th-century premises is a treasure trove of literary gems and hidden surprises. It's been in business for six decades and loyal customers swear by it, while knowledgeable booksellers spill forth with well-read pointers and helpful advice.

Pickett   Gifts & Souvenirs

(Map p250; ☏020-7823 5638; www.pickett.co.uk; cnr Sloane St & Sloane Tce, SW1; ⊙9.30am-6.30pm Mon-Tue & Thu-Fri, 10am-7pm Wed, 10am-6pm Sat; ☒Sloane Sq) ✔ Walking into Pickett as an adult is a bit like walking into a sweets shop as a child: the exquisite leather goods are all so colourful and beautiful, you don't really know where to start. Choice items include the perfectly finished handbags, the exquisite roll-up backgammon sets and the men's grooming sets. All leather goods are made in Britain.

Jo Loves   Cosmetics

(Map p250; ☏020-7730 8611; www.joloves.com; 42 Elizabeth St, SW1; ⊙10am-6pm Mon-Wed & Fri-Sat, to 7pm Thu, noon-5pm Sun; ☒Victoria) Famed British scent-maker Jo Malone opened Jo Loves in 2013 on a street where she once had a Saturday job as a young florist. The shop features the entrepreneur's signature candles, fragrances and bath products in a range of delicate scents – Arabian amber, white rose and lemon leaves, oud and mango. All products come exquisitely wrapped in red boxes with black bows.

Conran Shop   Design

(Map p250; ☏020-7589 7401; www.conranshop.co.uk; Michelin House, 81 Fulham Rd, SW3; ⊙10am-6pm Mon, Tue & Fri, to 7pm Wed & Thu, to 6.30pm Sat, noon-6pm Sun; ☒South Kensington)

★ Vintage Fashion

The realm of vintage apparel has moved from being sought out by those looking for something off-beat and original, to an all-out mainstream shopping habit. Vintage designer garments and odd bits and pieces from the 1920s to the 1980s are all gracing the rails in some surprisingly upmarket boutique vintage shops.

The less self-conscious charity shops – especially those in areas such as Chelsea, Kensington and Islington – are your best bets for real bargains on designer wear (usually, the richer the area, the better the secondhand shops).

Clockwise from top: A classic car boot sale; Camden Lock Market (p162); Vintage clothes stall at Broadway Market (p159)

The original design store (going strong since 1987), the Conran Shop is a treasure trove of beautiful things – from radios to sunglasses, kitchenware to children's toys and books, bathroom accessories to greeting cards. Browsing bliss. Spare some time to peruse the magnificent art nouveau/deco Michelin House the shop belongs to.

Harvey Nichols   Department Store
(Map p250; www.harveynichols.com; 109-125 Knightsbridge, SW1; ⊙10am-8pm Mon-Sat, 11.30am-6pm Sun; ⊖Knightsbridge) At London's temple of high fashion, you'll find Chloé and Balenciaga bags, the city's best denim range, a massive make-up hall with exclusive lines and great jewellery. The food hall and in-house restaurant, **Fifth Floor**, are, you guessed it, on the 5th floor. From 11.30am to midday, it's browsing time only.

British Red Cross   Vintage
(☏020-7376 7300; 69-71 Old Church St, SW3; ⊙10am-6pm Mon-Sat; ⊖Sloane Sq) The motto 'One man's rubbish is another man's treasure' couldn't be truer in this part of London, where the 'rubbish' is made up of designer gowns, cashmere jumpers and perhaps a

first edition or two. Obviously the price tags are a little higher than in your run-of-the-mill charity shop (£40 rather than £5 for a jumper or jacket) but it's still a bargain for the quality and browsing is half the fun.

❻ North London

Camden Lock Market   Market
(Map p254; www.camdenmarket.com; 54-56 Camden Lock Pl, NW1; ⊙10am-6pm; ⊖Camden Town) Right next to the canal lock, this is the original Camden Market, with diverse food stalls, ceramics, furniture, oriental rugs, musical instruments and clothes.

Stables Market   Market
(Map p254; www.camdenmarket.com; Chalk Farm Rd, NW1; ⊙10am-6pm; ⊖Chalk Farm) Connected to the Lock Market, the Stables is the best part of the Camden Market complex, with antiques, Asian artefacts, rugs, retro furniture and clothing. As the name suggests, it used to be an old stables complex, complete with horse hospital, where up to 800 horses (who worked hauling barges on Regent's Canal) would have been housed.

From left: Cambridge Satchel Company (p165); Harvey Nichols; Harry Potter Shop at Platform 9¾; South Bank Book Market (p165)

Harry Potter Shop
at Platform 9¾   Gifts & Souvenirs

(Map p254; www.harrypotterplatform934.com;
King's Cross Station, N1; ⏰8am-10pm Mon-Sat,
9am-9pm Sun; ⬤King's Cross St Pancras) With
Pottermania refusing to wind down and
Diagon Alley impossible to find, take your
junior witches and wizards to King's Cross
Station instead. This little wood-panelled
store also stocks jumpers sporting the colours of Hogwarts' four houses (Gryffindor
having pride of place) and assorted mer-
chandise, including, of course, the books.

⊙ The City

Silver Vaults   Arts & Crafts

(Map p245; 📞020-7242 3844; http://
silvervaultslondon.com; 53-63 Chancery Lane,
WC2; ⏰9am-5.30pm Mon-Fri, to 1pm Sat;
⬤Chancery Lane) The 30-odd shops that
work out of these secure subterranean
vaults make up the world's largest
collection of silver under one roof in the
world. The different businesses tend to
specialise in particular types of silverware –

from cutlery sets to picture frames and lots
of jewellery.

⊙ The South Bank

Lovely & British   Gifts & Souvenirs

(Map p245; 📞020-7378 6570; www.facebook.
com/LovelyandBritish; 132a Bermondsey St, SE1;
⏰10am-6pm; ⬤London Bridge) As the name
suggests, this gorgeous Bermondsey boutique prides itself on stocking prints, jewellery and homewares (crockery especially)
from British designers. It's an eclectic mix
of wares, with very reasonable prices, which
make lovely presents or souvenirs.

Southbank Centre
Shop   Homewares

(Map p245; www.southbankcentre.co.uk;
Festival Tce, SE1; ⏰10am-9pm Mon-Fri, to 8pm
Sat, noon-8pm Sun; ⬤Waterloo) This is the
place to come for quirky London books,
'50s-inspired homewares, original prints
and creative gifts for children. The shop is
eclectic but you're sure to find unique gifts
or souvenirs to take home.

Top Five London Souvenirs

Tea

The British drink par excellence, with plenty of iconic names to choose from. For lovely packaging too, try Fortnum & Mason (p165; pictured above) or Harrods (p160).

Vintage Clothes & Shoes

Your London vintage fashion finds will forever be associated with your trip to the city. Start your search at the Sunday UpMarket (p158).

British Design

With its cool and understated chic, British design has made a name for itself worldwide. Try the Conran Shop (p160; pictured above) or Monocle (p167).

Music

The city that produced legends from The Clash to Amy Winehouse is a brilliant place to buy records. Try Rough Trade East (p158) or Sister Ray (p167; pictured above).

London Toys

Double-decker buses, Paddington bears, guards in bearskin hats – London's icons make for great souvenirs. Hamleys (p129; pictured above) is the place to go.

South Bank Book Market Market
(Map p245; Riverside Walk, SE1; ⊙11am-7pm, shorter hours winter; ⊖Waterloo) The South Bank Book Market sells prints and secondhand books daily under the arches of Waterloo Bridge. You'll find anything here, from fiction to children's books, comics to classics.

⊕ The West End

For more, see Shopping in the West End (p128).

Fortnum & Mason Department Store
(Map p248; ☑020-7734 8040; www.fortnumandmason.com; 181 Piccadilly, W1; ⊙10am-8pm Mon-Sat, 11.30am-6pm Sun; ⊖Piccadilly Circus) With its classic eau-de-Nil (pale green) colour scheme, 'the Queen's grocery store' established 1707 refuses to yield to modern times. Its staff – men and women – still wear old-fashioned tailcoats and its glamorous food hall is supplied with hampers, cut marmalade, speciality teas, superior fruitcakes and so forth. Fortnum and Mason remains the quintessential London shopping experience.

Hatchards Books
(Map p248; ☑020-7439 9921; www.hatchards.co.uk; 187 Piccadilly, W1; ⊙9.30am-8pm Mon-Sat, noon-6.30pm Sun; ⊖Green Park or Piccadilly Circus) London's oldest bookshop dates to 1797. Holding three royal warrants, it's a stupendous bookshop now in the Waterstones stable, with a solid supply of signed editions and bursting at its smart seams with very browsable stock. There's a strong selection of first editions on the ground floor and regularly scheduled literary events.

Cadenhead's Whisky & Tasting Shop Drinks
(Map p250; ☑020-7935 6999; www.whiskytastingroom.com; 26 Chiltern St, W1; ⊙10.30am-6.30pm Mon-Thu, 11am-8.30 Fri, 10.30am-6pm Sat; ⊖Baker St) This shop is Scotland's oldest independent bottler of pure, nonblended whisky from local distilleries and a joy for anyone with a passion for *uisge-beatha* ('water of life', the

Scots Gaelic word for 'whisky'), though don't expect a warm welcome. All bottled whiskies derive from individually selected casks, without any filtrations, additions or colouring. Regular whisky tastings are held downstairs.

Cambridge Satchel Company Fashion & Accessories
(Map p248; ☑020-3077 1100; www.cambridgesatchel.com; 31 James St, WC2; ⊙10am-7pm Mon-Sat, 11am-6pm Sun; ⊖Covent Garden) The classic British leather satchel concept has morphed into a trendy and colourful array of backpacks, totes, clutches, work and music bags, mini satchels and more for men and women.

Skoob Books Books
(Map p254; ☑020-7278 8760; www.skoob.com; 66 The Brunswick, off Marmont St, WC1; ⊙10.30am-8pm Mon-Sat, to 6pm Sun; ⊖Russell Sq) Skoob (you work out the name) has got to be London's largest secondhand bookshop, with some 60,000 titles spread over 2000 sq ft of floor space (plus more than a million further books in a warehouse outside town). If you can't find it here, it probably doesn't exist.

Penhaligon's Perfume
(Map p248; ☑020-7629 1416; www.penhaligons.com; 16-17 Burlington Arcade, W1; ⊙10am-6pm Mon-Fri, 9.30am-6.30pm Sat, 11.30am-5.30pm Sun; ⊖Piccadilly Circus, Green Park) Located in the historic Burlington Arcade, Penhaligon's is a classic British perfumery. Attendants inquire about your favourite smells, take you on an exploratory tour of the shop's signature range and help you discover new scents in their traditional perfumes, home fragrances and bath and body products. Everything is produced in England.

Foyles Books
(Map p248; ☑020-7434 1574; www.foyles.co.uk; 107 Charing Cross Rd, WC2; ⊙9.30am-9pm Mon-Sat, 11.30am-6pm Sun; ⊖Tottenham Court Rd) This is London's most legendary bookshop, where you can bet on finding even the most obscure of titles. Once synonymous with chaos, Foyles got its act together and in 2014 moved just down the road into the

spacious former home of Central St Martins art school. Thoroughly redesigned, its stunning new home is a joy to explore.

Stanford's   Books, Maps

(Map p248; ☏020-7836 1321; www.stanfords. co.uk; 12-14 Long Acre, WC2; ☺9am-8pm Mon-Sat, 11.30am-6pm Sun; ☻Leicester Sq or Covent Garden) Trading from this address since 1853, this granddaddy of travel bookshops and seasoned seller of maps, guides, globes and literature is a destination in its own right. Ernest Shackleton and David Livingstone and, more recently, Michael Palin and Brad Pitt have all popped in and shopped here.

Molton Brown   Cosmetics

(Map p248; ☏020-7240 8383; www.moltonbrown. co.uk; 18 Russell St, WC2; ☺10am-7pm Mon-Sat, 11am-6pm Sun; ☻Covent Garden) A fabulously fragrant British natural beauty range, Molton Brown is *the* choice for boutique hotel, posh restaurant and 1st-class airline bathrooms. Its skincare products offer plenty of pampering for both men and women. In this store you can also pick up home accessories.

Gay's the Word   Books

(Map p254; ☏020-7278 7654; www.gaystheword. co.uk; 66 Marchmont St, WC1; ☺10am-6.30pm Mon-Sat, 2-6pm Sun; ☻Russell Sq) This London gay institution has been selling books nobody else stocks since 1979, with a superb range of gay- and lesbian-interest books and magazines plus a real community spirit. Used books available as well.

Cath Kidston   Fashion & Accessories

(Map p250; ☏020-7935 6555; www.cathkidston. com; 51 Marylebone High St, W1; ☺10am-7pm Mon-Sat, 11am-5pm Sun; ☻Baker St) If you favour the preppy look, you'll love Cath Kidston's signature floral prints and vintage-inspired fashion. There is also a range of homewares and some delightful London-branded gift items.

Gosh!   Books

(Map p248; ☏020-7636 1011; www.goshlondon. com; 1 Berwick St, W1; ☺10.30am-7pm; ☻Piccadilly Circus) Make your way here for graphic novels, manga and children's books, such as the Tintin and Asterix series. It's also the perfect place for finding presents for kids and teenagers.

Reckless Records

Reckless Records — Music

(Map p248; ☎020-7437 4271; www.reckless.
co.uk; 30 Berwick St, W1; ⊙10am-7pm; ⊖Oxford
Circus, Tottenham Court Rd) This outfit hasn't
really changed in spirit since it first opened
its doors in 1984. It still stocks secondhand
records and CDs, from punk, soul, dance
and independent to mainstream.

Moomin Shop — Gifts & Souvenirs

(Map p248; ☎020-7240 7057; www.
themoominshop.com; 43 Market Bldg, Covent
Garden, WC2; ⊙10am-8pm Mon-Sat, to 7pm Sun;
⊖Covent Garden) This tiny shop in Covent
Garden's central market building is a temple
to all things Moomin, that weird hippo-like
character created by Finnish artist Tove
Jansson. Trays, coasters, enamel mugs,
plates, towels, lunchboxes – the whole works.

Monocle Shop — Fashion & Accessories

(Map p250; ☎020-7486 8770; www.monocle.
com; 2a George St, W1; ⊙11am-7pm Mon-Sat,
noon-5pm Sun; ⊖Bond St) Run by the people
behind the design and international
current-affairs magazine *Monocle,* this tiny
(and attitudy) shop stocks very costly clothing, bags, umbrellas and books (including
their own guides). But if you are a fan of
minimalist quality design, you'll want to
stop by. There's also the **Monocle Cafe**
(Map p250; http://cafe.monocle.com; 18 Chiltern
St, W1; mains from £5.50; ⊙7am-7pm Mon-Wed,
7am-8pm Thu & Fri, 8am-8pm Sat, 8am-7pm Sun;
⊙; ⊖Baker St) not far away on Chiltern St.

Sister Ray — Music

(Map p248; ☎020-7734 3297; www.sisterray.
co.uk; 75 Berwick St, W1; ⊙10am-8pm Mon-Sat,
noon-6pm Sun; ⊖Oxford Circus, Tottenham
Court Rd) If you were a fan of the late John
Peel on the BBC, this specialist in innovative, experimental and indie music is just
right for you. Those of you who have never
heard of him will probably also like the shop
that 'sells music to the masses'.

Benjamin Pollock's Toy Shop — Toys

(Map p248; ☎: 020-7379 7866; www.pol-
locks-coventgarden.co.uk; 1st fl, 44 Market Bldg,
Covent Garden, WC2; ⊙10.30am-6pm Mon-Wed,
10.30am-6.30pm Thu-Sat, 11am-6pm Sun;

🛍 Chain Stores

Many bemoan the fact that chains have
taken over the main shopping centres,
leaving independent shops struggling
to balance the books. But since these
stores are cheap, fashionable and
always conveniently located, Londoners
(and others) keep going back for more.
As well as familiar overseas retailers,
such as Gap, H&M, Urban Outfitters and
Zara, you'll find plenty of home-grown
chains, including luxury womenswear
brand **Reiss** (www.reiss.com) and shoe
designer **L.K. Bennett** (www.lkben-
nett.com) – both regularly worn by
Catherine, Duchess of Cambridge – and
global giant Topshop (p130), for whom
super model Kate Moss has designed a
number of limited-edition collections.

Topshop on the Strand
ELENA ROSTUNOVA/SHUTTERSTOCK ©

⊖Covent Garden) This traditional toy shop
is stuffed with the things that kids of all
ages love: Victorian paper theatres, wooden
marionettes and finger puppets, and antique teddy bears (that look far too fragile
to cuddle, much less play with).

🔒 West London

Rough Trade West — Music

(Map p250; ☎020-7229 8541; www.roughtrade.
com; 130 Talbot Rd, W11; ⊙10am-6.30pm Mon-
Sat, 11am-5pm Sun; ⊖Ladbroke Grove) With
its underground, alternative and vintage
rarities, this home of the eponymous punk-
music label remains a haven for vinyl junkies.

BAR OPEN

Afternoon pints, all-night clubbing
and beyond

Bar Open

There is little Londoners like to do more than drink: from Hogarth's 18th-century Gin Lane prints to former mayor Boris Johnson's decision to ban all alcohol on public transport in 2008, the capital's history has been shot through with the population's desire to imbibe as much alcohol as possible and party into the night.

The metropolis offers a huge variety of venues at which to wet your whistle, from neighbourhood pubs to all-night clubs and everything in between. Note that when it comes to clubbing, a little planning will help you keep costs down and skip queues.

In This Section

Opening Hours

Pubs usually open at 11am or midday and close at 11pm, with a slightly earlier closing on a Sunday. On Friday and Saturday, some bars and pubs remain open to around 2am or 3am.

Clubs generally open at 10pm and close between 3am and 7am.

North London
Atmospheric pubs and
live music (p178)

**Clerkenwell, Shoreditch
& Spitalfields**
Edgy clubs and
hip bars (p174)

West London
Traditional pubs, river
views, relaxed evenings
(p183)

The City
Post-work punters,
quiet after 10pm
(p178)

East London
Increasingly trendy,
with excellent
bars (p175)

The West End
Legendary establishments,
up-for-it crowds (p179)

The South Bank
Franchises and
good ol' boozers
(p179)

**Greenwich &
South London**
Vibrant parties and
old-school pubs
(p177)

River Thames

Costs & Tipping

Many clubs are free or cheaper mid-week. If you want to go to a famous club on a Saturday night (the night for clubbing), expect to pay around £20. Some places are considerably cheaper if you arrive earlier in the night.

Tipping isn't customary.

Useful Websites

London on the Inside (www.londontheinside.com)

Skiddle (www.skiddle.com) Comprehensive info on nightclubs, DJs and events.

Time Out (www.timeout.com/london) Has details of bars, pubs and nightlife.

The Best...

Experience London's finest drinking establishments

Best Cocktail Bars

Worship St Whistling Shop (p175) Molecular cocktails at a Victorian-style drinking den.

Dukes London (p179) Bond-perfect martinis in gentleman's-club surroundings.

Swift (p181) Bespoke cocktails at a new Soho favourite.

Zetter Townhouse Cocktail Lounge (p174) Wonderfully quirky boudoir surroundings and devilishly good drinks.

Best Pubs

Dove Freehouse (p176) Great beers, great atmosphere – just how a pub should be.

Dove Freehouse bar(p174) A delightfully cosy 16th-century pub in a hidden alleyway.

Prospect of Whitby (p175; pictured above) London's oldest river pub, with Thames views and an open fire in winter.

Princess Louise (p182) A splendid Victorian pub with decorated tiles, etched mirrors and wood panelling.

Best for Clubbing

XOYO (p174) Excellent and varied gigs, club nights and art events.

Dalston Superstore (p176) Part bar, part club, straight and gay. It works.

Heaven (p182; pictured above) A longstanding favourite on the gay clubbing circuit.

Roof Gardens (p183) Clubbing cum roof gardens and flamingos. Obviously.

Best for Views

Madison (p178) Look into the heart of St Paul's and beyond from One New Change.

Oblix (p179) It's not even halfway up the Shard, but the views are legendary.

Netil360 (p175) Fab city views from hip rooftop bar – croquet, anyone?

Best Beer Gardens

Windsor Castle (p183; pictured above) Come summer, regulars abandon the Windsor's historic interior for the chilled-out garden.

Edinboro Castle (p178) A festive place to stretch out on a summer evening.

Greenwich Union (p177) Work your way through the Meantime brews from a garden table.

Best Bars

Gordon's Wine Bar (p182) A classic and long-standing London institution in darkened vaults.

Bar Pepito (p178) A delightful, pocket-sized Andalusian bar dedicated to lovers of sherry.

French House (p182) Soho's best boozer, with a steady supply of pastis and local eccentrics.

★ Lonely Planet's Top Choices

Princess Louise (p182) A stunner of a Victorian pub with snugs and a riot of etched glass.

Worship St Whistling Shop (p175) Fine-dining sophistication in liquid form.

Cat & Mutton (p175) Simultaneously traditional and hip, and always up for a party.

Trafalgar Tavern (p177) Riverside tavern oozing history.

The Pub

The pub (public house) is at the heart of London life and is one of the capital's great social levellers. Virtually every Londoner has a 'local' and looking for your own is a fun part of any visit.

Pubs in central London are mostly after-work drinking dens, busy from 5pm onwards with the postwork crowd during the week and revellers at weekends. In more residential areas, pubs come into their own at weekends, when long lunches turn into sloshy afternoons and groups of friends settle in for the night. Many also run popular quizzes on week nights. Other pubs entice punters through the doors with live music or comedy. Some have developed such a reputation for the quality of their food that they've been dubbed 'gastropubs'.

You'll be able to order almost anything you like in a pub, from beer to wine, soft drinks, spirits and sometimes hot drinks too. Some specialise in craft beer, offering drinks from local microbreweries, including real ale, fruit beers, organic ciders and other rarer beverages. Others, particularly the gastropubs, have invested in a good wine list.

In winter, some pubs offer mulled wine; in summer the must-have drink is Pimms and lemonade (if it's properly done it should have fresh mint leaves, citrus, strawberries and cucumber).

🍷 Clerkenwell, Shoreditch & Spitalfields

Ye Olde Mitre   Pub
(Map p253; www.yeoldemitreholborn.co.uk; 1 Ely Ct, EC1N; ⊙11am-11pm Mon-Fri; 🛜; ⊖Farringdon) A delightfully cosy historic pub with an extensive beer selection, tucked away in a backstreet off Hatton Garden. Ye Olde Mitre was built in 1546 for the servants of Ely Palace. There's no music, so rooms echo only with amiable chit-chat. Queen Elizabeth I danced around the cherry tree by the bar, they say.

Zetter Townhouse
Cocktail Lounge   Cocktail Bar
(Map p253; ☎020-7324 4545; www.thezettertownhouse.com; 49-50 St John's Sq, EC1V; ⊙7.30am-12.45am; 🛜; ⊖Farringdon) Tucked away behind an unassuming door on St John's Sq, this ground-floor bar is decorated with plush armchairs, stuffed animal heads and a legion of lamps. The cocktail list takes its theme from the area's distilling history – recipes of yesteryear plus homemade tinctures and cordials are used to create interesting and unusual tipples. House cocktails are all £10.50.

Fabric   Club
(Map p253; www.fabriclondon.com; 77a Charterhouse Street, EC1M; £5-25; ⊙11pm-7am Fri-Sun; ⊖Farringdon or Barbican) London's leading club, Fabric's three separate dance floors in a huge converted cold store opposite Smithfield meat market draws impressive queues (buy tickets online). FabricLive (on selected Fridays) rumbles with drum and bass and dubstep, while Fabric (usually on Saturdays but also on selected Fridays) is the club's signature live DJ night. Sunday's WetYourSelf! delivers house, techno and electronica.

XOYO   Club
(Map p253; www.xoyo.co.uk; 32-37 Cowper St, EC2A; ⊙9pm-4am Fri & Sat, hours vary Sun-Thu; ⊖Old St) This fantastic Shoreditch warehouse club throws together a pulsing and popular mix of gigs, club nights and

Dove Freehouse (p176)

art events. It has a varied line-up of indie bands, hip hop, electro, dub-step and much in between, and attracts a mix of clubbers, from skinny-jeaned hipsters to more mature hedonists (but no suits).

Worship St Whistling Shop
Cocktail Bar

(Map p253; 020-7247 0015; www. whistlingshop.com; 63 Worship St, EC2A; 5pm-midnight Mon & Tue, to 1am Wed & Thu, to 2am Fri & Sat; Old St) While the name is Victorian slang for a place selling illicit booze, this subterranean drinking den's master mixologists explore the experimental limits of cocktail chemistry and aromatic science, and they also concoct the classics. Many ingredients are made with rotary evaporators in the on-site lab. Also runs cocktail masterclasses.

East London

Netil360
Bar

(Map p255; www.netil360.com; 1 Westgate St, E8; 10am-10pm Wed-Fri, noon-11pm Sat & Sun Apr-

Nov; 55) Perched atop Netil House, this uber-hip rooftop cafe/bar offers incredible views over London, with brass telescopes enabling you to get better acquainted with workers in the Gherkin. In between drinks you can knock out a game of croquet on the AstroTurf, or perhaps book a hot tub for you and your mates to stew in.

Cat & Mutton
Pub

(Map p255; 020-7249 6555; www. catandmutton.com; 76 Broadway Market, E8; noon-midnight Sun-Fri, 10am-1pm Sat; 394) At this fabulous Georgian pub, Hackney hipsters sup pints under the watchful eyes of hunting trophies, black-and-white photos of old-time boxers and a large portrait of Karl Marx. If it's crammed downstairs, as it often is, head up the spiral staircase to the comfy couches. DJs spin funk, disco and soul on the weekends.

Prospect of Whitby
Pub

(57 Wapping Wall, E1; noon-11pm; Wapping) Once known as the Devil's Tavern, the Whitby is said to date from 1520, making it the oldest riverside pub in London.

From left: Trafalgar Tavern; Counting House (p178); Cutty Sark Tavern

Famous patrons have included Charles Dickens and Samuel Pepys so it's firmly on the tourist trail. There's a smallish terrace overlooking the Thames, a restaurant upstairs, open fires in winter and a pewter-topped bar.

Dove Freehouse   Pub
(Map p255; ☎020-7275 7617; www.dovepubs. com; 24-28 Broadway Market, E8; ☻noon-11pm Sun-Fri, 11am-11pm Sat; ☏; ☐394) Alluring at any time, the Dove has a rambling series of rooms and a wide range of Belgian Trappist, wheat and fruit-flavoured beers. Drinkers spill on to the street in warmer weather, or hunker down in the low-lit back room with board games when it's chilly.

Carpenter's Arms   Pub
(Map p255; ☎020-7739 6342; www.carpentersarmsfreehouse.com; 73 Cheshire St, E2; ☻4-11.30pm Mon-Wed, noon-11.30pm Thu-Sun; ☏; ☻Shoreditch High St) Once owned by infamous gangsters the Kray brothers (who bought it for their old ma to run), this chic yet cosy pub has been beautifully restored and its many wooden surfaces positively

gleam. A back room and small yard provide a little more space for the convivial drinkers. There's a huge range of draught and bottled beers and ciders.

Draughts   Bar
(Map p253; www.draughtslondon.com; 337 Acton Mews, E8; ☻10am-5pm & 6pm-11pm Mon-Thu & Sun, to midnight Fri, 10am-midnight Sat; ☐Haggerston) London's first board-game theme bar – it has over 500 to choose from – offers a delightfully geeky way to while away an afternoon. Food, wine and ale are served all day and there is even a 'game guru' on hand to explain rules and advise which games are best suited to your group's wants.

Dalston Superstore   Gay
(Map p255; ☎020-7254 2273; www. dalstonsuperstore.com; 117 Kingsland High St, E8; ☻11.45am-late; ☻Dalston Kingsland) Bar, club or diner? Gay or straight? Dalston Superstore is hard to pigeonhole, which we suspect is the point. This two-level industrial space is open all day but really comes into its own after dark when there are club nights in the basement.

D HALE SUTTON/ALAMY STOCK PHOTO ©

🟢 Greenwich & South London

Cutty Sark Tavern   Pub

(Map p256; 📞020-8858 3146; www.
cuttysarkse10.co.uk; 4-6 Ballast Quay, SE10;
⏲11.30am-11pm Mon-Sat, noon-10.30pm Sun;
🛜; 🚈DLR Cutty Sark) Housed in a delightful
bow-windowed, wood-beamed Georgian
building directly on the Thames, the Cutty
Sark is one of the few independent pubs
left in Greenwich. Half a dozen cask-
conditioned ales on tap line the bar, there's
an inviting riverside seating area opposite
and an upstairs dining room looking out on
to glorious views. It's a 10-minute walk from
the DLR station.

Greenwich Union   Pub

(Map p256; www.greenwichunion.com; 56 Royal
Hill, SE10; ⏲noon-11pm Mon-Fri, 10am-11pm
Sat, 10am-10.30pm Sun; 🚈DLR Greenwich) The
award-winning Union plies six or seven
Meantime microbrewery beers, including
raspberry and wheat varieties, and has a
strong list of ales and bottled international
brews. It's a handsome place, with duffed-
up leather armchairs and a welcoming long,
narrow aspect that leads to a conservatory
and beer garden at the rear.

Trafalgar Tavern   Pub

(Map p256; 📞020-8858 2909; www.
trafalgartavern.co.uk; 6 Park Row, SE10; ⏲noon-
11pm Mon-Thu, noon-midnight Fri, 10am-midnight
Sat, 10am-11pm Sun; 🚈DLR Cutty Sark) This
elegant tavern with big windows overlooking
the Thames is steeped in history. Dickens
apparently knocked back a few here – and
used it as the setting for the wedding
breakfast scene in *Our Mutual Friend* – and
prime ministers Gladstone and Disraeli used
to dine on the pub's celebrated whitebait.

🟢 Kensington & Hyde Park

Queen's Arms   Pub

(Map p250; www.thequeensarmskensington.
co.uk; 30 Queen's Gate Mews, SW7; ⏲noon-11pm
Mon-Sat, to 10.30pm Sun; 🚇Gloucester Rd) Just
around the corner from the Royal Albert
Hall, this godsend of a blue-grey painted
pub in an adorable cobbled mews setting
off bustling Queen's Gate beckons with a

cosy interior and a right royal selection of ales – including selections from small, local cask brewers – and ciders on tap. In warm weather, drinkers stand outside in the mews (only permitted on one side).

⊖ North London

Bar Pepito   Wine Bar
(Map p254; www.barpepito.co.uk; 3 Varnishers Yard, The Regent's Quarter, N1; ☺5pm-midnight Mon-Sat; ⊖King's Cross St Pancras) This tiny, intimate Andalusian bodega specialises in sherry and tapas. Novices fear not: the staff are on hand to advise. They're also experts at food pairings (top-notch ham and cheese selections). To go the whole hog, try a tasting flight of selected sherries with snacks to match.

Proud Camden   Bar
(Map p254; www.proudcamden.com; Stables Market, Chalk Farm Rd, NW1; ☺11am-1.30am Mon-Sat, to midnight Sun; ⊖Chalk Farm) Proud occupies a former horse hospital within Stables Market, with private booths in the old stalls, fantastic artworks on the walls (the main bar acts as a gallery during the day) and a kooky garden terrace complete with a hot tub. It's also one of Camden's best music venues, with live bands and DJs most nights (entry free to £15).

Edinboro Castle   Pub
(Map p254; www.edinborocastlepub.co.uk; 57 Mornington Tce, NW1; ☺11am-11pm; ☎; ⊖Camden Town) Large and relaxed Edinboro offers a refined atmosphere, gorgeous furniture perfect for slumping into, a fine bar and a full menu. The highlight, however, is the huge beer garden, complete with warm-weather BBQs and lit up with colour-ed lights on long summer evenings. Patio heaters come out in winter.

⊖ The City

Madison   Cocktail Bar
(Map p245; ☎020-3693 5160; www.madisonlondon.net; Rooftop Terrace, One New Change, EC4; ☺11am-midnight Mon-Wed, to 1am Thu-Sat, to 9pm Sun; ⊖St Paul's) Perched atop One New Change with a drop-dead view of St Paul's and beyond, Madison offers one of the largest public open-air roof terraces you'll ever encounter. There's a full restaurant and bar on one side and a cocktail bar with outdoor seating on the other. We come for the latter. Drinkers must be over 21; dress code is smart casual.

Blackfriar   Pub
(Map p245; ☎020-7236 5474; www.nicholsonspubs.co.uk/theblackfriarblackfriarslondon; 174 Queen Victoria St, EC4V; ☺9am-11pm Mon-Fri, noon-10.30pm Sun; ⊖Blackfriars) It may look like the corpulent friar above the entrance just stepped out of this olde-worlde pub just north of Blackfriars station, but the interior is actually an art-nouveau makeover from 1905. Built on the site of a monastery of Dominicans (who wore black robes), the theme is appealingly celebrated throughout the pub. It has a good selection of ales.

Ye Olde Cheshire Cheese   Pub
(Map p245; ☎020-7353 6170; Wine Office Court, 145 Fleet St, EC4; ☺11.30am-11pm Mon-Fri, noon-11pm Sat; ⊖Chancery Lane) The entrance to this historic pub is via a narrow alley off Fleet St. Over its long history, locals have included Dr Johnson, Thackeray and Dickens. Despite (or possibly because of) this, the Cheshire can feel a bit like a museum. Nevertheless it's one of London's most famous and historic pubs and well worth popping in for a pint.

Counting House   Pub
(Map p245; ☎020-7283 7123; www.the-counting-house.com; 50 Cornhill, EC3; ☺10am-11pm Mon-Fri; ☎; ⊖Bank) With its counters and basement vaults, this award-winning pub certainly looks and feels comfortable in the former headquarters of NatWest Bank (1893) with its domed skylight and beautifully appointed main bar. This is a favourite of City boys and girls, who come for the good range of real ales and the speciality pies (from £12).

📍 The South Bank

Oblix   Bar

(Map p245; www.oblixrestaurant.com; 32nd fl, Shard, 31 St Thomas St, SE1; ⊘noon-11pm; ⊖London Bridge) On the 32nd floor of the Shard (p79), Oblix offers mesmerising vistas of London. You can come for anything from a coffee (£3.50) to a cocktail (from £10) and enjoy virtually the same views as the official viewing galleries of the Shard (but at a reduced cost and with the added bonus of a drink). Live music every night from 7pm.

Little Bird Gin   Cocktail Bar

(Map p245; www.littlebirdgin.com; Maltby St, SE1; ⊘10am-4pm Sat, from 11am Sun; ⊖London Bridge) This South London–based distillery opens a pop-up bar in a workshop at Maltby Street Market (p146) to ply merry punters with devilishly good cocktails (£5 to £7), served in jam jars or apothecary's glass bottles.

Scootercaffe   Bar

(Map p245; 132 Lower Marsh, SE1; ⊘8.30am-11pm Mon-Fri, 10am-midnight Sat, to 11pm Sun; ⊛; ⊖Waterloo) A well-established fixture on the up-and-coming Lower Marsh road, this funky cafe-bar and former scooter repair shop with a Piatti scooter in the window serves killer hot chocolates, coffee and decadent cocktails. Unusually, you're allowed to bring in takeaway food. The tiny patio at the back is perfect for soaking up the sun.

📍 The West End

Dukes London   Cocktail Bar

(Map p248; ☎020-7491 4840; www.dukeshotel.com/dukes-bar; Dukes Hotel, 35 St James's Pl, SW1; ⊘2-11pm Mon-Sat, 4-10.30pm Sun; ⊛; ⊖Green Park) Sip to-die-for martinis in a gentleman's-club-like ambience at this tucked-away classic bar where white-jacketed masters mix up some awesomely good preparations. Ian Fleming used to frequent the place, perhaps perfecting his 'shaken, not stirred' James Bond maxim. Smokers can ease into the secluded Cognac and Cigar Garden to light up cigars purchased here.

🍺 Beer

The *raison d'être* of a pub is first and foremost to serve beer – be it lager, ale or stout in a glass or a bottle. On draught (drawn from the cask), it is served by the pint (570mL) or half-pint (285mL) and, more occasionally, third-of-a-pint for real ale tasting.

Pubs generally serve a good selection of lager (highly carbonated and drunk cool or cold) and a smaller selection of real ales or 'bitter' (still or only slightly gassy, drunk at room temperature, with strong flavours). The best-known British lager brand is Carling, although you'll find everything from Fosters to San Miguel.

Among the multitude of ales on offer in London pubs, London Pride, Courage Best, Burton Ale, Adnam's, Theakston (in particular Old Peculiar) and Old Speckled Hen are among the best. Once considered something of an old man's drink, real ale is enjoying a renaissance among young Londoners keen to sample flavours from the country's brewing tradition. Staff at bars serving good selections of real ales are often hugely knowledgeable, just like a sommelier in a restaurant with a good cellar, so ask them for recommendations if you're not sure what to order.

Stout, the best known of which is Irish Guinness, is a slightly sweet, dark beer with a distinct flavour that comes from malt that is roasted before fermentation.

London in a Glass

Beer begins with four core ingredients: water, malt, hops and yeast

English beer is often served at room temperature

Beer that's brewed and served traditionally is called 'real ale' to distinguish it from the mass-produced brands

It typically ranges from dark brown to bright amber in colour

BEER PINT/GETTY IMAGES ©

Know Your Craft Beer

Craft beer in London

The growing interest in small-batch or artisan beer over the past five to 10 years has been spectacular. It is now de rigueur for virtually every pub to serve at least a couple of craft beers. London has also a raft of microbreweries, many of which you can visit; popular brews to try include Camden Town, Beavertown, London Fields, Redchurch and Meantime.

Equipment in a boutique microbrewery
ZSTOCK/SHUTTERSTOCK ©

★ Top Three Places for a Pint

Anspach & Hobday (Map p245; www.anspachandhobday.com; 118 Druid St, SE1; ☺5-9pm Fri, 10.30am-5.30pm Sat, 12.30-5pm Sun; ⊖London Bridge) **Beer aficionados will also love trying brews from the experimental range.**

Howling Hops (Map p255; www.howlinghops.co.uk; Queen's Yard, White Post Lane, E9; ☺noon-11pm Mon-Thurs & Sun, noon-midnight Fri & Sat; ⊠Hackney Wick) **The tank bar at the Howling Hops brewery is the first of its kind in the UK, and as such serves arguably the freshest beer not just in London, but the country.**

Euston Tap (Map p254; ☏020-3137 8837; www.eustontap.com; 190 Euston Rd, NW1; ☺noon-11pm; ⊖Euston) **At this specialist boozery, craft beer devotees can choose between seven cask ales, 20 keg beers and 150 by the bottle.**

American Bar   Cocktail Bar

(Map p248; ☑020-7836 4343; www.fairmont.
com/savoy-london/dining/americanbar; Savoy,
The Strand, WC2; ☺11.30am-midnight Mon-Sat,
noon-midnight Sun; ⊖Covent Garden) Home
of the Hanky Panky, White Lady and other
classic infusions created en situ, the
seriously dishy and elegant American Bar
is an icon of London, with soft blue and rust
art-deco lines and live piano music. Cocktails
start at £16.50 and peak at a stupefying
£5000 (The Original Sazerac, containing
Sazerac de Forge cognac from 1857).

Dog & Duck   Pub

(Map p248; ☑020-7494 0697; www.
nicholsonspubs.co.uk/restaurants/london/
thedoganducksoholondon; 18 Bateman St,
W1; ☺11am-11pm Mon-Sat, noon-10pm Sun;
⊖Tottenham Court Rd) With a fine array of
real ales, some stunning Victorian glazed
tiling and garrulous crowds spilling onto the
pavement, the Dog & Duck has attracted a
host of famous regulars, including painters
John Constable and pre-Raphaelite Dante
Gabrielle Rossetti, dystopian writer George
Orwell and musician Madonna.

She Soho   Lesbian

(Map p248; ☑020-7287 5041; www.she-soho.
com; 23a Old Compton St, W1D; ☺4-11.30pm
Mon-Thu, noon-midnight Fri & Sat, noon-10.30pm
Sun; ⊖Leicester Sq) This intimate and dimly
lit basement bar has DJs, comedy, cabaret,
burlesque, live music and party nights.
Open till 3am on the last Friday and Saturday of the month. Everybody is welcome at
this friendly place.

Draft House   Bar

(Map p248; ☑020-7323 9361; www.drafthouse.
co.uk; 43 Goodge St, W1; ☺noon-11pm Mon-Thu,
to midnight Fri & Sat; ☎; ⊖Goodge St) Although
you can line your tummy with decent nosh,
Draft House (and its nine other branches
strewn throughout London) is largely about
the beer choice it crams into its pea-sized
premises. This is a public house for ale
aficionados, where you can happily corner
Sambook's from Battersea or choose from
several cask and a dozen keg ales.

Terroirs   Wine Bar

(Map p248; ☑020-7036 0660; www.
terroirswinebar.com; 5 William IV St, WC2;
☺noon-11pm Mon-Sat; ☎; ⊖Charing Cross Rd)
A fab two-floor spot for a pretheatre glass
and some expertly created charcuterie,
with informative staff, tempting and
affordable £10 lunch specials, a lively,
convivial atmosphere and a breathtaking
list of organic, natural and biodynamic
wines.

Swift   Cocktail Bar

(Map p248; ☑020-7437 7820; www.barswift.
com; 12 Old Compton St, W1; ☺3pm-midnight
Mon-Sat, to 10.30pm Sun; ⊖Leicester Sq or Tottenham Court Rd) Our favourite new place for
cocktails, Swift (as in the bird) has a black-
and-white, candlelit Upstairs Bar designed
for those who want a quick tipple before
dinner or the theatre, while the Downstairs
Bar (open from 5pm), with its sit-down bar
and art deco sofas, is a place to hang out.
There's live jazz and blues at the weekend.

Queen's Larder   Pub

(Map p254; ☑020-7837 5627; www.queenslarder.
co.uk; 1 Queen Sq, WC1; ☺11.30am-11pm Mon-Fri,
noon-11pm Sat, noon-10.30pm Sun; ⊖Russell
Sq) In a lovely square southeast of Russell
Sq is this cosy pub, so called because
Queen Charlotte, wife of 'Mad' King George
III, rented part of the pub's cellar to store
special foods for her husband while he
was being treated nearby for what is now
believed to have been the genetic disease
porphyria. There are benches outside and a
dining room upstairs.

Lamb & Flag   Pub

(Map p248; ☑020-7497 9504; www.
lambandflagcoventgarden.co.uk; 33 Rose St,
WC2; ☺11am-11pm Mon-Sat, noon-10.30pm Sun;
⊖Covent Garden) Everybody's favourite pub
in central London, pint-sized Lamb & Flag
is full of charm and history. It's on the site
of a pub that dates to at least 1772. Rain
or shine, you'll have to elbow your way to
the bar through the merry crowd drinking
outside. Inside are brass fittings and creaky
wooden floors.

Clubbing

When it comes to clubbing, London is up there with the best of them. You'll probably know what you want to experience – it might be big clubs or sweaty shoebox clubs with the freshest DJ talent – but there's plenty to tempt you to branch out from your usual tastes and try something new.

There are clubs across town. The East End is the top area for cutting-edge clubs, especially Shoreditch. Dalston and Hackney are popular for makeshift clubs in restaurant basements and former shops – so it's great for night-fun hunters. Camden Town still favours the indie crowd, while King's Cross has a bit of everything. The gay party crowd mainly gravitates to the south of the river, especially Vauxhall, although gay clubs still maintain a toehold in the West and East End.

Fabric (p174)
PYMCA/CONTRIBUTOR/GETTY IMAGES ©

Gordon's Wine Bar   Bar

(Map p248; ☑020-7930 1408; www.
gordonswinebar.com; 47 Villiers St, WC2; ☺11am-11pm Mon-Sat, noon-10pm Sun; ⊖Embankment or Charing Cross) Cavernous, candlelit and atmospheric, Gordon's (founded in 1890) is a victim of its own success – it's relentlessly busy and unless you arrive before the office crowd does (around 6pm), forget about landing a table. The French and New World wines are heady and reasonably priced; buy by the glass, the beaker (12cl), the schooner (15cl) or the bottle.

Princess Louise   Pub

(Map p248; ☑020-7405 8816; http://
princesslouisepub.co.uk; 208 High Holborn, WC1; ☺11am-11pm Mon-Fri, noon-11pm Sat, noon-6.45pm Sun; ⊖Holborn) The ground-floor saloon of this pub dating from 1872 is spectacularly decorated with a riot of fine tiles, etched mirrors, plasterwork and a stunning central horseshoe bar. The old Victorian wood partitions give drinkers plenty of nooks and alcoves to hide in and the frosted-glass 'snob screens' add further period allure.

French House Soho   Pub

(Map p248; ☑020-7437 2477; www.
frenchhousesoho.com; 49 Dean St, W1; ☺noon-11pm Mon-Sat, to 10.30pm Sun; ⊖Leicester Sq) French House is Soho's legendary boho boozer with a history to match: this was the meeting place of the Free French Forces during WWII. De Gaulle is said to have drunk here often, while Dylan Thomas, Peter O'Toole and Francis Bacon all ended up on the wooden floor at least once.

Heaven   Club, Gay

(Map p248; http://heaven-live.co.uk; Villiers St, WC2; ☺11pm-5am Mon, Thu & Fri, 10pm-5am Sat; ⊖Embankment or Charing Cross) This perennially popular gay club under the arches beneath Charing Cross station since 1979 is host to excellent live gigs and club nights. Monday's Popcorn (mixed dance party, all-welcome door policy) offers some of the best weeknight clubbing in the capital. The celebrated G-A-Y takes place here on Thursday (G-A-Y Porn Idol), Friday (G-A-Y Camp Attack) and Saturday (plain ol' G-A-Y).

Lamb   Pub

(Map p254; ☑020-7405 0713; www.thelamblondon.
com; 94 Lamb's Conduit St, WC1; ☺11am-11pm Mon-Wed, to midnight Thu-Sat, noon-10.30pm Sun; ⊖Russell Sq) The Lamb's central mahogany bar with beautiful Victorian 'snob screens' (so-called as they allowed the well-to-do to drink in private) has been a favourite with locals since 1729. Nearly three centuries later, its popularity hasn't waned, so come early to bag a booth and sample its good selection of Young's bitters and genial atmosphere.

Yard — Gay
(Map p248; ✏020-7437 2652; www.yardbar.
co.uk; 57 Rupert St, W1; ⏱4-11.30pm Mon & Tue,
noon-11.30pm Wed & Thu, noon-midnight Fri &
Sat, 1-10.30pm Sun; ⊖Piccadilly Circus) This
Soho favourite attracts a cross-section of
the great and the good. It's fairly attitude-
free, perfect for preclub drinks or just an
evening out. There are DJs upstairs in the
renovated Loft Bar most nights as well as
a friendly crowd in the open-air (heated in
season) Courtyard Bar below.

⊖ West London

Roof Gardens — Club
(Map p250; www.roofgardens.virgin.com; 99
Kensington High St, W8; club £20, gardens free;
⏱club 10pm-2am Fri & Sat, garden 9am-5pm (on
selected dates); 📶; ⊖High St Kensington) Atop
the former Derry and Toms building is this
enchanting venue – a nightclub with 0.6
hectares of gardens and resident flamingos. The wow-factor requires £20 entry,
you must register on the guest list (http://
gls.roofgardens.com/) before going and

drinks are £10 a pop. Open to over-21s, the
dress code is 'no effort, no entry' (leave the
onesie at home).

Windsor Castle — Pub
(Map p250; www.thewindsorcastlekensington.
co.uk; 114 Campden Hill Rd, W11; ⏱noon-11pm
Mon-Sat, to 10.30pm Sun; 📶; ⊖Notting Hill Gate)
A classic tavern on the brow of Campden
Hill Rd, this place has history, nooks and
charm on tap. It's worth the search for its
historic compartmentalised interior, roaring fire (in winter), delightful beer garden
(in summer) and affable regulars (most
always). According to legend, the bones of
Thomas Paine (author of *Rights of Man*) are
in the cellar.

Notting Hill Arts Club — Club
(Map p250; www.nottinghillartsclub.com; 21
Notting Hill Gate, W11; ⏱6pm-late Mon-Fri, 4pm-
late Sat & Sun; 📶; ⊖Notting Hill Gate) London
simply wouldn't be what it is without places
like NHAC. Cultivating the underground
music scene, this small basement club attracts a musically curious and experimental crowd. Dress code: no suits and ties.

Windsor Castle pub

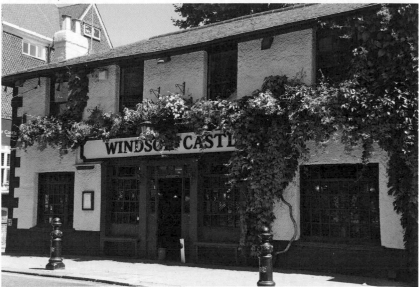

SHOWTIME

From a night out at the theatre
to live-music venues

Showtime

Whatever it is that sets your spirits soaring or your booty shaking, you'll find it in London. The city's been a world leader in theatre ever since a young man from Stratford-upon-Avon set up shop here in the 16th century. And if London started swinging in the 1960s, its live rock and pop scene has barely let up since.

The trick to bag tickets to high-profile events and performances is to book ahead – or hope there will be standby tickets on the day. And don't worry if you miss out: there are literally hundreds of smaller gigs and performances every night and the joy is to stumble upon them.

In This Section

Tickets

Book well ahead for live performances and if you can, buy directly from the venue.

On the day of performance, you can buy discounted tickets, sometimes up to 50% off, for West End productions from **Tkts Leicester Sq** (www.tkts.co.uk/leicester-square).

GUS STEWART/REDFERNS/GETTY IMAGES ©

All Time Low perform at the O2 Brixton Academy

The Best...

Theatre

Shakespeare's Globe (p190) Shakespeare, as it would have been 400 years ago.

National Theatre (p191) Contemporary theatre on the South Bank.

Wilton's (p188) The Victorian music-hall tradition lives on.

Live Music

Royal Albert Hall (p189) Gorgeous, grand and spacious, yet strangely intimate.

KOKO (p189) Fabulously glitzy venue showcasing original indie rock.

O2 Academy Brixton (p188) Legendary concert hall.

Royal Opera House (p194) One of the world's great opera venues.

✪ Clerkenwell, Shoreditch & Spitalfields

Sadler's Wells   Dance
(Map p253; ✆020-7863 8000;
www.sadlerswells.com; Rosebery Ave, EC1R;
◉Angel) A glittering modern venue that
was, in fact, first established in 1683,
Sadler's Wells is the most eclectic
modern-dance and ballet venue in town,
with experimental dance shows of all
genres and from all corners of the globe.
The Lilian Baylis Studio stages smaller
productions.

✪ East London

Vortex Jazz Club   Jazz
(Map p255; ✆020-7254 4097; www.vortexjazz.
co.uk; 11 Gillet Sq, N16; ◷8pm-midnight;
🚇Dalston Kingsland) With a fantastically
varied menu of jazz, the Vortex hosts an
outstanding line-up of musicians, singers
and songwriters from the UK, US, Europe,
Africa and beyond. It's a small venue so
make sure you book if there's an act you
particularly fancy.

Wilton's   Theatre
(Map p245; ✆020-7702 2789; www.wiltons.
org.uk; 1 Graces Alley, E1; tour £6; ◷tours 6pm
most Mon, bar 5-11pm Mon-Sat; ◉Tower Hill)
A gloriously atmospheric example of one
of London's Victorian public-house music
halls, Wilton's hosts a variety of shows,
from comedy and classical music to
theatre and opera. One-hour guided tours
offer an insight into its fascinating history.
The Mahogany Bar is a great way to get a
taste of the place if you're not attending a
performance.

Hackney Empire   Theatre
(Map p255; ✆020-8985 2424; www.
hackneyempire.co.uk; 291 Mare St, E8;
◉Hackney Central) One of London's
most beautiful theatres, this renovated
Edwardian music hall (1901) offers an
extremely diverse range of performances
– from hard-edged political theatre to

musicals, opera and comedy. It's one of the
very best places to catch a pantomime at
Christmas.

✪ Greenwich & South London

O2 Academy Brixton   Live Music
(www.o2academybrixton.co.uk; 211 Stockwell Rd,
SW9; ◷doors open 7pm most nights; ◉Brixton)
It's hard to have a bad night at the Brixton
Academy, even if you leave with your
soles sticky with beer, as this cavernous
former-5000-capacity art-deco theatre
always thrums with bonhomie. There's a
properly raked floor for good views, as well
as plenty of bars and an excellent mixed bill
of established and emerging talent. Most
shows are 14-plus.

Up the Creek   Comedy
(Map p256; www.up-the-creek.com; 302 Creek
Rd, SE10; admission £5-15; ◷7-11pm Thu & Sun,
to 2am Fri & Sat; 🚇DLR Cutty Sark) Bizarre-
ly enough, the hecklers can be funnier
than the acts at this great club. Mischief,
rowdiness and excellent comedy are the
norm, with the Blackout open-mic night on
Thursdays (www.the-blackout.co.uk, £5)
and Sunday specials (www.sundayspecial.
co.uk, £7). There's an after-party disco on
Fridays and Saturdays.

O2 Arena   Live Music
(www.theo2.co.uk; Peninsula Sq, SE10; 📶;
◉North Greenwich) One of the city's major
concert venues, hosting all the biggies –
the Rolling Stones, Paul Simon and Sting,
One Direction, Ed Sheeran and many
others – inside the 20,000-capacity arena.
It's also a popular venue for sporting
events.

✪ Kensington & Hyde Park

606 Club   Blues, Jazz
(✆020-7352 5953; www.606club.co.uk; 90 Lots
Rd, SW10; ◷7-11.15pm Sun-Thu, 8pm-12.30am
Fri & Sat; 🚇Imperial Wharf) Named after its

old address on King's Rd that cast a spell over jazz lovers London-wide back in the '80s, this fantastic, tucked-away basement jazz club and restaurant gives centre stage to contemporary British-based jazz musicians nightly. The club can only serve alcohol to nonmembers who are dining and it is highly advisable to book to get a table.

Royal Albert Hall   Concert Venue
(Map p250; ☎0845 401 5034; www. royalalberthall.com; Kensington Gore, SW7; ⊖South Kensington) This splendid Victorian concert hall hosts classical-music, rock and other performances, but is famously the venue for the BBC-sponsored Proms. Booking is possible, but from mid-July to mid-September Proms punters queue for £5 standing (or 'promenading') tickets that go on sale one hour before curtain-up. Otherwise, the box office and prepaid-ticket collection counter are through door 12 (south side of the hall).

✪ North London

Cecil Sharp House   Traditional Music
(Map p254; www.cecilsharphouse.org; 2 Regent's Park Rd, NW1; ⊖Camden Town) If you've ever fancied clog stamping, hanky waving or bell jingling, this is the place for you. Home to the English Folk Dance and Song Society, this institute keeps all manner of wacky folk traditions alive, with performances and classes held in its gorgeous mural-covered Kennedy Hall. The dance classes are oodles of fun; no experience necessary.

KOKO   Live Music
(Map p254; www.koko.uk.com; 1a Camden High St, NW1; ⊖Mornington Cres) Once the legendary Camden Palace, where Charlie Chaplin, the Goons and the Sex Pistols performed, and where Prince played surprise gigs, KOKO is maintaining its reputation as one of London's better gig venues. The theatre has a dance floor

 **Live Music**

Musically diverse and defiantly different, London is a hotspot of musical innovation and talent. It leads the world in articulate indie rock, in particular, and tomorrow's guitar heroes are right this minute paying their dues on sticky-floored stages in Camden Town, Shoreditch and Dalston.

Monster international acts see London as an essential stop on their transglobal stomps, but be prepared for tickets selling out faster than you can find your credit card. The city's beautiful old theatres and music halls play host to a constant roster of well-known names in more intimate settings. In summer, giant festivals take over the city's parks, while smaller, more localised events such as the **Dalston Music Festival** (www.dalstonmusicfestival.com) showcase up-and-comers in multiple spaces.

If jazz or blues are your thing, London has some truly excellent clubs and pubs where you can catch classics and contemporary tunes. The city's major jazz event is the **London Jazz Festival** (www.londonjazzfestival.org.uk) in November.

Ice-T and Ron McCurdy perform at the London Jazz Festival
JOSEPH OKPAKO / CONTRIBUTOR / GETTY IMAGES ©

and decadent balconies, and attracts an indie crowd. There are live bands most nights and hugely popular club nights on Saturdays.

Scala   Live Music

(Map p254; ☑020-7833 2022; www.scala.
co.uk; 275 Pentonville Rd, N1; ⊖King's Cross St
Pancras) Opened in 1920 as a salubrious
golden-age cinema, Scala slipped into
porn-movie hell in the 1970s only to be
reborn as a club and live-music venue in
the noughties. It's one of the best places in
London to catch an intimate gig and is also
a great dance space that hosts a diverse
range of club nights.

Regent's Park Open Air
Theatre   Theatre

(Map p254; ☑0844 826 4242; www.
openairtheatre.org; Queen Mary's Gardens,
Regent's Park, NW1; ⊙May-Sep; ⛐; ⊖Baker
St) A popular and very atmospheric
summertime fixture in London, this
1250-seat outdoor auditorium plays host
to four productions a year: famous plays
(Shakespeare often features), new works,
musicals and usually one production aimed
at families.

Roundhouse   Concert Venue

(www.roundhouse.org.uk; Chalk Farm Rd, NW1;
⊖Chalk Farm) Built as a railway-repair

shed in 1847, this unusual Grade II–listed
round building became an arts centre in
the 1960s and hosted legendary bands
before falling into near-dereliction in 1983.
Its 21st-century resurrection as a creative
hub has been a great success and it now
hosts everything from big-name concerts
to dance, circus, stand-up comedy, poetry
slam and improvisation.

✪ The City

Barbican   Performing Arts

(Map p253; ☑box office 020-7638 8891; www.
barbican.org.uk; Silk St, EC2; ⊙box office
10am-8pm Mon-Sat, from 11am Sun; ⊖Bar-
bican) Home to the wonderful London
Symphony Orchestra and its associate
orchestra, the lesser-known BBC Symphony Orchestra, the arts centre also
hosts scores of other leading musicians,
focusing in particular on jazz, folk, world
and soul artists. Dance is another strong
point here, while film covers recent
releases as well as film festivals and
seasons.

From left: Scala (p189); 100 Club (p194); Royal Festival
Hall; London Wonderground

⚙ The South Bank

Shakespeare's Globe — Theatre
(Map p245; ☎020-7401 9919; www.
shakespearesglobe.com; 21 New Globe Walk,
SE1; seats £20-45, standing £5; ⊜Blackfriars
or London Bridge) If you love Shakespeare
and the theatre, the Globe (p85) will knock
your theatrical socks off. This authentic
Shakespearean theatre is a wooden 'O'
without a roof over the central stage area,
and although there are covered wooden
bench seats in tiers around the stage, many
people (there's room for 700) do as 17th-
century 'groundlings' did, standing in front
of the stage.

Because the building is quite open to
the elements, you may have to wrap up.
Groundlings note: umbrellas are not allowed, but cheap raincoats are on sale. Unexpected aircraft noise is unavoidable, too.

The theatre season runs from late April
to mid-October and includes works by
Shakespeare and his contemporaries such
as Christopher Marlowe.

If you don't like the idea of standing in
the rain or sitting in the cold, opt for an
indoor candlelit play in the **Sam Wanamak-
er Playhouse**, a Jacobean theatre similar
to the one Shakespeare would have used
in winter. The programming also includes
opera.

National Theatre — Theatre
(Royal National Theatre; Map p245; ☎020-7452
3000; www.nationaltheatre.org.uk; South Bank,
SE1; ⊜Waterloo) England's flagship theatre
showcases a mix of classic and contemporary plays performed by excellent casts
in three theatres (Olivier, Lyttelton and
Dorfman). Artistic director Rufus Norris,
who started in April 2015, made headlines
in 2016 for announcing plans to stage a
Brexit-based drama.

Southbank Centre — Concert Venue
(Map p245; ☎0844 875 0073; www.
southbankcentre.co.uk; Belvedere Rd, SE1;
⊜Waterloo) The Southbank Centre
comprises several venues – **Royal Festival
Hall** (Map p245; ☎020-7960 4200; www.
southbankcentre.co.uk; Southbank Centre,
Belvedere Rd, SE1; 🛜; ⊜Waterloo), Queen
Elizabeth Hall and Purcell Room – hosting
a wide range of performing arts. As well

as regular programming, it organises fantastic festivals, including **London Wonderground** (circus and cabaret), **Udderbelly** (a festival of comedy in all its guises) and **Meltdown** (a music event curated by the best and most eclectic names in music).

Old Vic   Theatre

(Map p245; ☎0844 871 7628; www.oldvictheatre. com; The Cut, SE1; ⊖Waterloo) American actor Kevin Spacey took the theatrical helm of this London theatre in 2003, giving it a new lease of life. He was succeeded in April 2015 by Matthew Warchus (who directed *Matilda the Musical* and the film *Pride*), whose aim is to bring an eclectic programming to the theatre: expect new writing, as well as dynamic revivals of old works and musicals.

Young Vic   Theatre

(Map p245; ☎020-7922 2922; www.youngvic.org; 66 The Cut, SE1; ⊖Southwark or Waterloo) This ground-breaking theatre is as much about showcasing and discovering new talent as it is about people discovering theatre. The Young Vic features actors, directors and plays from across the world, many tackling contemporary political and cultural issues, such as the death penalty, racism or corruption, and often blending dance and music with acting.

✪ The West End

Pizza Express Jazz Club   Jazz

(Map p248; ☎020-7439 4962; www. pizzaexpresslive.com/venues/soho-jazz-club; 10 Dean St, W1; admission £15-40; ⊖Tottenham Court Rd) Pizza Express has been one of the best jazz venues in London since opening in 1969. It may be a strange arrangement, in a basement beneath a branch of the chain restaurant, but it's highly popular. Lots of big names perform here and promising artists such as Norah Jones, Gregory Porter and the late Amy Winehouse played here in their early days.

★ Theatre

A night out at the theatre is as much a must-do London experience as a trip on the top deck of a double-decker bus. London's Theatreland in the dazzling West End – from Aldwych in the east, past Shaftesbury Ave to Regent St in the west – has a concentration of theatres only rivalled by New York's Broadway. It's a thrillingly diverse scene, encompassing Shakespeare's classics performed with old-school precision, edgy new works, raise-the-roof musicals and some of the world's longest-running shows.

Clockwise from top: National Theatre (p191); Old Vic; A performance at Young Vic

Classical Music, Ballet & Opera

With multiple world-class orchestras and ensembles, quality venues, reasonable ticket prices and performances covering the whole musical gamut from traditional crowd-pleasers to innovative compositions, London will satisfy even the fussiest classical music buff. The Southbank Centre (p191), Barbican (p190) and Royal Albert Hall (p189) all maintain an alluring program of performances, further gilding London's outstanding reputation as a cosmopolitan centre for classical music. The Proms (p12) is the festival calendar's biggest event.

Opera and ballet lovers should make an evening at the **Royal Opera House** a priority – the setting and quality of the programming are truly world class.

Paul Hamlyn Hall, Royal Opera House
CHRISTIAN MUELLER / SHUTTERSTOCK ©

Wigmore Hall   Classical Music
(Map p250; www.wigmore-hall.org.uk; 36 Wigmore St, W1; ⊖Bond St) This is one of the best and most active (more than 400 concerts a year) classical-music venues in town, not only because of its fantastic acoustics, beautiful art-nouveau hall and great variety of concerts and recitals, but also because of the sheer standard of the performances. Built in 1901, it has remained one of the world's top places for chamber music.

Prince Charles Cinema   Cinema
(Map p248; www.princecharlescinema.com; 7 Leicester Pl, WC2; tickets £8-16; ⊖Leicester Sq) Leicester Sq cinema-ticket prices are very high, so wait until the first-runs have moved to the Prince Charles, central London's cheapest cinema, where non-members pay only £9 to £11.50 for new releases. Also on the cards are minifestivals, Q&As with film directors, classics, sleepover movie marathons and exuberant sing-along screenings of films like *Frozen, The Sound of Music* and *Rocky Horror Picture Show* (£16).

Royal Opera House   Opera
(Map p248; ☏020-7304 4000; www.roh.org.uk; Bow St, WC2; tickets £4-270; ⊖Covent Garden) Classic opera in London has a fantastic setting on Covent Garden Piazza and coming here for a night is a sumptuous – if pricey – affair. Although the program has been fluffed up by modern influences, the main attractions are still the opera and classical ballet – all are wonderful productions and feature world-class performers.

Ronnie Scott's   Jazz
(Map p248; ☏020-7439 0747; www.ronniescotts.co.uk; 47 Frith St, W1; ☺7pm-3am Mon-Sat, 1-4pm & 8pm-midnight Sun; ⊖Leicester Sq or Tottenham Court Rd) Ronnie Scott's jazz club opened at this address in 1965 and became widely known as Britain's best. Support acts are at 7pm, with main gigs at 8.15pm (8pm Sunday) and a second house at 11.15pm Friday and Saturday (check though). The more informal Late, Late Show runs from 1am till 3am.

Comedy Store   Comedy
(Map p248; ☏0844 871 7699; www.thecomedystore.co.uk; 1a Oxendon St, SW1; admission £8-22.50; ⊖Piccadilly Circus) This is one of the first (and still one of the best) comedy clubs in London. Wednesday and Sunday night's Comedy Store Players is the most famous improvisation outfit in town, with the wonderful Josie Lawrence, now a veteran of two decades. On Thursdays, Fridays and Saturdays, Best in Stand Up features the best on London's comedy circuit.

Prince Charles Cinema

100 Club

Live Music

(Map p248; ☎020-7636 0933; www.the100club.
co.uk; 100 Oxford St, W1; admission £8-20; ☺check
website for gig times; ☻Oxford Circus or Tottenham
Court Rd) This heritage London venue at the
same address for over a half-century started
off as a jazz club but now leans toward rock.
Back in the day it showcased Chris Barber,
BB King and the Rolling Stones, and it was
at the centre of the punk revolution and the
'90s indie scene. It hosts dancing gigs, the
occasional big name, where-are-they-now
bands and top-league tributes.

Amused Moose Soho

Comedy

(Map p248; ☎box office 020-7287 3727; www.
amusedmoose.com; Sanctum Soho Hotel, 20
Warwick St, W1; ☻Piccadilly Circus, Oxford
Circus) One of the city's best clubs, the
peripatetic Amused Moose (the cinema in
the Sanctum Soho Hotel is just one of its
hosting venues) is popular with audiences
and comedians alike, perhaps helped along
by the fact that heckling is 'unacceptable'
and all the acts are 'first-date friendly' (ie
unlikely to humiliate the front row).

✪ West London

Electric Cinema

Cinema

(Map p250; ☎020-7908 9696; www.
electriccinema.co.uk; 191 Portobello Rd, W11;
tickets £8-22.50; ☻Ladbroke Grove) Having
notched up its first centenary in 2011, the
Electric is one of the UK's oldest cinemas,
updated. Avail yourself of the luxurious
leather armchairs, sofas, footstools and
tables for food and drink in the auditorium,
or select one of the six front-row double
beds! Tickets are cheapest on Mondays.

Opera Holland Park

Opera

(Map p250; ☎0300 999 1000; www.
operahollandpark.com; Holland Park, W8;
tickets £18-77; ☻High St Kensington, Holland
Park) Sit under the 1000-seat canopy,
temporarily erected every summer for
a nine-week season in the middle of
Holland Park (p127) for a mix of crowd
pleasers and rare (even obscure) works.
Five operas are generally performed
each year.

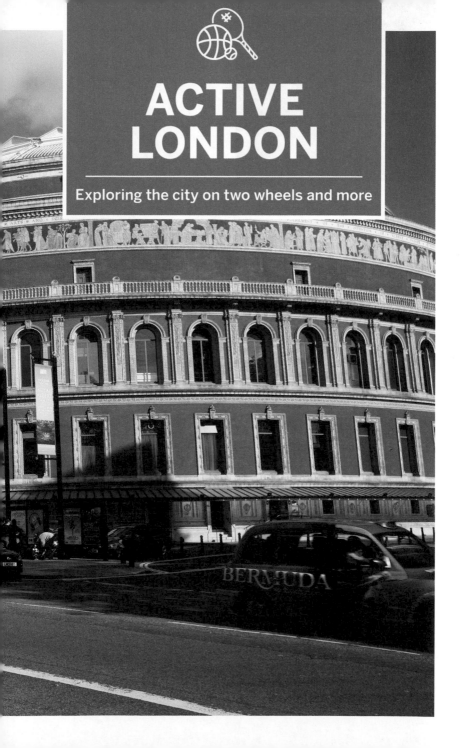

ACTIVE LONDON

Exploring the city on two wheels and more

Active London

The 2012 Olympic Games put a spring in London's step and left the city with a sudden embarrassment of world-class sports facilities in the east of town, some of which are now open to the public. The rest of London boasts a well-developed infrastructure for participatory and spectator sports to get your heart racing and the endorphins flowing.

Many events are free to watch; and if you've missed out on expensive ones, you can always watch in the pub or on a big screen somewhere. Active types will love the Santander Cycle Hire Scheme, which allows you to explore the city easily (and cheaply!) on two wheels.

In This Section

Sports Seasons

Football The season runs from mid-August to May.

Rugby The Six Nations (www.www.rbssixnations.com) is rugby's big annual tournament, spread over five weekends in February and March.

Tennis London is gripped by tennis fever during Wimbledon (July).

DRIMAFILM / SHUTTERSTOCK ©

People watching Wimbledon on an outdoor screen

The Best...

Free Spectator Sports

London Marathon (April) Watch runners pound the pavement from Blackheath to Buckingham Palace.

Oxford & Cambridge Boat Race (early April) Features the arch-rival universities on a course from Putney to Mortlake.

Head of the River Race (late March) Held along the same course as the Boat Race, but in reverse and with international crews.

Big-Screen Locations

Outdoor screens usually operate between April and October.

Trafalgar Square If there is anything big happening, you can be guaranteed there will be a big screen to watch it on at London's prime square.

Queen Elizabeth Olympic Park Given its legacy, it's hardly surprising big sporting events are broadcast here.

⊕ Walking Tours

Guide London — Tours
(Association of Professional Tourist Guides; ☑020-7611 2545; www.guidelondon.org.uk; half-/full-day £160/272) Hire a prestigious Blue Badge Tourist Guide: these know-it-all guides have studied for two years and passed a dozen written and practical exams to do their job. They can tell you stories about the sights that you'd only hear from them, or whisk you on a themed tour – from royalty and the Beatles to parks and shopping. Go by car, public transport, bike or on foot.

Unseen Tours — Walking
(☑07514 266 774; www.sockmobevents.org.uk; £12) See London from an entirely different angle on one of these award-winning neighbourhood tours led by the London homeless covering Camden Town, Brick Lane, Shoreditch and London Bridge. Sixty percent of the tour price goes to the guide.

London Walks — Walking
(☑020-7624 3978; www.walks.com; adult/child £10/free) A huge choice of themed walks, including Jack the Ripper, the Beatles, Sherlock Holmes, Harry Potter and ghost walks. Check the website for schedules – there are walks every day.

⊕ Bus Tours

Original Tour — Bus
(www.theoriginaltour.com; adult/child £30/15; ☺8.30am-8.30pm) A 24-hour hop-on, hop-off bus service with a river cruise thrown in, as well as three themed walks: Changing of the Guard, Rock 'n' Roll and Jack the Ripper. Buses run every five to 20 minutes; you can buy tickets on the bus or online. There's also a 48-hour ticket available (adult/child £40/19), with an extended river cruise.

Big Bus Tours — Bus
(☑020-7808 6753; www.bigbustours.com; adult/child £30/12.50; ☺every 20min 8.30am-6pm Apr-Sep, to 5pm Oct & Mar, to 4.30pm

Nov-Feb) Informative commentaries in 12 languages. The ticket includes a free river cruise with City Cruises and three thematic walking tours (Royal London, film locations, mysteries). Good online booking discounts available. Onboard wi-fi. The ticket is valid for 24 hours; for an extra £8 (£5 for children), you can upgrade to a 48-hour ticket.

⊕ Boat Tours

Thames River Services — Boating
(Map p256; ☑020-7930 4097; www.thamesriverservices.co.uk; adult/child 1-way £12.50/6.25, return £16.50/8.25) These cruise boats leave Westminster Pier for Greenwich, stopping at the Tower of London. Every second service from April to October continues on from Greenwich to the Thames Barrier (from Westminster, one-way adult/child £14/7, return £17/8.50, hourly 11.30am to 3.30pm) but does not land there; it passes the **O2** (www.theo2.co.uk; Peninsula Sq, SE10; ☒North Greenwich) along the way.

Lee & Stort Boats — Boating
(Map p255; ☑0845 116 2012; www.leeandstortboats.co.uk; Stratford Waterfront Pontoon, E20; adult/child £9/4; ☺Sat & Sun Mar, daily Apr-Sep, selected days Oct-Feb; ☒Stratford) Lee & Stort offers 45-minute tours on the waterways through Queen Elizabeth Olympic Park. Check the display boards in the park for departure times, which are usually on the hour from midday onwards.

Thames Rockets — Boating
(Map p245; ☑020-7928 8933; www.thamesrockets.com; Boarding Gate 1, London Eye, Waterloo Millennium Pier, Westminster Bridge Rd, SE1; adult/child £43.50/29.50; ☺10am-6pm; ☒) Feel like James Bond – or David Beckham en route to the 2012 Olympic Games – on this high-speed inflatable boat that flies down the Thames at 30 to 35 knots. Thames Rockets also does a Captain Kidd–themed trip between the London Eye and Canary Wharf for the same price.

London Waterbus Company
Cruise

(Map p250; ☎020-7482 2550; www.
londonwaterbus.co.uk; 32 Camden Lock Pl, NW1;
adult/child one-way £9/7.50, return £14/12;
☺hourly 10am-5pm Apr-Sep, weekends only
and less frequent departures other months;
☻Warwick Ave or Camden Town) This enclosed
barge runs enjoyable 50-minute trips on
Regent's Canal between Little Venice and
Camden Lock, passing by Regent's Park
and stopping at London Zoo. There are
fewer departures outside high season –
check the website for schedules. One-way
tickets (adult/child £25/18), including
entry to London Zoo, are also available
for passengers to disembark within the
zoo grounds. Buy tickets aboard the
narrowboats.

🌀 Pool & Spa

Hampstead Heath Ponds
Swimming

(www.cityoflondon.gov.uk; Hampstead Heath,
NW5; adult/child £2/1; ☻Hampstead Heath)
Set in the midst of the gorgeous heath,
Hampstead's three bathing ponds (men's,
women's and mixed) offer a cooling dip
in murky brown water. Despite what you
might think from its appearance, the water
is tested daily and meets stringent quality
guidelines.

Porchester Spa
Spa

(Map p250; ☎020-7313 3858; www.
porchesterspatreatments.co.uk; Porchester
Centre, Queensway, W2; admission £28.55;
☺10am-10pm; ☻Bayswater, Royal Oak)
Housed in a gorgeous art-deco building,
the Porchester is a no-frills spa run
by Westminster Council. With a 30m
swimming pool, a large Finnish-log sauna,
two steam rooms, three Turkish hot rooms
and a massive plunge pool, there are
plenty of affordable treatments on offer
including massages and male and female
pampering/grooming sessions.

It's women only on Tuesdays, Thursdays and Fridays all day and between

🏀 Football

Football is at the very heart of English
culture, with about a dozen league
teams in London and usually around
five or six in the Premier League.
Tickets for Premier League fixtures
(August to mid-May) can be impossible to secure for visitors. Stadiums
where you can watch matches (or,
more realistically, take tours) include
the city's landmark national stadium, **Wembley** (☎0800 169 9933;
www.wembleystadium.com; tours adult/
child £19/11; ☻Wembley Park); **Arsenal
Emirates Stadium** (☎020-7619 5000;
www.arsenal.com/tours; Hornsey Rd, N5;
tours self-guided adult/child £20/10, guided
£40; ☺10am-6pm Mon-Sat, to 4pm Sun;
☻Holloway Rd); **Chelsea** (☎0871 984
1955; www.chelseafc.com; Stamford Bridge,
Fulham Rd, SW6; tours adult/child £21/15;
☺museum 9.30am-5pm, tours 10am-3pm;
☻Fulham Broadway); and the **London
Stadium**, formerly known as the Olympic Stadium and now home of West
Ham United.

Numerous pubs across the capital
show Premier League games (as well as
international fixtures) and watching a
football game in a pub is an experience
in itself.

London Stadium
BBA PHOTOGRAPHY / SHUTTERSTOCK ©

10am and 2pm on Sundays; men only on
Mondays, Wednesdays and Saturdays.
Couples are welcome from 4pm to 10pm
on Sundays.

 **Santander Cycles**

Like Paris and other European cities, London has its own cycle-hire scheme, called Santander Cycles (p235), also variously referred to as 'Barclays Bikes' after their former sponsor, or 'Boris bikes' after the city's mayor, Boris Johnson (2008–16), who launched the initiative. The bikes have proved as popular with visitors as with Londoners.

The idea is simple: pick up a bike from one of the 700 docking stations dotted around the capital. Cycle. Drop it off at another docking station.

The access fee is £2 for 24 hours. All you need is a credit or debit card. The first 30 minutes are free. It's then £2 for any additional period of 30 minutes.

You can take as many bikes as you like during your access period (24 hours), leaving five minutes between each trip.

The pricing structure is designed to encourage short journeys rather than longer rentals; for those, go to a hire company. You'll also find that although easy to ride, the bikes only have three gears and are quite heavy. You must be 18 to buy access and at least 14 to ride a bike.

Santander Cycles docking station at Canary Wharf
SIXPIXX / SHUTTERSTOCK ©

Serpentine Lido   Swimming

(Map p250; ☑020-7706 3422; Hyde Park, W2; adult/child £4.80/1.80; ☺10am-6pm daily Jun-Aug, 10am-6pm Sat & Sun May; ☻Hyde Park Corner, Knightsbridge) Perhaps the ultimate London pool inside the Serpentine lake, this fabulous lido is open May to August. Sun loungers are available for £3.50 for the whole day.

London Aquatics Centre   Swimming

(www.londonaquaticscentre.org; Queen Elizabeth Olympic Park, E20; adult/child £4.95/2.50; ☺6am-10.30pm; ☻Stratford) The sweeping lines and wave-like movement of Zaha Hadid's award-winning Aquatics Centre make it the architectural highlight of Olympic Park. Bathed in natural light, the 50m competition pool beneath the huge undulating roof (which sits on just three supports) is an extraordinary place to swim. There's also a second 50m pool, a diving area, gym, creche and cafe.

❸ Cycling

Lee Valley VeloPark   Cycling

(Map p255; ☑0300 0030 610; www.visitleevalley.org.uk/velopark; Abercrombie Rd, E20; 1hr taster adult/child £40/30, pay & ride weekend/weekday £5/4, bike & helmet hire from £8; ☺9am-10pm; ☻Hackney Wick) An architectural highlight of Olympic Park, the cutting-edge velodrome is open to the public – either to wander through and watch the pros tear around the steep-sloped circuit, or to have a go yourself. Both the velodrome and the attached BMX park offer taster sessions. Mountain bikers and road cyclists can attack the tracks on a pay-and-ride basis.

London Bicycle Tour   Cycling

(Map p245; ☑020-7928 6838; www.londonbicycle.com; 1 Gabriel's Wharf, 56 Upper Ground, SE1; tour incl bike from adult/child £24.95/21.95, bike hire per day £20; ☻Southwark or Waterloo) Three-hour tours begin in the South Bank and take in London's highlights on both sides of the river; the classic tour is available in eight languages. A night ride is available. You can also hire traditional or speciality bikes, such as tandems and folding bikes, by the hour or day.

MITCH GUNN / SHUTTERSTOCK ©

London Aquatics Centre

🔂 Tennis

Wimbledon Championships
Spectator Sport

(☎020-8944 1066; www.wimbledon.com; Church Rd, SW19; grounds admission £8-25, tickets £41-190) For a few weeks each June and July, the sporting world's attention is fixed on the quiet southern suburb of Wimbledon, as it has been since 1877. Most show-court tickets for the Wimbledon Championships are allocated through public ballot, applications for which usually begin in early August of the preceding year and close at the end of December.

Entry into the ballot does not mean entrants will get a ticket. A quantity of show-court, outer-court, ground tickets and late-entry tickets are also available if you queue on the day of play, but if you want a show-court ticket it is recommended you camp the night before in the queue. See www.wimbledon.com for details.

🔂 Climbing

Up at The O2
Adventure Sports

(www.theo2.co.uk/upattheo2; The O2, Greenwich Peninsula, SE10; from £28; ⊙hours vary; ⊖North Greenwich) London isn't exactly your thrill-seeking destination, but this ascent of the O2 is not for the faint-hearted. Equipped with climbing suit and harness, you'll scale the famous entertainment venue to reach a viewing platform perched 52m above the Thames with sweeping views of Canary Wharf, the river, Greenwich and beyond. Hours vary depending on the season (sunset and twilight climbs also available).

REST YOUR HEAD

Top tips for the best accommodation

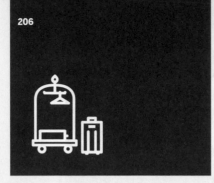

Rest Your Head

Landing the right accommodation is integral to your London experience, and there's no shortage of choice. There's some fantastic accommodation about – from party-oriented hostels to stately top-end hotels – so it's worth spending a little time ahead of your trip researching your options.

Budget is likely to be your number one consideration, given how pricey accommodation is in London, but you should also think about the neighbourhood you'd like to stay in. Are you a culture vulture? Would you like to be able to walk (or hop a quick cab ride) home after a night out? Are you after village charm or cool cachet? Make sure you think your options through and book ahead: London is busy year-round.

In This Section

Prices & Tipping

A 'budget hotel' in London generally costs up to £100 for a standard double room with bathroom. For a midrange option, plan on spending £100 to £200. Luxury options run £200 and higher.

Tipping isn't expected in hotels in London, except perhaps for porters in top-end hotels (although it remains discretionary).

POMPAEM GOGH / SHUTTERSTOCK ©

The Ritz Hotel

Reservations

o Book rooms as far in advance as possible, especially for weekends and holiday periods.

o The British Hotel Reservation Centre (www.bhrconline.com) has desks at airports and major train stations.

o Visit London (www.visitlondon.com) offers a free accommodation booking service and has a list of gay-friendly accommodation.

Useful Websites

Lonely Planet (www.lonelyplanet.com/london) Hundreds of properties, from budget hostels to luxury apartments.

London Town (www.londontown.com) Excellent last-minute offers on boutique hotels and B&Bs.

Alastair Sawdays (www.sawdays.co.uk) Hand-picked selection of bolt-holes in the capital.

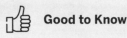

Good to Know

Value-added tax (VAT; 20%) is added to hotel rooms. Some hotels include this in their advertised rates, some don't.

Breakfast may be included in the room rate. Sometimes this is a continental breakfast; full English breakfast might cost extra.

Hotels

London has a grand roll call of stately hotels and many are experiences in their own right. Standards across the top end and much of the boutique bracket are high, but so are prices. Quirkiness and individuality can be found in abundance, alongside dyed-in-the-wool traditionalism. A wealth of budget boutique hotels has exploited a lucrative niche, while a rung or two down in overall quality and charm, midrange chain hotels generally offer good locations and dependable comfort. Demand can often outstrip supply – especially on the bottom step of the market – so book ahead, particularly during holiday periods and in summer.

B&Bs

Housed in good-looking old properties, bed and breakfasts come in a tier below hotels, often promising boutique-style charm and a more personal level of service. Handy B&B clusters appear in Paddington, South Kensington, Victoria and Bloomsbury.

Hostels

After B&Bs the cheapest form of accommodation are hostels: both the official Youth Hostel Association (YHA) ones and the usually hipper, more party-orientated independent ones. Hostels vary in quality so select carefully; most offer twins as well as dorms.

Rates & Booking

Deluxe hotel rooms will cost from around £350 per double but there's good variety at the top end, so you should find a room from about £200 offering superior comfort without the prestige. Some boutique hotels also occupy this bracket. There's a noticeable dip in quality below this price. Under £100 and you're at the more serviceable, budget end of the market. Look out for weekend deals that can put a better class of hotel within reach. Rates often slide in winter. Book through the hotels' websites for the best online deals or promotional rates.

Long-Term Rentals

If you're in London for a week or more, a short-term or serviced apartment may make sense: rates at the bottom end are comparable to a B&B, you can manage your budget more carefully by eating in, and you'll get to feel like a local.

Great neighbourhoods to consider for their vibe include Notting Hill, Hackney, Bermondsey, Pimlico and Camden, where you'll find plenty of food markets, great local pubs and lots of boutiques. **Airbnb** (www.airbnb.co.uk/london) is the go-to source for finding a London pad, but you can also try **Holiday Lettings** (www.holidaylettings.co.uk/london).

For something a little more hotel-like, serviced apartments are a great option. Try the following, which are all in the centre: **196 Bishopsgate** (☎020-7621 8788; www.196bishopsgate.com; 196 Bishopsgate, EC2; apt from £183; ❄️🛜; ⊖Liverpool St), **Number 5 Maddox Street** (☎020-7647 0200; www.living-rooms.co.uk/hotel/no-5-maddox-st; 5 Maddox St, W1; ste £250-925; ❄️🛜; ⊖Oxford Circus) and **Beaufort House** (☎020-7584 2600; www.beauforthouse.co.uk; 45 Beaufort Gardens, SW3; 1-4 bedroom apt £443-1350; ❄️🛜; ⊖Knightsbridge).

Where to Stay

Neighbourhood	Atmosphere
The West End	At the heart of London, with excellent transport links. Fantastic range of options, but expensive and busy. Numerous eating and nightlife options.
The City	Central and well connected, but geared toward business clientele; very quiet at weekends. Expensive on week nights, but good deals to be found at weekends.
The South Bank	Cheaper than the West End, but choice and transport connections more limited. Close to great sights such as the Tate Modern and Borough Market.
Kensington & Hyde Park	Stylish area, with gorgeous hotels, but expensive and with limited nightlife. Good transport links and easy connection to Heathrow.
Clerkenwell, Shoreditch & Spitalfields	Trendy area with great boutique hotels; excellent for restaurants and nightlife, but few top sights and transport options somewhat limited.
East London	Limited sleeping options, but great multicultural local feel; some areas less safe at night.
North London	Leafy area, with great sleeping options and a vibrant nightlife, but further from main sights and with fewer transport options.
West London	Lovely neighbourhood with village charm, great vibe at weekends; plenty of cheap but average hotels. Light on top sights.
Greenwich & South London	Village feel, but limited sleeping and transport options; great for Greenwich sights, but inconvenient for everything else.
Richmond, Kew & Hampton Court	Smart riverside hotels, semirural pockets, but sights spread out and far from central London.

In Focus

The financial district of London

London Today

*Britain's exit from the EU (Brexit) has put a damper
on London's spirit. With its multicultural population,
thriving financial sector and firm links with the
continent, the capital seems at odds ideologically with the
rest of the country. Its energy, however, remains second
to none; its creative juices are still in full flow with a lot
of exciting developments, such as the new Crossrail Line
and the regeneration of Battersea and King's Cross.*

London v the Rest?

London is the world's leading financial centre for international business and commerce and the fifth-largest city economy in the world. As the economic downturn of the last decade fades into memory, the UK is increasingly a nation of two halves: London (and the southeast) and the rest of the country. The capital generates more than 20% of Britain's income, a percentage that has been rising over the last 10 years. Employment in London is rosier than for the rest of the nation, with the jobless rate at just under 6%; the price of property is double the national average; and incomes are 30% higher in London than elsewhere in the country. Tourism continues to grow at 3.5% a year. There's a flip side, however: 28% of Londoners are living in poverty compared with just 21% in the rest of England.

Ethnicity & Multiculturalism

London is one of the most cosmopolitan place in which to live. According to the last census (2011), almost 37% of London's population is foreign born – with almost a quarter born outside Europe. Today an estimated 270 different ethnic groups speak 300 different languages and, despite some tensions, most get along well.

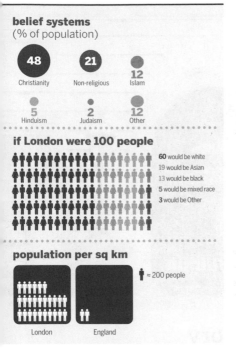

belief systems
(% of population)

48 Christianity
21 Non-religious
12 Islam
5 Hinduism
2 Judaism
12 Other

if London were 100 people

60 would be white
19 would be Asian
13 would be black
5 would be mixed race
3 would be Other

population per sq km

= 200 people

London   England

Building Boom

The huge rise in population – London is expected to have 9 million inhabitants by 2020, up from 8.3 million today – has led to a building boom not seen since the end of WWII. Church spires are now dwarfed by a forest of construction cranes working to build more than 230 high-rise condos and office buildings. East London is where most of the activity is taking place these days, but the building boom is evident along the entire stretch of the Thames. New landmark skyscrapers in the City include the 37-storey Walkie Talkie (20 Fenchurch St) and the 225m-tall Cheesegrater (Leadenhall Building), with many more on the cards or under construction south of the river.

All Change in Politics

Virtually no one foresaw the outcome of the 2015 national elections, in which the Conservative Party soundly beat Labour, gaining 28 seats and a narrow majority in Parliament. Always bucking the trend, however, London elected Labour candidate Sadiq Khan as its mayor a year later, convincingly defeating Conservative golden boy Zac Goldsmith.

Goodbye to Europe

On June 24 2016, Britain awoke to monumental news. By a slim referendum vote the UK had opted to leave the EU, cutting ties stretching back 43 years. Within hours of the so-called 'Brexit' (British exit) result, Prime Minister David Cameron, who'd campaigned to remain within the EU, announced his resignation.

Nationally, the referendum result was very close: 52% voted to leave the EU against 48% to remain, although unsurprisingly, the capital was strongly in favour of 'remain' (60%).

Brexit became law in March 2017, when Prime Minister Theresa May formally launched the two-year disentanglement process. Depending on the outcome of the negotiations, Brexit could have an enormous impact on London, especially the financial services industry and the millions of EU nationals living in the capital.

Guard on duty at Buckingham Palace (p46)

BENSON HE / SHUTTERSTOCK ©

History

London's history is a long and turbulent narrative spanning more than two millennia. Over those years there have been good times of strength and economic prosperity and horrific times of plague, fire and war. But even when down on its knees, London has always been able to get up, dust itself off and move on, constantly re-inventing itself along the way.

AD 43
The Romans invade Britain, led by Emperor Claudius; they mix with the local Celtic tribespeople and stay for almost four centuries.

852
Vikings settle in London; a period of great struggle between the kingdoms of Wessex and Denmark begins.

1066
Following his decisive victory at the Battle of Hastings, William, Duke of Normandy, is crowned in Westminster Abbey.

Statue of King George V, Westminster Abbey (p36)

ANIBAL TREJO / SHUTTERSTOCK ©

Londinium

The Celts were the first to arrive in the area that is now London, some time around the 4th century BC. It was the Romans, however, who established a real settlement in AD 43, the port of Londinium. They slung a wooden bridge over the Thames (near the site of today's London Bridge) and created a thriving colonial outpost before abandoning British soil for good in 410.

Saxon & Norman London

Saxon settlers, who colonised the southeast of England from the 5th century onwards, established themselves outside the city walls due west of Londinium in Lundenwic. This infant trading community grew in importance and attracted the attention of the Vikings in Denmark. They attacked in 842 and again nine years later, burning Lundenwic to the ground. Under the leadership of King Alfred the Great of Wessex, the Saxon population fought back, driving the Danes out in 886.

1215	1348	1605
King John signs the Magna Carta, an agreement forming the basis of constitutional law in England.	Rats on ships from Europe bring the 'Black Death', a plague that eventually wipes out almost two-thirds of the city's residents.	A Catholic plot to blow up James I is foiled; Guy Fawkes, one of the alleged plotters, is executed the following year.

Hampton Court Palace (p110)

PLUSONE/SHUTTERSTOCK ©

★ Best for Royal History

Saxon London grew into a prosperous and well-organised town segmented into 20 wards, each with its own alderman and resident colonies of German merchants and French vintners. But attacks by the Danes continued apace and the Saxon leadership was weakening; in 1016 Londoners were forced to accept the Danish leader Canute as king of England. With the death of Canute's brutal son Harthacanute in 1042, the throne passed to the Saxon Edward the Confessor, who went on to found a palace and an abbey at Westminster.

On his deathbed in 1066, Edward anointed Harold Godwinson, the Earl of Wessex, as his successor. This enraged William, Duke of Normandy, who claimed that Edward had promised him the throne. William mounted a massive invasion from France, and on 14 October defeated (and killed) Harold at the Battle of Hastings, before marching on London to claim his prize. William, now dubbed 'the Conqueror', was crowned king of England in Westminster Abbey on 25 December 1066, ensuring the Norman conquest was complete.

Medieval & Tudor London

Successive medieval kings were happy to let the City of London keep its independence as long as its merchants continued to finance their wars and building projects. During the Tudor dynasty, which coincided with the discovery of the Americas and thriving world trade, London became one of the largest and most important cities in Europe. Henry VIII reigned from 1509 to 1547, built palaces at Whitehall and St James's, and bullied his lord chancellor, Cardinal Thomas Wolsey, into giving him the one at Hampton Court.

The most momentous event of his reign, however, was his split with the Catholic Church in 1534 after the Pope refused to annul his marriage to Catherine of Aragon, who had borne him only one surviving daughter after 24 years of marriage.

The 45-year reign (1558–1603) of Henry's daughter Elizabeth I is still regarded as one of the most extraordinary periods in English history. During these four decades English literature reached new heights and religious tolerance gradually grew. With the defeat of the Spanish Armada in 1588, England became a naval superpower and London established itself as the premier world trade market with the opening of the Royal Exchange in 1570.

1666	1708	1838
The Great Fire of London burns for five days, leaving four-fifths of the metropolis in smoking ruins.	The last stone of Sir Christopher Wren's masterpiece, St Paul's Cathedral, is laid by his son and the son of his master mason.	The coronation of Queen Victoria ushers in a new era for London; the British capital becomes the economic centre of the world.

Civil Wars, Plague & Fire

Elizabeth was succeeded by her second cousin James I and then his son Charles I. The latter's belief in the 'divine right of kings' set him on a collision course with an increasingly confident parliament at Westminster and a powerful City of London. The latter two rallied behind Oliver Cromwell against Royalist Troops. Charles was defeated in 1646 and executed in 1649.

Cromwell ruled the country as a republic for the next 11 years. Under the Commonwealth of England, as the English republic was known, Cromwell banned theatre, dancing, Christmas and just about anything remotely fun.

After Cromwell's death, parliament restored the exiled Charles II to the throne in 1660. Charles II's reign witnessed two great tragedies in London: the Great Plague of 1665, which decimated the population, and the Great Fire of London, which swept ferociously through the city's densely packed streets the following year. The wreckage of the inferno at least allowed master architect Christopher Wren to build his 51 magnificent churches. The crowning glory of the 'Great Rebuilding' was his St Paul's Cathedral, completed in 1708. A masterpiece of English baroque architecture, it remains one of the city's most prominent and iconic landmarks.

Great Fire of London

The Great Fire of London broke out in Thomas Farriner's bakery in Pudding Lane on the evening of 2 September 1666. Initially dismissed by London's lord mayor as 'something a woman might pisse out', the fire spread uncontrollably and destroyed 89 churches and more than 13,000 houses, raging for days. Amazingly, fewer than a dozen people died. The fire destroyed medieval London, changing the city forever. Many Londoners left for the countryside or to seek their fortunes in the New World, while the city itself rebuilt its medieval heart with grand buildings such as Wren's St Paul's Cathedral. Wren's magnificent Monument (1677) near London Bridge stands as a memorial to the fire and its victims.

Georgian & Victorian London

While the achievements of the 18th-century Georgian kings were impressive (though 'mad' George III will forever be remembered as the king who lost the American colonies), they were overshadowed by those of the dazzling Victorian era, dating from Queen Victoria's ascension to the throne in 1837.

During the Industrial Revolution, London became the nerve centre of the largest and richest empire the world had ever witnessed, in an imperial expansion that covered a quarter of the earth's surface area and ruled over more than 500 million people. Queen Victoria lived to celebrate her Diamond Jubilee in 1897, but died four years later aged 81 and was laid to rest beside her beloved consort, Prince Albert, at Windsor. Her reign is seen as the climax of Britain's world supremacy, when London was the de facto capital of the world.

1851	**1940–41**	**1953**
The Great Exhibition, the brainchild of Victoria's consort, Albert, opens to great fanfare in the Crystal Palace in Hyde Park.	London is devastated by the Blitz, although St Paul's Cathedral and the Tower of London escape largely unscathed.	Queen Elizabeth II's coronation is broadcast live around the world on television; many English families buy their first TV.

KYRIEN / SHUTTERSTOCK ©

The World Wars

WWI broke out in August 1914 and became known as the Great War. The first German bombs fell from zeppelins near the Guildhall a year later, killing 39 people. Planes were soon dropping bombs on the capital, killing in all some 670 Londoners (half the national total of civilian deaths).

In the 1930s Prime Minister Neville Chamberlain's policy of appeasing Adolf Hitler eventually proved misguided, as the German Führer's lust for expansion appeared insatiable. When Nazi Germany invaded Poland on 1 September 1939, Britain declared war, having signed a mutual-assistance pact with Poland only a few days before. World War II (1939–45), which would prove to be Europe's darkest hour, had begun.

Winston Churchill, prime minister from 1940, orchestrated much of the nation's war strategy from the Cabinet War Rooms deep below Whitehall, lifting the nation's spirit from here with his stirring wartime speeches. By the time Nazi Germany capitulated in May 1945, up to a third of the East End and the City of London had been flattened, almost 30,000 Londoners had been killed and a further 50,000 seriously wounded.

Postwar London

Once the celebrations of Victory in Europe (VE) Day had died down, the nation began to confront the war's appalling toll and to rebuild. The years of austerity had begun, with rationing of essential items and high-rise residences sprouting up from bomb sites. Rationing of most goods ended in 1953, the year Elizabeth II was crowned following the death the year before of her father King George VI.

Immigrants from around the world – particularly the former colonies – flocked to postwar London, where a dwindling population had generated labour shortages, and the city's character changed forever. The place to be during the 1960s, 'Swinging London' became the epicentre of cool in fashion and music, its streets awash with colour and vitality.

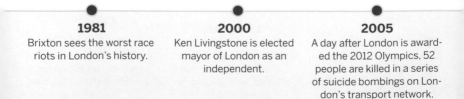

1981
Brixton sees the worst race riots in London's history.

2000
Ken Livingstone is elected mayor of London as an independent.

2005
A day after London is awarded the 2012 Olympics, 52 people are killed in a series of suicide bombings on London's transport network.

The ensuing 1970s brought glam rock, punk, economic depression and the country's first female prime minister in 1979. In power for the entire 1980s and pushing an unprecedented program of privatisation, the late Margaret Thatcher is easily the most significant of Britain's postwar leaders. Opinions about 'Maggie' still polarise the Brits today.

While poorer Londoners suffered under Thatcher's significant trimming back of the welfare state, things had rarely looked better for the wealthy, as London underwent explosive economic growth. In 1992, much to the astonishment of most Londoners, the Conservative Party was elected for their fourth successive term in government, despite Mrs Thatcher being jettisoned by her party a year and a half before. By 1995 the writing was on the wall for the Conservative Party, as the Labour Party, apparently unelectable for a decade, came back with a new face.

The Blitz

The Blitz (from the German Blitzkrieg, meaning 'lightning war') struck England between September 1940 and May 1941, when London and other parts of Britain were heavily bombed by the German Luftwaffe. Londoners responded with legendary resilience and stoicism. Underground stations were converted into giant bomb shelters, although this was not always safe – one bomb rolled down the escalator at Bank station and exploded on the platform, killing more than 100 people. Buckingham Palace took a direct hit during a bombing raid early in the campaign, famously prompting Queen Elizabeth (the present monarch's late mother) to announce that 'now we can look the East End in the face'.

London in the New Century

Invigorated by its sheer desperation to return to power, the Labour Party elected the thoroughly telegenic Tony Blair as its leader, who in turn managed to ditch some of the more socialist-sounding clauses in the party credo and reinvent it as New Labour, leading to a huge landslide win in the May 1997 general election. The Conservatives atomised nationwide; the Blair era had begun in earnest.

Most importantly for London, Labour recognised the demand the city had for local government and created the London Assembly and the post of mayor. In Ken Livingstone, London elected a mayor who introduced a congestion charge and sought to update the ageing public transport network. In 2008 he was defeated by his arch-rival, Conservative Boris Johnson.

Johnson won his second term in 2012, the year of the Olympic Games (overwhelmingly judged an unqualified success) and the Queen's Diamond Jubilee (the 60th anniversary of her ascension to the throne).

2008
Boris Johnson, a Conservative MP and journalist, beats Ken Livingstone to become London's new mayor.

2012
Boris Johnson narrowly beats Ken Livingstone to win his second mayoral election; London hosts the 2012 Olympics and Paralympics.

2014
The southern half of the Olympic site opens to the public as Queen Elizabeth Olympic Park.

Millennium Bridge before St Paul's Cathedral (p86)

TOMASSEREDA / GETTY IMAGES ©

Architecture

Unlike many other world-class cities, London has never been methodically planned. Rather, it has developed in an organic fashion. London retains architectural reminders from every period of its long history. This is a city for explorers; seek out part of a Roman wall enclosed in the lobby of a modern building, for example, or a coaching inn dating to the Restoration tucked away in a courtyard off Borough High St.

Ancient London Architecture

Traces of medieval London are hard to find thanks to the devastating Great Fire of 1666, but several works by the architect Inigo Jones (1573–1652) have endured, including Covent Garden Piazza in the West End.

There are a few even older treasures scattered around – including the mighty Tower of London in the City, parts of which date back to the late 11th century. Westminster Abbey and Temple Church are 12th- to 13th-century creations. Few Roman traces survive outside museums, though the Temple of Mithras, built in AD 240, was relocated to the eastern end of Queen Victoria St in the City when the Bloomberg headquarters were completed at Walbrook Sq in 2016. Stretches of the Roman wall remain as foundations to a medieval wall outside Tower Hill tube station and in a few sections below Bastion high walk, next to the Museum of London, all in the City.

The Saxons, who moved into the area after the decline of the Roman Empire, found Londinium too small, ignored what the Romans had left behind and built their communities further up the Thames. The best place to see in situ what the Saxons left behind is the church of All Hallows by the Tower, northwest of the Tower of London. The church boasts an important archway, the walls of a 7th-century Saxon church and fragments from a Roman pavement.

Noteworthy medieval secular structures include the 1365 Jewel Tower, opposite the Houses of Parliament, and Westminster Hall; both are surviving chunks of the medieval Palace of Westminster.

After the Great Fire

After the 1666 fire, Sir Christopher Wren was commissioned to oversee reconstruction, but his vision of a new city layout of broad, symmetrical avenues never made it past the planners. His legacy lives on, however, in St Paul's Cathedral (1708), in the maritime precincts at Greenwich and in numerous City churches.

Nicholas Hawksmoor joined contemporary James Gibb in taking Wren's English baroque style even further; one great example is St Martin-in-the-Fields in Trafalgar Sq.

Like Wren before him, Georgian architect John Nash aimed to impose some symmetry on unruly London and was slightly more successful in achieving this, through grand creations such as Trafalgar Sq and the elegantly curving arcade of Regent St. Built in similar style, the surrounding squares of St James's remain some of the finest public spaces in London – little wonder then that Queen Victoria decided to move into the recently vacated Buckingham Palace in 1837.

Toward Modernity

Pragmatism replaced grand vision with the Victorians, who desired ornate civic buildings that reflected the glory of empire but were open to the masses, too. The style's turrets, towers and arches are best exemplified by the flamboyant Natural History Museum (Alfred Waterhouse), St Pancras Chambers (George Gilbert Scott) and the Houses of Parliament (Augustus Pugin and Charles Barry), the latter replacing the Palace of Westminster that had largely burned down in 1834.

The Victorians and Edwardians were also ardent builders of functional and cheap terraced houses, many of which became slums but today house London's urban middle classes.

A flirtation with art deco and the great suburban residential building boom of the 1930s was followed by a utilitarian modernism after WWII, as the city rushed to build new housing to replace terraces lost in the Blitz. Low-cost developments and unattractive high-rise housing were thrown up on bomb sites; many of these blocks still fragment the London horizon today.

Brutalism – a hard-edged and uncompromising architectural style that flourished from the 1950s to the 1970s, favouring concrete and reflecting socialist utopian principles – worked better on paper than in real life, but made significant contributions to London's architectural melange. Denys Lasdun's National Theatre, begun in 1966, is representative of the style.

★ **Best Modern Architecture**

Shard (p79)

Tate Modern (p82)

30 St Mary Axe (p69)

Millennium Bridge (p91)

London Aquatics Centre (p202)

30 St Mary Axe (p69)

Postmodernism & Beyond

The next big wave of development arrived in the derelict wasteland of the former London docks, which were emptied of their terraces and warehouses and rebuilt as towering skyscrapers and 'loft' apartments. Taking pride of place in the Docklands was Cesar Pelli's 244m-high 1 Canada Square (1991), commonly known as Canary Wharf and easily visible from central London. The City was also the site of architectural innovation, including the centrepiece 1986 Lloyd's of London: Sir Richard Rogers' 'inside-out' masterpiece of ducts, pipes, glass and stainless steel.

Contemporary Architecture

There followed a lull in new construction until around 2000, when a glut of millennium projects unveiled new structures and rejuvenated others: the London Eye, Tate Modern and the Millennium Bridge all spiced up the South Bank, while Norman Foster's iconic 30 St Mary Axe, better known as the Gherkin, started a new wave of skyscraper construction in the City. Even the once-mocked Millennium Dome won a new lease on life as the 02 concert and sports hall.

By the middle of the decade, London's biggest urban development project ever was under way: the 200-hectare Queen Elizabeth Olympic Park in the Lea River Valley near Stratford in East London, where most of the events of the 2012 Summer Olympics and Paralympics took place. But the park would offer few architectural surprises – except for Zaha Hadid's stunning Aquatics Centre, a breathtaking structure suitably inspired by the fluid geometry of water; and the ArcelorMittal Orbit, a zany public work of art with viewing platforms designed by the sculptor Anish Kapoor.

The spotlight may have been shining on East London, but the City and South London have undergone energetic developments, too. Most notable is the so-called Shard, the EU's tallest building at 310m, completed in 2012. In the City, the Walkie Talkie has divided opinions, but its jungle-like Sky Garden on levels 35 to 37 are universally loved.

British Library (p118)

RON ELLIS / SHUTTERSTOCK ©

Literary London

For over six centuries, London has been the setting for works of prose. Indeed, the capital has been the inspiration for the masterful imaginations of such eminent wordsmiths as Shakespeare, Defoe, Dickens, Orwell, Conrad, Eliot, Greene and Woolf (even though not all were native to the city, or even British).

It's hard to reconcile the bawdy portrayal of London in Geoffrey Chaucer's *Canterbury Tales* with Charles Dickens' bleak hellhole in *Oliver Twist*, let alone Daniel Defoe's plague-ravaged metropolis in *Journal of the Plague Year* with Zadie Smith's multiethnic romp *White Teeth*. Ever-changing, yet somehow eerily consistent, London has left its mark on some of the most influential writing in the English language.

Chaucerian London

The first literary reference to London appears in Chaucer's *Canterbury Tales*, written between 1387 and 1400: the 29 pilgrims of the tale gather for their trip to Canterbury at the

Shakespeare's Globe (p190)

KAMIRA / SHUTTERSTOCK ©

Tabard Inn in Talbot Yard, Southwark, and agree to share stories on the way there and back. The inn burned down in 1676; a blue plaque marks the site of the building today.

Shakespearian London

Born in Warwickshire, William Shakespeare spent most of his life as an actor and playwright in London around the turn of the 17th century. He trod the boards of several theatres in Shoreditch and Southwark and wrote his greatest tragedies, among them *Hamlet, Othello, Macbeth* and *King Lear,* for the original Globe theatre on the South Bank. Although London was his home for most of his life, Shakespeare set nearly all his plays in foreign or imaginary lands. Only *Henry IV: Parts I & II* include a London setting – a tavern called the Boar's Head in Eastcheap.

Dickensian & 19th-Century London

Two early 19th-century Romantic poets drew inspiration from London. John Keats, born above a Moorgate public house in 1795, wrote 'Ode to a Nightingale' while living near Hampstead Heath in 1819 and 'Ode on a Grecian Urn' reportedly after viewing the Parthenon frieze in the British Museum the same year. William Wordsworth discovered inspiration for the poem 'Upon Westminster Bridge' while visiting London in 1802.

Charles Dickens was the definitive London author. When his father and family were interned at Marshalsea Prison in Southwark for not paying their debts, the 12-year-old Charles was forced to fend for himself on the streets. That grim period provided a font of experiences on which to draw. His novels most closely associated with London are *Oliver Twist,* with its gang of thieves led by Fagin in Clerkenwell, and *Little Dorrit,* whose hero was born in the Marshalsea. The house in Bloomsbury where he wrote *Oliver Twist* and two other novels now houses the expanded Charles Dickens Museum (p45).

Sir Arthur Conan Doyle (1858–1930) portrayed a very different London, his pipe-smoking, cocaine-snorting sleuth, Sherlock Holmes, coming to exemplify a cool and unflappable Englishness. Letters to the mythical hero and his admiring friend, Dr Watson, still arrive at 221b Baker St, where there's a **museum** (⌕020-7224 3688; www.sherlock-holmes.co.uk; 221b Baker St, NW1; adult/child £15/10; ⊙9.30am-6pm; ⊖Baker St) to everyone's favourite Victorian detective.

London at the end of the 19th century appears in many books, but especially those of Somerset Maugham. His first novel, *Liza of Lambeth,* was based on his experiences as an intern in the slums of South London, while *Of Human Bondage* provides a portrait of late-Victorian London.

American Writers & London in the 20th Century

Of Americans who wrote about London at the turn of the century, Henry James, who settled here, stands supreme with his *Daisy Miller* and *The Europeans*. St Louis–born TS Eliot moved to London in 1915, where he published his poems 'The Love Song of J Alfred Prufrock' and 'The Waste Land', in which London is portrayed as an 'unreal city'.

Interwar Developments

Between the world wars, PG Wodehouse depicted London high life with his hilarious lampooning of the English upper classes in the Jeeves stories. George Orwell's experience of living as a beggar in London's East End coloured his book *Down and Out in Paris and London* (1933).

The Modern Age

This period is marked by the emergence of multicultural voices. Hanif Kureishi explored London from the perspective of young Pakistanis in his best-known novels *The Black Album* and *The Buddha of Suburbia,* while Timothy Mo's *Sour Sweet* is a poignant and funny account of a Chinese family in the 1960s trying to adjust to English life.

The decades leading up to the turn of the millennium were great ones for British literature, bringing a dazzling new generation of writers to the fore, such as Martin Amis *(Money, London Fields)*, Julian Barnes *(Metroland, Talking it Over)*, Ian McEwan *(Enduring Love, Atonement)* and Salman Rushdie *(Midnight's Children, The Satanic Verses)*.

Millennium London

Helen Fielding's *Bridget Jones's Diary* and its sequel, *Bridget Jones: The Edge of Reason*, launched the 'chick lit' genre, one that transcended the travails of a young single Londoner to become a worldwide phenomenon.

Peter Ackroyd named the city as the love of his life; *London: the Biography* was his inexhaustible paean to the capital.

The Current Scene

Home to most of the UK's major publishers and its best bookshops, London remains a vibrant place for writers and readers alike. New London writers in recent years include Monica Ali *(Brick Lane),* Zadie Smith *(NW),* Jake Arnott *(The Long Firm)* and Gautam Malkani *(Londonstani).*

Every bookshop in town has a London section, where you will find many of these titles and lots more.

National Gallery (p54)

Art

*When it comes to art, London has traditionally been
overshadowed by other European capitals. Yet many
of history's greatest artists have spent time in London,
including the likes of Monet and Van Gogh, and in terms
of contemporary art, there's a compelling argument for
putting London at the very top of the European pack.*

Holbein to Turner

It wasn't until the rule of the Tudors that art began to take off in London. The German Hans Holbein the Younger (1497–1543) was court painter to Henry VIII; one of his finest works, *The Ambassadors* (1533), hangs in the National Gallery. A batch of great portrait artists worked at court during the 17th century, the best being Anthony Van Dyck (1599–1641), who painted *Charles I on Horseback* (1638), also in the National Gallery.

Local artists began to emerge in the 18th century, including landscapists Thomas Gainsborough (1727–88) and John Constable (1776–1837).

JMW Turner (1775–1851), equally at home with oils and watercolours, represented the pinnacle of 19th-century British art. His later works, including *Snow Storm – Steam-boat off a Harbour's Mouth* (1842) and *Rain, Steam and Speed – the Great Western Railway* (1844), now in the Tate Britain and the National Gallery, later inspired the Impressionist works of Claude Monet.

★ **Best for British Art**

Tate Britain (p52)

National Gallery (p54)

National Portrait Gallery (p55)

Fourth Plinth Project (p58)

The Pre-Raphaelites to Hockney

The brief but splendid flowering of the Pre-Raphaelite Brotherhood (1848–54) with the likes of William Holman Hunt and John Everett Millais took its inspiration from the Romantic poets. Tate Britain has the best selection of works from this period.

Sculptors Henry Moore (1898–1986) and Barbara Hepworth (1903–1975) both typified the modernist movement in British sculpture (you can see examples of their work in Kensington Gardens).

After WWII, art transformed yet again. In 1945, the tortured, Irish-born painter Francis Bacon (1909–92) caused a stir when he exhibited his *Three Studies for Figures at the Base of a Crucifixion* – now on display at the Tate Britain – and afterwards continued to spook the art world with his repulsive yet mesmerising visions.

Australian art critic Robert Hughes eulogised Bacon's contemporary, Lucian Freud (1922–2011), as 'the greatest living realist painter'. Freud's early work was often surrealist, but from the 1950s the bohemian Freud exclusively focused on pale, muted portraits.

London in the swinging 1960s was perfectly encapsulated by pop art, the vocabulary of which was best articulated by the brilliant David Hockney (b 1937). Two of his most famous works, *Mr and Mrs Clark and Percy* (1971) and *A Bigger Splash* (1974), are displayed at the Tate Britain.

Brit Art & Beyond

Brit Art sprang from a show called *Freeze*, which was staged in a Docklands warehouse in 1988, organised by artist and showman Damien Hirst and largely featuring his fellow graduates from Goldsmiths' College. Influenced by pop culture and punk, Brit Art was brash, decadent, ironic, easy to grasp and eminently marketable. Hirst's *Mother & Child (Divided)*, a cow and her calf sliced into sections and preserved in formaldehyde, and Tracey Emin's *My Bed*, the artist's unmade bed and the mess next to it, are seminal works from this era.

The best way to take the pulse of the British contemporary art scene is to attend the annual Summer Exhibition at the Royal Academy of Arts, which features works by established as well as unknown artists.

Canary Wharf underground station

Survival Guide

Directory A–Z

Customs Regulations

The UK distinguishes between goods bought duty-free outside the EU and those bought in another EU country, where taxes and duties will have already been paid.

If you exceed your duty-free allowance, you will have to pay tax on the items. For European goods, there is officially no limit to how much you can bring but customs use certain guidelines to distinguish between personal and commercial use.

Discount Cards

Of interest to visitors who want to take in lots of paid sights in a short time is the **London Pass** (www. londonpass.com; 1/2/3/6 days £59/79/95/129). The pass offers free entry and queue-jumping to all major attractions and can be altered to include use of the Underground and buses. Check the website for details. Child passes are available too.

Electricity

**Type G
230V/50Hz**

Emergency

Dial 999 to call the police, fire brigade or ambulance in the event of an emergency.

Gay & Lesbian Travellers

Protection from discrimination is enshrined in law, but that's not to say homophobia does not exist. Always report homophobic crimes to the **police** (🖉999).

Useful Websites

o **60by80** (www.60by80.com/london)

o **Ginger Beer** (www.gingerbeer.co.uk)

o **Jake** (www.jaketm.com)

o **Time Out London LGBT** (www.timeout.com/london/lgbt)

Health

EU nationals can obtain free emergency treatment (and, in some cases, reduced-cost healthcare) on presentation of a **European Health Insurance Card** (www.ehic.org.uk).

Reciprocal arrangements with the UK allow Australians, New Zealanders and residents and nationals of several other countries to receive free emergency medical treatment and subsidised dental care through the **National Health Service** (NHS; 🖉111; www.nhs.uk). They can use hospital emergency departments, GPs and dentists. For a full list click on 'Services near you' on the NHS website.

Hospitals

The following hospitals have 24-hour accident and emergency departments:
Guy's Hospital (🖉020-7188 7188; www.guysandstthomas.nhs.uk; Great Maze Pond, SE1; ⊖London Bridge) One of central

Practicalities

Smoking Forbidden in all enclosed public places nationwide. Most pubs have some sort of smoking area outside.

Weights & Measures The UK uses a confusing mix of metric and imperial systems.

London's busiest hospitals, near London Bridge.

University College London Hospital (☏020-3456 7890, 0845 155 5000; www.uclh. nhs.uk; 235 Euston Rd. NW1; ☻Warren St or Euston) A large hospital in Euston.

Insurance

Travel insurance is advisable for non-EU residents as it offers greater flexibility over where and how you're treated and covers expenses for an ambulance and repatriation that will not be picked up by the NHS.

Pharmacies

The main pharmacy chains in London are Boots and Superdrug; a branch of either – or both – can be found on virtually every high street.

The **Boots** (☏020-7734 6126; www.boots.com; 44-46 Regent St, W1; ⊗8am-11pm Mon-Fri, 9am-11pm Sat, 12.30-6.30pm Sun; ☻Piccadilly Circus) in Piccadilly Circus is one of the biggest and most centrally located and has extended opening times.

Internet Access

❍ Virtually every hotel in London now provides wi-fi free of charge (only a couple of budget places have it as an add-on).

❍ A huge number of cafes and an increasing number of restaurants offer free wi-fi to customers, including chains such as Starbucks, Costa, Pret A Manger and McDonald's. Cultural venues such as the Barbican or the Southbank Centre also have free wi-fi.

Legal Matters

Should you face any legal difficulties while in London, visit a branch of the Citizens Advice Bureau (www. citizensadvice.org.uk), or contact your embassy.

Drugs

Illegal drugs of every type are widely available in London, especially in clubs. Nonetheless, all the usual drug warnings apply. If you're caught with pot today, you're likely to be arrested. Possession of harder drugs, including heroin and cocaine, is always treated seriously. Searches on entering clubs are common.

Fines

In general you rarely have to pay on the spot for an offence. The exceptions are trains, the tube and buses, where people who can't produce a valid ticket for the journey when asked to by an inspector can be fined then and there.

Money

❍ The pound sterling (£) is the unit of currency.

❍ One pound sterling is made up of 100 pence (called 'pee', colloquially).

❍ Notes come in denominations of £5, £10, £20 and £50, while coins are 1p ('penny'), 2p, 5p, 10p, 20p, 50p, £1 and £2.

ATMs

ATMs are everywhere and will generally accept Visa, MasterCard, Cirrus or Maestro cards, as well as more obscure ones. There is almost always a transaction surcharge for cash withdrawals with foreign cards.

Changing Money

○ The best place to change money is in any local post-office branch, where no commission is charged.

○ You can also change money in most high-street banks and some travel agencies, as well as at the numerous bureaux de change throughout the city.

Credit & Debit Cards

○ Credit and debit cards are accepted almost universally in London, in restaurants, bars, shops and even by some taxis.

○ American Express and Diners Club are far less widely used than Visa and MasterCard.

○ Contactless cards and payments (which do not require a chip and pin or a signature) are increasingly widespread (watch for the wi-fi-like symbol on cards and in shops). Transactions are limited to a maximum of £30.

Opening Hours

The following are standard opening hours:

Banks 9am–5pm Monday to Friday
Pubs & Bars 11am–11pm
Restaurants noon–2.30pm & 6–11pm
Sights 10am–6pm

Shops 9am–7pm Monday to Saturday, noon–6pm Sunday

Public Holidays

Most attractions and businesses close for a couple of days over Christmas and sometimes Easter. Places that normally shut on Sunday will probably close on bank-holiday Mondays.

New Year's Day 1 January
Good Friday Late March/April
Easter Monday Late March/April
May Day Holiday First Monday in May
Spring Bank Holiday Last Monday in May
Summer Bank Holiday Last Monday in August
Christmas Day 25 December
Boxing Day 26 December

Safe Travel

London is a fairly safe city for its size, so exercising common sense should keep you secure.

If you're getting a cab after a night's clubbing, make sure you go for a black cab or a licensed minicab firm.

Pickpocketing does happen in London, so keep an eye on your handbag and wallet, especially in bars and nightclubs and in crowded areas such as the Underground.

Telephone

Mobile Phones

Buy local SIM cards for European and Australian phones, or a pay-as-you-go phone. Set other phones to international roaming.

Useful Numbers

Directory Enquiries (International) 118 505
Directory Enquiries (Local & National) 118 118, 118 500
International dialing code 00
Premium rate applies 09
Reverse Charge/Collect Calls 155
Special rates apply 084 and 087
Toll-free 0800

Time

London is on GMT; during British Summer Time (BST; late March to late October), London clocks are one hour ahead of GMT.

Toilets

It's an offence to urinate in the streets. Train stations, bus terminals and attractions generally have good facilities, providing also for people with disabilities and those with young children.

You'll also find public toilets across the city; most charge 50p.

Tourist Information

City of London Information Centre (www.visitthecity.co.uk; St Paul's Churchyard, EC4; ⊘9.30am-5.30pm Mon-Sat, 10am-4pm Sun; ☏; ⊖St Paul's) Multilingual tourist information, fast-track tickets to City attractions and guided walks (adult/child £7/6).

Greenwich Tourist Office (☑0870 608 2000; www.visitgreenwich.org.uk; Pepys House, 2 Cutty Sark Gardens, SE10; ⊘10am-5pm; ⍰DLR Cutty Sark) Has a wealth of information about Greenwich and the surrounding areas. Free daily guided walks leave at 12.15pm and 2.15pm.

Visit London (www.visitlondon.com) Visit London can fill you in on everything from tourist attractions and events (such as the Changing of the Guard and Chinese New Year parade) to river trips and tours, accommodation, eating, theatre, shopping, children's London, and gay and lesbian venues. There are helpful kiosks at **Heathrow Airport** (www.visitlondon.com/tag/tourist-information-centre; Terminal 1, 2 & 3 Underground station concourse; ⊘7.30am-8.30pm), **King's Cross St Pancras Station** (www.visitlondon.com/tag/tourist-information-centre; Western Ticket Hall, Euston Rd N1; ⊘8am-6pm), **Liverpool Street Station** (www.visitlondon.com/tag/tourist-information-centre; Liverpool Street Station; ⊘8am-6pm), **Piccadilly Circus Underground Station** (www.visitlondon.com/tag/tourist-information-centre; Piccadilly Circus Underground Station; ⊘9.30am-4pm), The City, Greenwich and **Victoria Station** (www.visitlondon.com/tag/tourist-information-centre; Victoria Station; ⊘7.15am-9.15pm Mon-Sat, 8.15am-8.15pm Sun).

Travellers with Disabilities

For travellers with disabilities, London is an odd mix of user-friendliness and downright disinterest. New hotels and modern tourist attractions are legally required to be accessible to people in wheelchairs, but many historic buildings are hard to adapt.

Transport is equally hit and miss, but slowly improving:

○ Only 66 of London's 270 tube stations have step-free access; the rest have escalators or stairs.

○ The above-ground DLR is entirely accessible for wheelchairs.

○ All buses can be lowered to street level when they stop; wheelchair users travel free.

○ Guide dogs are universally welcome on public transport and in hotels, restaurants, attractions etc.

Transport for London (www.tfl.gov.uk) publishes the *Getting Around London* guide, which contains the latest information on accessibility for passengers with disabilities.

Download Lonely Planet's free Accessible Travel guide from http://lptravel.to/accessibletravel.

Climate Change & Travel

Every form of transport that relies on carbon-based fuel generates CO_2, the main cause of human-induced climate change. Modern travel is dependent on aeroplanes, which might use less fuel per kilometre per person than most cars but travel much greater distances. The altitude at which aircraft emit gases (including CO_2) and particles also contributes to their climate change impact. Many websites offer 'carbon calculators' that allow people to estimate the carbon emissions generated by their journey and, for those who wish to do so, to offset the impact of the greenhouse gases emitted with contributions to portfolios of climate-friendly initiatives throughout the world. Lonely Planet offsets the carbon footprint of all staff and author travel.

Visas

Visas are not required for US, Canadian, Australian, or New Zealand visitors for stays of up to six months. European Union nationals can stay indefinitely for the time being (Brexit pending). Check the website of the **UK Border Agency** (www.gov. uk/check-uk-visa) or with your local British embassy or consulate for the most up-to-date information.

Women Travellers

Female visitors to London are unlikely to have many problems, provided they take the usual big-city precautions. Don't get into an Underground carriage with no one else in it or with just one or two men. And if you feel unsafe, you should take a taxi or licensed minicab.

Transport

Arriving in London

Most people arrive in London by air, but an increasing number of visitors coming from Europe let the Eurostar (the Channel Tunnel train) take the strain, while buses from across the continent are a further option.

The city has five airports: Heathrow, Gatwick, Stansted, Luton and London City. Most transatlantic flights land at Heathrow and Gatwick. Visitors from Europe are more likely to arrive at Gatwick, Stansted or Luton (the latter two are used exclusively by low-cost airlines such as easyJet and Ryanair).

Flights, cars and tours can be booked online at lonelyplanet.com.

Heathrow Airport

Some 15 miles west of central London, **Heathrow** (LHR; www.heathrowairport. com) is one of the world's busiest international airports and counts four terminals (numbered 2 to 5).

Train

Underground (www.tfl.gov.uk; one-way £5.10) Three Underground stations on the Piccadilly line serve Heathrow: one for Terminals 2 and 3, another for Terminal 4, and the terminus for Terminal 5. The Underground, commonly referred to as 'the tube', is the cheapest way of getting to Heathrow (from central London one hour, every three to nine minutes). It runs from around 5am to midnight. Buy tickets at the station.

Crossrail (www.crossrail.co.uk) The western branch of this new line is due to open in May 2018, linking London Paddington with Heathrow Terminal 4 in 30 minutes.

Heathrow Express (www. heathrowexpress.com; 1-way/ return £22/36) This high-speed train whisks passengers from Heathrow Central station (serving Terminals 2 and 3) and Terminal 5 to Paddington in 15 minutes. Terminal 4 passengers should take the free interterminal shuttle train to Heathrow Central and board there. Trains run every 15 minutes from just after 5am in both directions to between 11.25pm (from Paddington) and 11.40pm (from the airport).

Bus

National Express (www.nationalexpress.com) coaches (one-way from £6, 35 to 90 minutes, every 30 minutes to one hour) link the Heathrow Central bus station with Victoria coach station.

Taxi

A metered black-cab trip to/from central London will cost between £45 and £85 and take 45 minutes to an hour, depending on traffic and your departure point.

Gatwick Airport

Located some 30 miles south of central London, **Gatwick** (LGW; www. gatwickairport.com) is Britain's number-two airport. The North and South Terminals are linked by a 24-hour shuttle train, with the journey time about three minutes.

Train

Gatwick Express (www.gatwickexpress.com; 1-way/return adult £19.90/34.90, 1-way/return child £9.95/17.45) This dedicated train service links the station near the South Terminal with Victoria station in central London every 15 minutes. From the airport, there are services between 4.35am and 12.50am. From Victoria, they leave between 3.30am and 12.32am. The journey takes 30 minutes.

National Rail (www.nationalrail.co.uk) has regular train services to/from London Bridge (30 minutes, every 15 to 30 minutes), London King's Cross (55 minutes, every 15 to 30 minutes) and London Victoria (30 minutes, every 10 to 15 minutes). Fares vary depending on the time of travel and the train company, but allow £10 to £20 for a single.

Bus

National Express (www.nationalexpress.com) coaches (one-way from £6, 80 minutes to two hours) run throughout the day from Gatwick to Victoria Coach station. Services leave hourly around the clock.

Taxi

A metered black-cab trip to/from central London costs around £100 and takes just over an hour. Minicabs are usually cheaper.

Stansted Airport

Stansted (STN; www.stanstedairport.com) is 35 miles northeast of central London in the direction of Cambridge.

Train

Stansted Express (☎0845 8500150; www.stanstedexpress.com; one-way/return £19/32) This rail service (one-way/return £19.10/31, 45 minutes, every 15 to 30 minutes) links the airport and Liverpool St station. From the airport, the first train leaves at 5.30am, the last at 12.30am. Trains depart Liverpool St station from 3.40am to 11.25pm.

Bus

National Express (www.nationalexpress.com) Run around the clock, offering well over 100 services per day. The A6 runs to Victoria coach station (one-way from £12, 85 minutes to more than two hours, every 20 minutes) via North London. The A9 runs to Liverpool St station (one-way from £10, 60 to 80 minutes, every 30 minutes).

EasyBus (www.easybus.co.uk) Runs services to Baker St and Old St tube stations every 15 minutes. The journey (one-way from £4.95) takes one hour from Old St, 1¼ hour from Baker St.

Terravision (www.terravision.eu) Coaches link Stansted to both Liverpool St train station (bus A51, one-way/return from £8/14, 55 minutes) and Victoria coach station (bus A50, one-way/return from

£9/15, 75 minutes) every 20 to 40 minutes between 6am and 1am.

Taxi

A metered black-cab trip to/from central London costs around £130. Minicabs are cheaper.

Luton Airport

A smallish airport 32 miles northwest of London, **Luton** (LTN; www.london-luton.co.uk) generally caters for cheap charter flights and discount airlines.

Train

National Rail (www.nationalrail.co.uk) services (one-way from £10, 35 to 50 minutes, every six to 30 minutes, from 7am to 10pm) run from London Bridge and London King's Cross stations to Luton Airport Parkway station, from where an airport shuttle bus (one-way £1.60) will take you to the airport in 10 minutes.

Bus

EasyBus (www.easybus.co.uk) minibuses run between Victoria coach station and Luton (one-way from £4.95) every half-hour round the clock. Another route links the airport with Liverpool St station (buses every 15 to 30 minutes).

Taxi

A metered black-cab trip to/from central London costs about £110.

London City Airport

Its proximity to central London, which is just 6 miles to the west, as well as to the commercial district of the Docklands, means **London City Airport** (LCY; www.londoncityairport.com; 🛜) is predominantly a gateway airport for business travellers.

Train

The **Docklands Light Railway** (DLR; www.tfl.gov.uk/dlr) stops at the London City Airport station (one-way £2.80 to £3.30). The journey to Bank takes just over 20 minutes.

Taxi

A metered black-cab trip to or from the City/Oxford St/Earl's Court costs about £25/35/50.

St Pancras International Train Station

St Pancras International, the arrival point for **Eurostar** (📞03432 186186; www.eurostar.com) trains from Europe is connected by many underground lines to other parts of the city.

Getting Around

Public transport in London is extensive, often excellent and always pricey. It is managed by **Transport for London** (www.tfl.gov.uk),

Oyster Card & Contactless

The Oyster Card is a smart card on which you can store credit towards 'prepay' fares, as well as Travelcards valid for periods from a day to a year. Oyster Cards are valid across the entire public transport network in London. All you need to do when entering a station is touch your card on one of the readers (which have a yellow circle with the image of an Oyster Card on them) and then touch again on your way out. The system will then deduct the appropriate amount of credit from your card, as necessary. For bus journeys, you only need to touch once upon boarding.

Oyster Cards can be bought (£5 refundable deposit required) and topped up at any Underground station, travel information centre or shop displaying the Oyster logo. To get your deposit back along with any remaining credit, simply return your Oyster Card at a ticket booth.

Contactless cards (which do not require chip and pin or a signature) can now be used directly on Oyster Card readers and are subject to the same Oyster fares. The advantage is that you don't have to bother with buying, topping up and then returning an Oyster Card, but bear in mind the cost of card transactions.

which has a user-friendly, multilingual website with a journey planner, maps, detailed information on every mode of transport in the capital and live updates on traffic.

The cheapest way to get around London is with an Oyster Card or a UK contactless card (foreign card holders should check for contactless charges first). Paper tickets still exist but aren't as cheap or convenient.

The tube, DLR and Overground network are ideal for zooming across different parts of the city; buses and the **Santander**

Cycles (📞0343 222 6666; www.tfl.gov.uk/modes/cycling/santander-cycles) are great for shorter journeys.

Left-luggage facility **Excess Baggage** (www.left-baggage.co.uk) operates at London's main train stations and airports. The pricing structure varies but allow £10 per 24-hour slot.

London Underground

The London Underground ('the tube'; 11 colour-coded lines) is part of an integrated-transport system that also includes the Docklands Light Railway (a driverless overhead train operating in the eastern part of the city) and Overground network (mostly outside of Zone 1 and sometimes underground). It is the quickest and easiest way of getting around the city, if not the cheapest.

The first trains operate from around 5.30am Monday to Saturday and 6.45am Sunday. The last trains leave around 12.30am Monday to Saturday and 11.30pm Sunday.

Additionally, selected lines (the Victoria and Jubilee lines, plus most of the Piccadilly, Central and Northern lines) run all night on Fridays and Saturdays to get revellers home, with trains every 10 minutes or so.

During weekend closures, schedules, maps and alternative route suggestions are posted in every station and staff are at hand to help redirect you.

Some stations, most famously Leicester Sq and Covent Garden, are much closer in reality than they appear on the map.

Fares

- London is divided into nine concentric fare zones.

- It will always be cheaper to travel with an Oyster Card or a contactless card than a paper ticket.

- Children under the age of 11 travel free; 11- to 15-year-olds are half-price if regis-

tered on an accompanying adult's Oyster Card (register at Zone 1 or Heathrow tube stations).

Bus

London's ubiquitous red double-decker buses afford great views of the city but be aware that the going can be slow. Bus services normally operate from 5am to 11.30pm.

There are excellent bus maps at every stop detailing all routes and destinations served from that particular area.

Night Bus

- More than 50 night-bus routes (prefixed with the letter 'N') run from around 11.30pm to 5am.

- There are also another 60 bus routes operating 24 hours; the frequency decreases between 11pm and 5am.

Fares

- Cash cannot be used on London's buses. Pay with an Oyster Card, Travelcard or a contactless payment card.

- Bus fares are a flat £1.50, no matter the distance travelled.

- Children under 11 travel free; 11- to 15-year-olds are half-price if registered on an accompanying adult's Oyster Card (register at Zone 1 or Heathrow tube stations)

Taxi

Black Cabs

The **black cab** is as much a feature of the London cityscape as the red double-decker bus.

- Cabs are available for hire when the yellow sign above the windscreen is lit; just stick your arm out to signal one.

- Fares are metered, with the flagfall charge of £2.60 (covering the first 248m during a weekday), rising by increments of 20p for each subsequent 124m.

- Fares are more expensive in the evenings and overnight.

- Apps such as **Hailo** (www.hailocab.com) use your smartphone's GPS to locate the nearest black cab. You only pay the metered fare.

Minicabs

- Minicabs, which are licensed, are cheaper (usually) competitors of black cabs.

- Unlike black cabs, minicabs cannot be hailed on the street; they must be hired by phone or through a dispatcher.

- Minicabs don't have meters; there's usually a fare set by the dispatcher. Make sure you ask before setting off.

- Your hotel or host will be able to recommend a

reputable minicab company in the neighbourhood. Or phone a large 24-hour operator such as **Addison Lee** (☑020-7387 8888; www. addisonlee.com).

○ Apps such as **Uber** (www. uber.com) or **Kabbee** (www. kabbee.com) allow you to book a minicab in double-quick time.

Boat

Thames Clippers (www. thamesclippers.com; all zones adult/child £8.20/4.10) One of several companies operating boats along the River Thames, Thames Clippers offers proper commuter services. It's fast, pleasant and you're almost always guaranteed a seat and a view. Boats run every 20 minutes from 6am to between 10pm and 11pm. The route goes from London Eye Millennium Pier to Woolwich Arsenal Pier, with boats west to Putney too.

Bicycle

The Santander Cycle Hire Scheme is a great and affordable way to get around London.

Behind the Scenes

Acknowledgements

Climate map data adapted from Peel MC, Finlayson BL & McMahon TA (2007) 'Updated World Map of the Köppen-Geiger Climate Classification', *Hydrology and Earth System Sciences*, 11, 163344.

This Book

This book was curated by Emilie Filou, who also researched and wrote for it along with Peter Dragicevich, Steve Fallon and Damian Harper.

The previous edition was also researched and written by Emilie Filou, Peter Dragicevich, Steve Fallon and Damian Harper.

This guidebook was produced by the following:

Destination Editor James Smart

Product Editor Will Allen

Senior Cartographer Mark Griffiths

Book Designer Michael Buick

Assisting Editors Imogen Bannister, Katie Connolly, Kellie Langdon, Kathryn Rowan, Maja Vatrić

Assisting Book Designer Virginia Moreno

Cover Researcher Wibowo Rusli

Thanks to Grace Dobell, Sasha Drew, Victoria Harrison, Anne Mason, Lauren O'Connell, Lyahna Spencer

Send Us Your Feedback

We love to hear from travellers – your comments keep us on our toes and help make our books better. Our well-travelled team reads every word on what you loved or loathed about this book. Although we cannot reply individually to postal submissions, we always guarantee that your feedback goes straight to the appropriate authors, in time for the next edition. Each person who sends us information is thanked in the next edition, the most useful submissions are rewarded with a selection of digital PDF chapters.

Visit lonelyplanet.com/contact to submit your updates and suggestions or to ask for help. Our award-winning website also features inspirational travel stories, news and discussions.

Note: We may edit, reproduce and incorporate your comments in Lonely Planet products such as guidebooks, websites and digital products, so let us know if you don't want your comments reproduced or your name acknowledged. For a copy of our privacy policy visit lonelyplanet.com/privacy.

A–Z
Index

ENGEL CHING / SHUTTERSTOCK ©

London Maps

City & South Bank

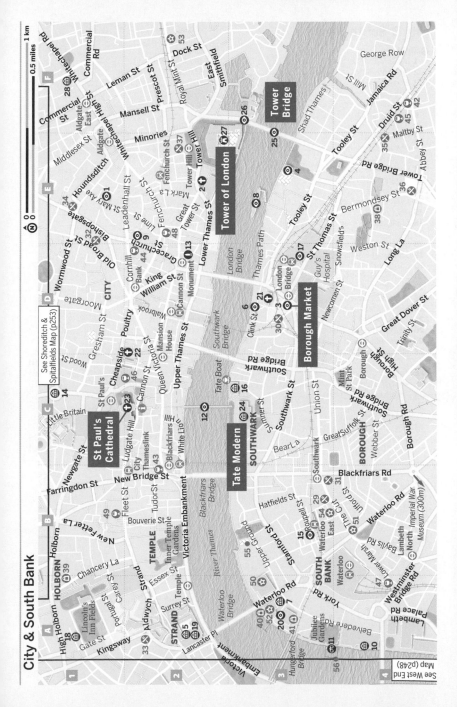

See Shoreditch & Spitalfields Map (p253)

See West End Map (p248)

Tower Bridge

Tower of London

St Paul's Cathedral

Borough Market

Tate Modern

George Row

CITY

HOLBORN

TEMPLE

STRAND

SOUTHWARK

BOROUGH

SOUTH BANK

City & South Bank

◉ **Sights**

1	30 St Mary Axe	E1
2	All Hallows by the Tower	E2
3	Borough Market	D3
4	City Hall	E3
5	Courtauld Gallery	A2
6	Golden Hinde	D3
7	Hayward Gallery	A3
8	HMS Belfast	E3
9	Leadenhall Market	E2
10	London Dungeon	A4
11	London Eye	A3
12	Millennium Bridge	C2
13	Monument	D2
14	Museum of London	C1
15	Roupell St	B3
16	Shakespeare's Globe	C3
17	Shard	D3
18	Sir John Soane's Museum	A1
19	Somerset House	A2
20	Southbank Centre	A3
21	Southwark Cathedral	D3
22	St Mary-le-Bow	D2
23	St Paul's Cathedral	C2
24	Tate Modern	C3
25	Tower Bridge	F3
26	Tower Bridge Exhibition	F3
27	Tower of London	E2
28	Whitechapel Gallery	F1

🍴 **Eating**

29	Anchor & Hope	B3
30	Arabica Bar & Kitchen	D3
31	Baltic	B3
	Café Below	(see 22)
32	City Social	E1
33	Counter at the Delaunay	A2
	Crypt Café	(see 23)
	Delaunay	(see 33)
34	Duck & Waffle	E1
35	Maltby Street Market	E4
	Padella	(see 3)
36	Watch House	E4
37	Wine Library	E2

🛍 **Shopping**

38	Lovely & British	E4
39	Silver Vaults	A1
40	South Bank Book Market	A3
41	Southbank Centre Shop	A3

🍷 **Drinking & Nightlife**

42	Anspach & Hobday	F4
43	Blackfriar	B2
44	Counting House	D2
45	Jensen	F4
	Little Bird Gin	(see 35)
46	Madison	C2
	Oblix	(see 17)
47	Scootercaffe	A4
48	Sky Pod	E2
49	Ye Olde Cheshire Cheese	B1

🎭 **Entertainment**

50	National Theatre	A3
51	Old Vic	B4
52	Queen Elizabeth Hall	A3
	Royal Festival Hall	(see 20)
	Shakespeare's Globe	(see 16)
	Southbank Centre	(see 20)
53	Wilton's	F2
54	Young Vic	B3

🎨 **Activities, Courses & Tours**

55	London Bicycle Tour	B3
56	Thames Rockets	A4

West End

⊚ Sights
1	Big Ben	F7
2	Buckingham Palace	B7
3	Changing of the Guard	B8
4	Chinatown	D3
5	Churchill War Rooms	E7
6	College Garden	E8
7	Covent Garden Piazza	F3
8	Fourth Plinth Project	E5
9	Horse Guards Parade	E6
10	House of Commons	F8
11	House of Lords	F8
12	Houses of Parliament	F8
13	Jewel Tower	E8
14	London Film Museum	F3
15	London Transport Museum	F3
16	National Gallery	E4
17	National Portrait Gallery	E4
18	No 10 Downing Street	E6
19	Queen's Gallery	B8
20	Royal Academy of Arts	B5
21	Royal Mews	A8
22	Royal Opera House	F3
23	Soho	D3
24	Soho Square	D2
25	St James's Park	C7
26	St Martin-in-the-Fields	E4
	Summer Exhibition	(see 20)
27	Trafalgar Square	E5
28	Westminster Abbey	E8
29	Westminster Abbey Museum	E8

⊗ Eating
30	Barrafina	E4
31	Brasserie Zédel	C4
32	Cafe Murano	B5
33	Cellarium	E8
34	Dishoom	E3
35	Great Queen Street	F2
36	Gymkhana	B5
37	Kanada-Ya	E2
38	National Dining Rooms	D5
39	Palomar	D4
40	Pollen Street Social	B3
	Portrait	(see 17)
41	Shoryu	D5
42	Spuntino	D3
43	Yauatcha	C3

⊜ Shopping
44	Benjamin Pollock's Toy Shop	F3
45	Cambridge Satchel Company	F3
46	Fortnum & Mason	C5
47	Foyles	D2
48	Gosh!	C3
	Grant & Cutler	(see 47)
49	Hamleys	B3
50	Hatchards	C5
51	Liberty	B3
52	Molton Brown	F3
53	Moomin Shop	F3
54	Penhaligon's	B5
	Ray's Jazz	(see 47)
55	Reckless Records	C3
56	Sister Ray	C3
57	Stanford's	E3
58	Stella McCartney	A4
59	Topshop	B2
60	We Built This City	C3

⊖ Drinking & Nightlife
61	American Bar	F4
62	Dog & Duck	D3
63	Draft House	C1
64	Dukes London	B6
65	French House Soho	D3
66	Gordon's Wine Bar	F5
67	Heaven	F5
68	Lamb & Flag	E3
69	Princess Louise	F1
70	She Soho	D3
71	Swift	D3
72	Terroirs	E4
73	Yard	D3

⊛ Entertainment
74	100 Club	C2
75	Amused Moose Soho	C3
76	Comedy Store	D4
77	Pizza Express Jazz Club	D2
78	Prince Charles Cinema	D4
79	Ronnie Scott's	D3
	Royal Opera House	(see 22)

⊕ Activities, Courses & Tours
	Houses of Parliament Tours	(see 12)
80	Westminster Passenger Services Association	F7

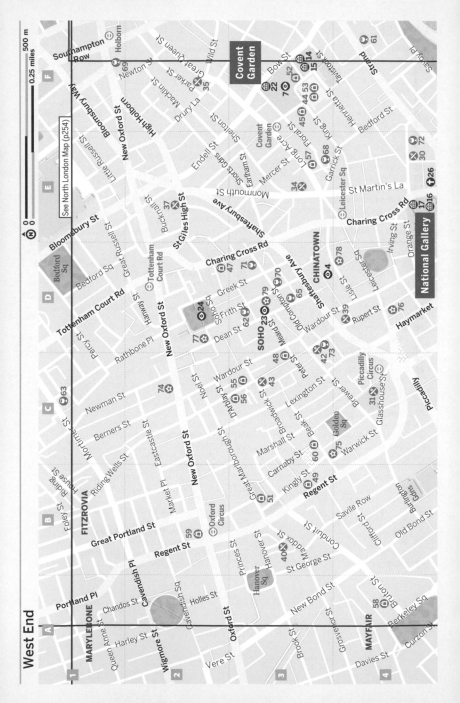

West End

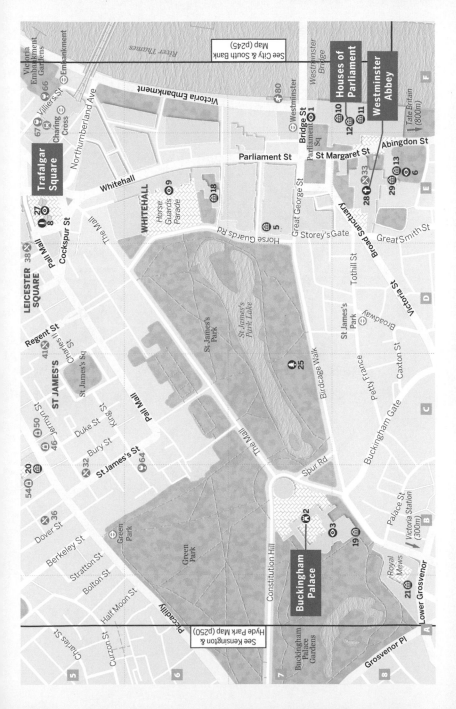

Kensington & Hyde Park

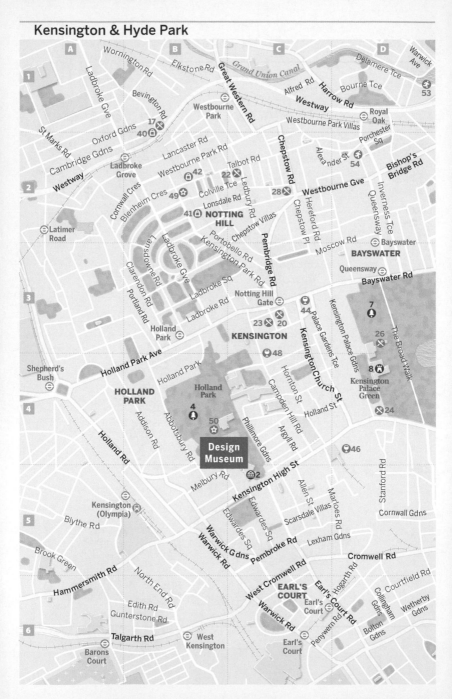

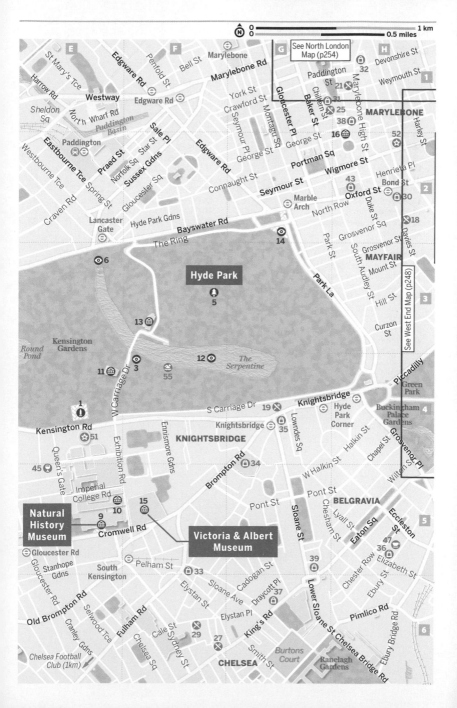

Kensington & Hyde Park

◎ Sights
1	Albert Memorial	E4
2	Design Museum	C5
3	Diana, Princess of Wales Memorial Fountain	F4
4	Holland Park	B4
5	Hyde Park	F3
6	Italian Gardens	E3
7	Kensington Gardens	D3
8	Kensington Palace	D4
9	Natural History Museum	E5
10	Science Museum	E5
11	Serpentine Galleries	E4
12	Serpentine Lake	F4
13	Serpentine Sackler Gallery	F3
14	Speakers' Corner	G2
15	Victoria & Albert Museum	F5
16	Wallace Collection	H2

⊗ Eating
17	Acklam Village Market	B1
18	Claridge's Foyer and Reading Room	H2
19	Dinner by Heston Blumenthal	G4
20	Geales	C3
21	La Fromagerie	H1
22	Ledbury	C2
	Magazine	(see 13)
23	Mazi	C3
24	Min Jiang	D4
25	Monocle Cafe	G1
26	Orangery	D3
27	Rabbit	F6
28	Taquería	C2
29	Tom's Kitchen	F6

	V&A Café	(see 15)
	Wallace	(see 16)

⊙ Shopping
30	Browns	H2
31	Cadenhead's Whisky & Tasting Shop	G1
32	Cath Kidston	H1
33	Conran Shop	F5
34	Harrods	G4
35	Harvey Nichols	G4
36	Jo Loves	H5
37	John Sandoe Books	G6
38	Monocle Shop	H1
39	Pickett	G5
40	Portobello Green Arcade	B2
41	Portobello Road Market	B2
42	Rough Trade West	B2
43	Selfridges	H2

⊙ Drinking & Nightlife
44	Notting Hill Arts Club	C3
45	Queen's Arms	E5
46	Roof Gardens	D4
47	Tomtom Coffee House	H5
48	Windsor Castle	C3

⊙ Entertainment
49	Electric Cinema	B2
50	Opera Holland Park	B4
51	Royal Albert Hall	E4
52	Wigmore Hall	H2

⊙ Activities, Courses & Tours
53	London Waterbus Company	D1
54	Porchester Spa	D2
55	Serpentine Lido	F4

Shoreditch & Spitalfields

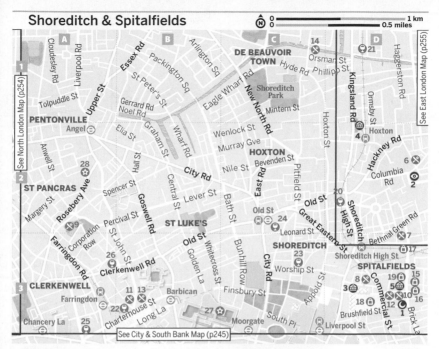

◎ Sights
1 Brick Lane Great Mosque D3
2 Columbia Road Flower Market D2
3 Dennis Severs' House D3
4 Geffrye Museum D2
5 Old Truman Brewery D3

✕ Eating
6 Brawn D2
7 Brick Lane Beigel Bake D3
8 Hawksmoor D3
9 Morito A2
10 Nude Espresso D3
11 Polpo B3
12 Poppies D3
13 St John B3
14 Towpath C1

◎ Shopping
15 Backyard Market D3

16 Blitz London D3
17 Brick Lane Market D3
18 Old Spitalfields Market D3
19 Rough Trade East D3
Sunday UpMarket .... (see 19)

◎ Drinking & Nightlife
93 Feet East .... (see 15)
20 Cargo D2
21 Draughts D1
22 Fabric B3
23 Worship St Whistling Shop C3
24 XOYO C2
25 Ye Olde Mitre A3
26 Zetter Townhouse Cocktail
Lounge A3

◎ Entertainment
27 Barbican B3
28 Sadler's Wells A2

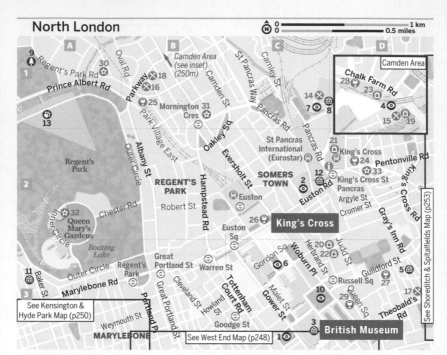

Sights
1	Bedford Square	C3
2	British Library	C2
3	British Museum	C3
4	Camden Market	D1
5	Charles Dickens Museum	D3
6	Gordon Square	C3
7	Granary Square	C1
8	House of Illustration	C1
9	Primrose Hill	A1
10	Russell Square	C3
11	Sherlock Holmes Museum	A3
12	St Pancras Station & Hotel	C2
13	ZSL London Zoo	A1

Eating
14	Caravan	C1
15	Chin Chin Labs	D1
	Grain Store	(see 14)
16	Hook Camden Town	B1
17	Lady Ottoline	D3
18	Market	B1

Shopping
19	Camden Lock Market	D1
20	Gay's the Word	C3
21	Harry Potter Shop at Platform 9¾	D2
22	Skoob Books	D3
23	Stables Market	D1

Drinking & Nightlife
24	Bar Pepito	D2
25	Edinboro Castle	B1
26	Euston Tap	C2
27	Lamb	D3
28	Proud Camden	D1
29	Queen's Larder	D3

Entertainment
30	Cecil Sharp House	A1
31	KOKO	B1
32	Regent's Park Open Air Theatre	A2
33	Scala	D2

East London

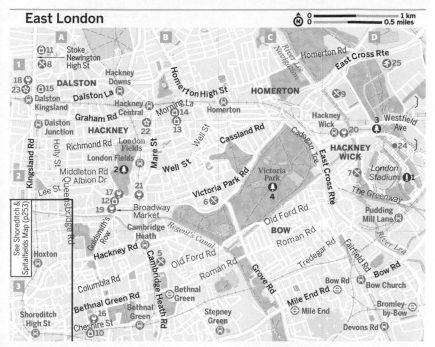

Greenwich

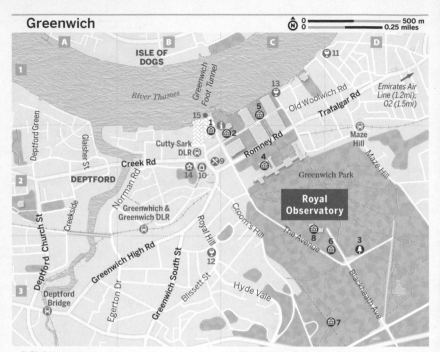

⊙ Sights
1 Cutty Sark	B2
2 Discover Greenwich	C2
3 Greenwich Park	D3
4 National Maritime Museum	C2
5 Old Royal Naval College	C1
6 Peter Harrison Planetarium	D3
7 Ranger's House (Wernher Collection)	D3
8 Royal Observatory	C2

⊗ Eating
9 Greenwich Market	B2

🔒 Shopping
Arty Globe	(see 9)
10 Casbah Records	B2
Greenwich Market	(see 9)

⊜ Drinking & Nightlife
11 Cutty Sark Tavern	D1
12 Greenwich Union	B3
13 Trafalgar Tavern	C1

⊛ Entertainment
14 Up the Creek	B2

⊘ Activities, Courses & Tours
15 Thames River Services	B1

Symbols & Map Key

Look for these symbols to quickly identify listings:

- ◉ Sights
- ✈ Activities
- ☯ Courses
- 🎯 Tours
- ✹ Festivals & Events
- ✗ Eating
- ☕ Drinking
- ✪ Entertainment
- 🛍 Shopping
- ℹ Information & Transport

These symbols and abbreviations give vital information for each listing:

🌱 Sustainable or green recommendation

FREE No payment required

- ☎ Telephone number
- ☺ Opening hours
- P Parking
- ⊘ Nonsmoking
- ❄ Air-conditioning
- @ Internet access
- 📶 Wi-fi access
- 🏊 Swimming pool
- 🚍 Bus
- ⛴ Ferry
- 🚊 Tram
- 🚆 Train
- ⊖ Tube
- 🗎 English-language menu
- 🌿 Vegetarian selection
- 👪 Family-friendly

Find your best experiences with these Great For... icons.

- Art & Culture
- Beaches
- Budget
- Cafe/Coffee
- Cycling
- Detour
- Drinking
- Entertainment
- Events
- Family Travel
- Food & Drink
- History
- Local Life
- Nature & Wildlife
- Photo Op
- Scenery
- Shopping
- Short Trip
- Sport
- Walking
- Winter Travel

Sights

- ◉ Beach
- ◉ Bird Sanctuary
- ◉ Buddhist
- ◉ Castle/Palace
- ◉ Christian
- ◉ Confucian
- ◉ Hindu
- ◉ Islamic
- ◉ Jain
- ◉ Jewish
- ◉ Monument
- ◉ Museum/Gallery/ Historic Building
- ◉ Ruin
- ◉ Shinto
- ◉ Sikh
- ◉ Taoist
- ◉ Winery/Vineyard
- ◉ Zoo/Wildlife Sanctuary
- ◉ Other Sight

Points of Interest

- © Bodysurfing
- ◬ Camping
- ☕ Cafe
- ◐ Canoeing/Kayaking
- ● Course/Tour
- ◒ Diving
- ◓ Drinking & Nightlife
- ✗ Eating
- ☯ Entertainment
- ♨ Sento Hot Baths/ Onsen
- 🛍 Shopping
- ⛷ Skiing
- ◎ Sleeping
- ◑ Snorkelling
- ◔ Surfing
- ◕ Swimming/Pool
- ◖ Walking
- ◗ Windsurfing
- ☯ Other Activity

Information

- $ Bank
- ◉ Embassy/Consulate
- ✚ Hospital/Medical
- @ Internet
- ◉ Police
- ◉ Post Office
- ✆ Telephone
- ◉ Toilet
- ℹ Tourist Information
- ● Other Information

Geographic

- ◉ Beach
- ◂ Gate
- ◉ Hut/Shelter
- ◉ Lighthouse
- ◉ Lookout
- ▲ Mountain/Volcano
- ◉ Oasis
- ◉ Park
-)(Pass
- ◉ Picnic Area
- ◉ Waterfall

Transport

- ◉ Airport
- Ⓑ BART station
- ◉ Border crossing
- Ⓣ Boston T station
- ◉ Bus
- ◉ Cable car/Funicular
- ◉ Cycling
- ◉ Ferry
- Ⓜ Metro/MRT station
- ◉ Monorail
- Ⓟ Parking
- ◉ Petrol station
- Ⓢ Subway/S-Bahn/ Skytrain station
- ◉ Taxi
- ◉ Train station/Railway
- ◉ Tram
- ◉ Tube Station
- Ⓤ Underground/ U-Bahn station
- ● Other Transport

258

Our Story

A beat-up old car, a few dollars in the pocket and a sense of adventure. In 1972 that's all Tony and Maureen Wheeler needed for the trip of a lifetime – across Europe and Asia overland to Australia. It took several months, and at the end – broke but inspired – they sat at their kitchen table writing and stapling together their first travel guide, *Across Asia on the Cheap*. Within a week they'd sold 1500 copies. Lonely Planet was born.

Today, Lonely Planet has offices in Franklin, London, Melbourne, Oakland, Dublin, Beijing, and Delhi, with more than 600 staff and writers. We share Tony's belief that 'a great guidebook should do three things: inform, educate and amuse'.

Our Writers

Emilie Filou

Emilie was born in Paris, where she lived until she was 18. Following her three-year degree and three gap years, she found herself in London, fell in love with the place and never really left. She now works as a journalist specialising in Africa and makes regular trips to the region from her home in northeast London. You can see her work on www.emiliefilou.com; she tweets at @EmilieFilou.

Peter Dragicevich

After a dozen years reviewing music and restaurants for publications in New Zealand and Australia, London's bright lights and loud guitars could no longer be resisted. Like all good Kiwis, Peter got to know the city while surfing his way between friends' flats all over London before finally putting down roots in North London.

Steve Fallon

After a full 15 years living in the centre of the known universe – East London – Steve cockney-rhymes in his sleep, eats jellied eel for brekkie, drinks lager by the bucketful and dances around the occasional handbag. As always, he did everything the hard/fun way: walking the walks, seeing the sights, taking (some) advice from friends, colleagues and the odd taxi driver and digesting everything in sight. Steve is a qualified London Blue Badge Tourist Guide (www.steveslondon.com).

Damian Harper

Born off the Strand within earshot of Bow Bells (favourable wind permitting), Damian grew up in Notting Hill way before it was discovered by Hollywood. A onetime Shakespeare and Company bookseller and radio presenter, Damian has been authoring guidebooks for Lonely Planet since the late 1990s. He lives in South London with his wife and two kids, frequently returning to China (his second home).

STAY IN TOUCH LONELYPLANET.COM/CONTACT

AUSTRALIA The Malt Store, Level 3, 551 Swanston St, Carlton, Victoria 3053 ☏ 03 8379 8000, fax 03 8379 8111

IRELAND Unit E, Digital Court. The Digital Hub, Rainsford St, Dublin 8, Ireland

USA 124 Linden Street, Oakland, CA 94607 ☏ 510 250 6400, toll free 800 275 8555, fax 510 893 8572

UK 240 Blackfriars Road, London SE1 8NW ☏ 020 3771 5100, fax 020 3771 5101

 twitter.com/lonelyplanet   facebook.com/lonelyplanet   instagram.com/lonelyplanet youtube.com/lonelyplanet lonelyplanet.com/newsletter

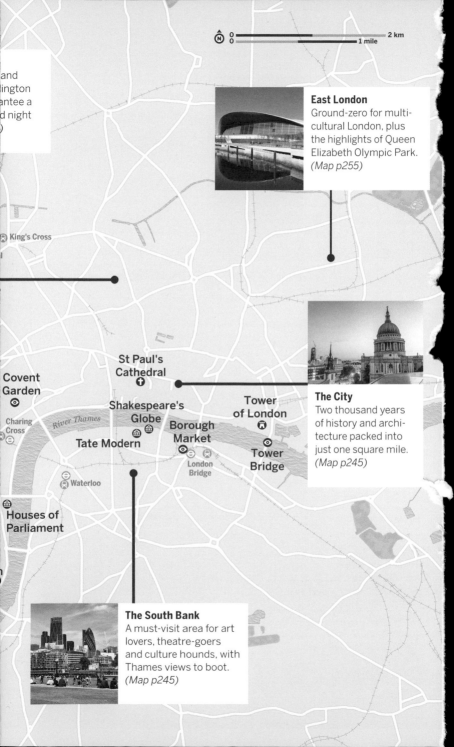

and
ington
antee a
d night

King's Cross

East London
Ground-zero for multi-cultural London, plus the highlights of Queen Elizabeth Olympic Park.
(Map p255)

Covent Garden

Charing Cross

St Paul's Cathedral

River Thames

Shakespeare's Globe

Borough Market

Tate Modern

Tower of London

London Bridge

Tower Bridge

Waterloo

Houses of Parliament

The City
Two thousand years of history and architecture packed into just one square mile.
(Map p245)

The South Bank
A must-visit area for art lovers, theatre-goers and culture hounds, with Thames views to boot.
(Map p245)

0 — 2 km
0 — 1 mile